BIG
DUNC

BIG DUNC

THE UPFRONT AUTOBIOGRAPHY

DUNCAN FERGUSON
with *Henry Winter*

CENTURY

UK | USA | Canada | Ireland | Australia
India | New Zealand | South Africa

Century is part of the Penguin Random House group of companies
whose addresses can be found at global.penguinrandomhouse.com

Penguin Random House UK,
One Embassy Gardens, 8 Viaduct Gardens, London SW11 7BW

penguin.co.uk
global.penguinrandomhouse.com

First published 2025
003

Copyright © Duncan Ferguson, 2025
Foreword copyright © Carlo Ancelotti, 2025

The moral right of the author has been asserted

Penguin Random House values and supports copyright. Copyright fuels creativity, encourages diverse voices, promotes freedom of expression and supports a vibrant culture. Thank you for purchasing an authorised edition of this book and for respecting intellectual property laws by not reproducing, scanning or distributing any part of it by any means without permission. You are supporting authors and enabling Penguin Random House to continue to publish books for everyone. No part of this book may be used or reproduced in any manner for the purpose of training artificial intelligence technologies or systems. In accordance with Article 4(3) of the DSM Directive 2019/790, Penguin Random House expressly reserves this work from the text and data mining exception.

Set in 12/15.5pt Goudy Oldstyle Std
Typeset by Jouve (UK), Milton Keynes

Printed and bound in Great Britain by Clays Ltd, Elcograf S.p.A.

The authorised representative in the EEA is Penguin Random House Ireland,
Morrison Chambers, 32 Nassau Street, Dublin D02 YH68

A CIP catalogue record for this book is available from the British Library

ISBN: 978–1–529–93928–6 (hardback)
ISBN: 978–1–529–96398–4 (trade paperback)

Penguin Random House is committed to a sustainable future
for our business, our readers and our planet. This book is made
from Forest Stewardship Council® certified paper.

'You get knocked down.
Get back up.
End of.'

'When you play for Everton, you forget about the rest.
The rest mean nothing.'

Duncan Ferguson

CONTENTS

Foreword		ix
Prologue: Welcome to Hell		1
Introduction		11
1	The Barlinnie Letters	17
2	The Targetman Targeted	34
3	Ifs and Butts	44
4	The End of the Affair	55
5	Remembering Bannockburn	57
6	Chasing My Goals	66
7	Tyranny at Tannadice	77
8	Pigeons, Ferrets and Other Creatures	100
9	Scotland the Grave	107
10	Tapping Up and Stepping Up	117
11	Rangers Dangers	125
12	Doomsday	134
13	Escape to Everton	136
14	By Royle Command	140

CONTENTS

15	Banged Up and Banging Them In	158
16	Seeing Red	162
17	Leaving Home	172
18	Going Home	182
19	Taken to the Collina's	200
20	Endgame	202
21	The Love of My Life	215
22	My Dad, My Hero	221
23	Burglars	228
24	Mates	232
25	Sobering Up	241
26	Skint	245
27	Absent Friends	251
28	New Coach	253
29	Koeman	264
30	Stockmanship	273
31	Big Sam	277
32	Marco	284
33	Caretaking and Taking Care	289
34	Carlo Fantastico	301
35	Benítez	313
36	Heartache	318
37	Just About Managing	328
38	Inverness	335
39	Brothers and Sisters	343
Acknowledgements		346
Index		347

FOREWORD
BY CARLO ANCELOTTI

Duncan was very supportive when I arrived at Everton Football Club as manager in December 2019. He was really, *really* good with me. Duncan helped me a lot to know the culture of Everton and to understand the structure of the club. That was so important. He's a legend there. He talked to me about the passion the supporters have, which I soon saw myself. Everton is a special football club. One of the reasons it is special is because of Duncan Ferguson. I could see he was respected by everyone there and he showed respect to all.

That included me. Since that day when I arrived on Merseyside, Duncan's become a good friend of mine. During my eighteen months there, Duncan and I built a great relationship personally and professionally. He always helped me. I remember one freezing-cold night at Goodison. We were playing Tottenham Hotspur in the FA Cup and my body was numb. The game was in extra time and I was standing in the technical area and I couldn't move or react. I just stood there. Duncan saw I was struggling in the cold so he brought me a steaming cup of coffee. I gripped it, drank it and felt the warmth spreading through me again. It was like a life-saver! It would also turn out to be a lucky charm. At just the

FOREWORD

same moment that Duncan brought me the drink, our Brazilian player Bernard scored the winner. Duncan's coffee got an assist!

Duncan is a manager. OK, he was an assistant coach for me, but he's a manager. Duncan has all the passion for football to be a good manager. He has great knowledge of the game. He played for sixteen years. He played internationally. He knows football.

I saw how good he was when we had training at Finch Farm. Duncan knew how to prepare an excellent training session properly and how to manage it. Some people can prepare a training session, but after that they have difficulty in keeping it going. Duncan has absolutely no problem in that department. I left him to manage training sometimes and it went well because Duncan has good energy. I knew the players enjoyed his sessions.

I remember when he became caretaker after Rafa Benítez left in 2022, we swapped messages. I told him he was ready and he knew what he was doing. I'd seen that on the training ground. I've always believed in him.

Duncan has a huge personality. He's a good guy, a nice guy. We had a lot of special moments together. I remember at the end of the first season, I hired a boat and we met up in Croatia. Duncan was on a boat with a friend of his. We had a great time talking and eating together. Honestly, every day was fun with Duncan. He's a really funny guy but also serious. That's a great quality. He's able to share an amusing moment with a sincere one.

I still have a good relationship with him. We talk a lot about his son Cameron, who was playing at Newcastle, then up in Scotland and then Wales. I always wish the best for Duncan and his family. And I wish him the best with this book.

PROLOGUE: WELCOME TO HELL

I believe I'm a brave man, tough physically and mentally, but when I got led handcuffed into HMP Barlinnie on 11 October 1995, my blood ran cold. My life was on hold, even at risk. I was entering Britain's most notorious prison with its huge stone walls, barbed wire wound around the top and forbidding metal doors that had all the charm of the brass plate on a coffin. Outside, I was Big Dunc, Everton and Scotland targetman. Inside, I was the target. And I was terrified.

I'd just lost my appeal against a three-month sentence for what the courts claimed was an assault on Raith Rovers' John McStay at Ibrox on 16 April 1994. I hardly grazed the boy, I promise you. I was playing for Rangers at the time and I just ended up feeling like some people in the Scottish judiciary didn't like the club. They were probably delighted to see me banged up in Barlinnie. As I entered the prison, I thought, 'What on earth is happening to me? What's happening to my life? How has it come to this?' Yes, I connected with the lad, but to face this hell because of that incident felt terribly unfair.

I was marched through the small, dingy reception area and into the holding cubicles, known as doggy boxes. I sat for several hours on a bench inside, with food and cigarette butts on the floor, and graffiti on the walls, surrounded by men with 'Mars bars' – scars. Everywhere I looked I sensed menace.

My stomach knotted with tension as I completed the cold, clinical elements of being processed. Clothes off. An invasive inspection. A lingering sense of humiliation. Unsmiling guards gave me my number – 12718 – and handed me my gear, a red shirt with white stripes and blue denim trousers. Every part of the process dehumanised me further.

Earlier in the day I'd handed my watch, rings and some money to my dad as I left the courtroom in Edinburgh. God only knows what my mum and dad were feeling, with everything I was putting them through. All I had in my pocket was £5 to buy some phonecards – prison currency – as I was taken by guards from the doggy box towards my cell in D Hall. My new home was directly opposite the hanging shed where the gallows once wrung the life out of the condemned.

It was late afternoon, early evening in 'The Big Hoose' or 'Bar L' as Barlinnie was known, and processing had taken about three hours. I was classed as a Category D prisoner, which meant I was considered unlikely to make an effort to escape. The only effort I made was not to betray the fear growing inside me as I stepped on to the metal spiral staircase connecting the ground floor to the four floors above it.

I was only twenty-three, still a kid in many ways.

It was terrifying for anybody going into Barlinnie but just imagine what it was like for someone who'd been a Rangers centre-forward and had played for Scotland and was a current Premiership player. A big target.

Going through the doors of Barlinnie and hearing the keys clanking and the locks rattling shut was terrifying. I'd just lost my

PROLOGUE: WELCOME TO HELL

freedom but I was determined not to lose my mind. I'm strong, I told myself. And I needed to be.

Silence. As intimidating a sound as I've heard in my life. The dead quiet inside Barlinnie that first day was only disturbed by the clank, clank, clank of our feet walking the floors on the metal staircase.

Finally, two voices broke the silence. Scouse voices! Would you believe it? I'd only been with Everton a year since I left Rangers,* but the people of Liverpool, and the accent, already felt like home.

'All right, la'!' said the voice.

'All right, big man! How you getting on?' said another.

Even more amazingly, I knew the dad of one of them, who ran a nightclub in one of the estates in Merseyside. These Barlinnie boys had been up in Glasgow for the drugs, and had got caught. Everton fans. I had support.

Everyone in Barlinnie knew I was coming. It was all over the news that I'd lost my appeal against the guilty verdict. I was the first British footballer imprisoned for something that had happened on the pitch. Three months. The 'brevity' of my sentence meant I couldn't be transferred to an open prison or an English jail. I still questioned this. Why not an open prison? Why Barlinnie in the middle of Glasgow? Why? But Barlinnie, one of the toughest square miles in Britain, it was, which deepened my anger at the verdict. I felt it was more than unfair, disgusting really, but my new neighbours weren't bothered about the rights and wrongs of the decision. They just wanted to see this famous footballer. The one who'd broken the British transfer record with a £4 million move to

---

* I was charged for the 'assault' on John McStay while I was still at Rangers, but I was sentenced after I had moved to and was playing for Everton.

Rangers from Dundee United. The one who'd played for Scotland. And the one who had helped Everton win the FA Cup within a year of coming to the club. What a fall from grace.

After a brief chat with the Barlinnie Evertonians, no one else spoke for a while. I was relieved when I made it behind my 'wood', the cell door. The guards – never 'screws' to me – turned the key, leaving me alone with my thoughts and the crude graffiti on the wall of the dirty little cell that stank of shit. I looked around, and quickly took in the window with metal bars, a bed, a rickety little table and a pot in the corner. (I honestly didn't know what the pot was for at first; I would find out the next morning. No en suite here.) I'd been in Barlinnie scarcely four hours and already I felt like I'd been stitched up.

I put my blanket down on the bed and tried to rest, but the prison hadn't issued me with any sheets and the bed scratched like hell, as the wiry bedding dug into my skin. 'How am I going to sleep like this for three months?' I thought. I knew I probably wasn't being singled out. It was all part of the initiation. When I asked the other boys in the following days how they managed to get any sleep at all on the wire beds they laughed and told me, 'Big man, you need to get a sheet!'

On that first evening, lights out came at 10 p.m. prompt, but then the night sounds began. It wasn't long before a thick, sinister Glaswegian voice cut the atmosphere like a knife.

'Ya dirty Orange bastard, Ferguson, I'm gonna fuckin' kill ya!'

Several more brave boys took up the cudgels.

'Ya'll get it in the mornin', ya big Orange cunt!'

'We're gonna slash your fuckin' face!' I sat at the end of my bed listening to all these threats, shaking.

'Yer gettin' cut tomorra, Billy Boy! You'll get a fuckin' hidin'!'

'Come out yer cell, ya Hun, and we'll knife ya!'

On it went. I'm Protestant, I played for a Protestant club in

PROLOGUE: WELCOME TO HELL

Rangers. Being in a prison in Glasgow, with half the joint supporting the Catholic club Celtic, meant that sectarianism flowed through Barlinnie like sewage from a broken pipe. In fairness, if I'd been a Celtic player the Rangers fans would have been just as tough on me. Still, it was hard to deal with, because it wasn't how I was brought up by my mum and dad. Sectarian songs weren't the soundtrack of my life in my home town of Stirling, not like they can be in Glasgow. Sectarianism just wasn't me, but it's how I was identified that first night. The jeers echoed around D Hall and even into C Hall, where more inmates joined in.

'Which cell is he in, Jimmy?'

'O'er from the hanging shed. Right opposite.'

The threats kept coming.

'Ya'll get it right in the throat when we see ya tomorra, Ferguson, ya shit!'

The dire warnings of me getting slashed and cut to bits continued unchecked until all of a sudden a single heavy Glaswegian voice boomed out with all the authority of a man accustomed to being listened to.

'Shut up, the lot of ya. I want to get my head down and sleep, so fuckin' keep it shut. The next fucker who opens his mouth, he'll answer to me in the mornin' . . .'

The whole nick went quiet. Bang, dead. It must have been one of the top boys from across the hall. I never found out who he was, and I would learn that those boys tend to protect their anonymity. But I would also discover that during my time in Barlinnie there were certain people looking after me inside. I never heard another word directed at me that night, not a peep. But, believe me, it was the longest night of my life. Never mind the wiry bed, it was images of a blade that kept me awake.

Welcome to hell.

*

My daily prison routine began the next morning with no frills. Prisoners woke up at 6.30 a.m. and headed to the communal shower area. Nothing could have prepared me for discovering what that pot in the corner of my room was really for, as I stood in line watching men depositing shit and piss from their chamber pots into big sinks. What did I expect? Proper sanitation? A disgrace, it was. Dehumanising. Some boys threw their shit and piss at others. I would get used to this. From that morning onwards I would worry about who was standing at my back. It could be anybody and I had to be wary. I couldn't turn around or show weakness. I needed eyes in the back of my head to avoid some scarface pouring his piss and shit on me.

They all had scars inside Barlinnie. Big, long, thick scars that (I would come to understand) had come from gaping wounds that couldn't properly be stitched. I would discover that you could get cut to ribbons for £2 of credit on a phonecard. Or sometimes for no reason. Weapons, needles and syringes had been confiscated from incoming prisoners the day before in the doggy boxes where nurses assessed us before we were taken to our cells. But once inside, I was warned that the hard cases always found a way to slash you. In the lines that day I was told about toothbrushes with razor blades moulded into the plastic – the weapon of choice. Along with heavy-duty PP9 batteries wrapped inside socks, used as a bludgeoning tool to the back of the head. You learned quickly always to look behind you. I would soon see boys get hit or cut. I would see a lot of bloodletting inside Barlinnie. But that was to come.

After slopping out, it was breakfast at 7 a.m. back in our cells. I had a boiled egg sat on the edge of my bed – there was no communal eating in D Hall – and then the cell doors were opened and those who were working stepped out on to the galleries at

PROLOGUE: WELCOME TO HELL

8 a.m. Cleaning jobs, laundry, ground maintenance, joinery, the library – there was a range of work.

I hadn't been assigned a job yet on my first day, and not everyone worked. The rest of the day's itinerary was as follows. Lunch in cells at 12.30 p.m. An hour's recreation from 1, and then back to work at 2. Tea in your cell at 4.30 and back to work again at 5.30. Evening recreation would start at 8 and then the cell doors would finally be slammed shut at 9.30, lights out half an hour later. I would realise that some prisoners remained locked up for twenty-three hours a day. Day after day.

I was told that at weekends we weren't allowed out of our cells for more than an hour. To avoid being overwhelmed by the stench of our own excrement, I would learn that if you had to shit in your cell you used newspaper, laid it out on the floor, squatted down and shat on the paper, then rolled it up and lobbed it through the metal bars of the window on to the courtyard down below. Some boys would set the paper on fire and send it flying out of their cells, shouting, 'Bombs away!' The boys on the bottom floor, many of them coming off drugs and spending hours on end banging the cell walls, were known as the bomb squad. It fell on them, in every sense, to clean up all the shit off the yard that piled up against their windows.

It was after returning to my cell on that first morning that I had to confront the reality of Barlinnie and its violent undercurrent, which could swell into a full-on bloodbath in a split-second. Being back behind my 'wood' was a protective feeling. I knew I was safe in my cell. Outside, it was a bear pit, a jungle. Swirling around my head were the intimidating cries from the night before: 'We're gonna slash your fuckin' face! Ya'll get it in the mornin'!'

So I steeled myself, not knowing what was going to happen. Should I leave my cell? I sat on the edge of my bed thinking of the knives that might be waiting. Come on, Dunc, take that step. That was a moment that tested me. Do you go forward or do you go back? In my career to that point, I had always gone forward. In my life, too, I had probably gone forward more than I had gone back. Take the step, I thought.

But don't go near anybody, I told myself as I walked out on to the gallery, feeling like every last man in that godforsaken place was looking at me. Mind your own business and let everyone else mind theirs.

I heard whispering – 'There's Dunc.' And then a louder voice from across the landing.

'D'ya want your hair cut, big fella?'

A boy wearing the regulation red shirt with white stripes and blue denim trousers stood there, holding a pair of scissors. Now everybody was looking.

What do I say? What do I do? The night before everyone's telling me I'm going to get cut to pieces and this boy has scissors.

The whole place fell silent again. I felt all eyes on me. How would I react?

I either bottle it and retreat to my cell or I step forward. Come on, Dunc. Ready. Forward.

'Yes, no problem, mate,' I said, and I walked across the gallery and over to the chair where I sat down in front of him.

I felt sick to the pit of my stomach. This guy could stick his scissors in my throat. Everything I'd told myself beforehand – don't go near anybody, mind your own business and let everyone else mind theirs – I'd just gone and screwed up within seconds of walking out of my cell. Now I had a boy at my back with a pair of scissors in his hand, and I was completely defenceless. It was the most frightened I've ever been in my life. My heart was jumping out of my shirt, absolutely pumping.

All of a sudden his hands dropped down on my shoulders and

PROLOGUE: WELCOME TO HELL

grabbed hold of me like a clamp and I could see the scissors out of the corner of my eye. Just one stabbing motion away from my jugular.

'What will it be, big fella?'

'Short back and sides, wee man.'

And he began to cut. My hair. It broke the ice. If I was going to get slashed in jail, at least it wouldn't be by the barber of Barlinnie. I survived, and my pulse settled a bit, but I would never relax in Barlinnie, not even close. For every one of the slow-moving days I was in there, I was always on edge.

INTRODUCTION

Barlinnie is a hellish memory I will take to my grave. Even now, thirty years on, I can still smell the piss, shit and disinfectant. I will never forget the staring eyes, some sadistic, some soulless, none too welcoming.

That grim experience is one of the reasons why I'm writing this book. But there are others. You might have read some of the headlines about me over the years, which have followed me around my career. I can't really argue with some of them, can I? 'Duncan Disorderly' was right at the time in the nineties because I was going out, drinking and mounting up a lot of offences, wasn't I? The press write what they want and I gave them a fair bit of material to work with. What pisses me off is that they're still talking about some of the things that happened when I was eighteen. I'm fifty-three now. I'm writing this book because I've never given my side of what happened and I've never put a stop to the lies.

I've rarely done interviews, I rarely speak in public. In fact, Everton once organised a talking Christmas card with my voice on it, to wish fans well over the festive period. The club ended up having thousands of people phoning in to the Christmas hotline just to hear what I sounded like. I really had never done interviews. Of course, the internet has changed things a bit these days, but even now, when I chat to fans on the street they'll often say, 'It's the first time I've heard you speak.'

Throughout my playing days I was always wary of talking to the press. I had a reputation, and a lot of that reputation was stirred up by the papers. Some journalists I've come to like but not many. Particularly around the time of Barlinnie, when I was in my early twenties and naive, I thought everybody was against me, so I just didn't open up. Maybe that helped the media to create an aura around me.

Years later there was even this Scottish journalist, Alan Pattullo, who wrote a 90,000-word book about my life without speaking to me. I wouldn't have helped him anyway, to be honest. I've met him a few times since. He seems a nice fella, but I've never read a page of his book. I hope it's done well for him. He came to Forest Green a couple of years ago, in 2023 when I was managing there. I didn't know it was him when we first met. It wasn't until a bit later on that somebody said, 'This is Pattullo,' and I said, 'Oh, hello, how are you doing?' That was it.

I understand there's a fascination that some people have about me. Some Finnish composer once wrote an opera about my life. It was on the radio. The BBC. Classical music inspired by me was on the radio! It's called *Barlinnie Nine*. Not even David Beckham's had an orchestral work written about him, I like to think. But, then again, not many players have been in prison or, more to the point, Barlinnie.

So, you may think you know me, but I've hidden so much of myself from the public down the years. Here, for the first time, I want to give you the real story. To explain. That's really why I'm doing the book. Yes, there were a few years that weren't great periods in my life. Take, for example, when I was a young lad from

INTRODUCTION

Stirling, trying to find my way in the world. I'd started going out young. I was drinking with my friends at thirteen, getting bottles of Woodpecker and Merrydown cider for a pound by asking older kids to buy them for us in supermarkets. We would look for fag packets on the ground, hoping we found a smoke inside. When I reached the age of sixteen I started going to nightclubs: McQ's in Bannockburn, Rainbow Rocks in Stirling – I remember that, the big one. That's if we could get in. I was underage, trying to get past the bouncers and into the clubs for a wee dance.

It was around that time when the trouble started. I took a couple of drags on a joint when I was around sixteen or seventeen, and was sick. But mainly the problems came from drink. At the end of a night I'd be standing in a taxi rank, waiting to go home. People were drunk, I was standing at the back of the rank, keeping my head down, and before I knew it there was aggro. Local people recognised me. I was becoming known as a footballer. I became a target, a name. It was difficult to deal with. I never started a row in my life. I might have finished a few, even by throwing the first punch, but I never sought trouble. I've had violence in my life, but I've never seen myself as a violent man. Most of that trouble was between seventeen and twenty, a part of my life I'm not proud about. As you'll discover in this book, some of my youthful scraps would follow me all the way to Barlinnie. My troubles with the law began long before my confrontation with John McStay.

Most of all, though, in this book I want to be honest about the events in my life that have been significant, and the forces that have shaped me. And there have been many.

An old-school father who worked incredibly hard to give his family a better life. A refusal to walk away when threatened that has led to fights on and off the field. A hunger for football so deep that I played much of my career injured. A manager in

Jim McLean at Dundee United that I wanted to punch most days. A joy playing alongside Ally McCoist at Rangers, Mikel Arteta and Wayne Rooney at Everton, and Alan Shearer at Newcastle United. An anger at the Italian referee Pierluigi Collina, who denied Everton a crack at the Champions League and one of our greatest moments. These are some of the stories we'll explore.

You'll learn about my passion for coaching and improving players like Romelu Lukaku, John Stones, Richarlison, James Rodríguez and Dominic Calvert-Lewin. My love of working for managers like Ronald Koeman and one of the true greats in Carlo Ancelotti, and then managing in the Premier League myself briefly. I want to set the record straight on so many points: giving up Scotland, which was my biggest regret, and giving up booze, almost burning a hotel down, surviving bankruptcy and finding burglars in my home. Twice. I have so many tales to tell you. About why I love pigeons, about my hatred of injustice and why I occasionally fell out with refs as well as judges, about my relationship with Everton managers like Roberto Martínez, Sam Allardyce, Marco Silva, Rafa Benítez and Frank Lampard. And about why I became critical of Everton's recruitment of players and had issues with the board.

In my words, in these pages, I also want to pay tribute to the most important people in my life: my wife and three children. They saved me. And I want you to appreciate my other great love, Everton Football Club, and my heartache at leaving them for Newcastle on a crazy night at Goodison, and then the sweet feeling of returning home two years later. When I finally left as a player, and as a coach, the club handled it badly. Leaving hurt so much because I loved Everton so much. Still do. Because in my darkest hour inside Barlinnie, Everton stood by me, from fans to directors. Sitting in my cell, desperately alone, I knew there were

INTRODUCTION

people out there who cared for me. That kept me going during what turned out to be the forty-four-day-long nightmare of being banged up in Barlinnie. In writing this book, I've had to confront again many of the demons I faced inside.

Let's go back there to pick up the story.

1

THE BARLINNIE LETTERS

The name Barlinnie carried a grim association with condemned men imprisoned for crimes ranging from gangland violence to multiple murders, the Lockerbie bombing to paedophile depravity. The name alone was enough to send a chill down the spine. Mine, anyway.

Ten men convicted of murder walked from their cells to the hangman's scaffold in D Hall between 1946 and 1960. I'd look out the tiny window over their unmarked graves in the yard outside. Barlinnie is home, they say, to Europe's busiest methadone clinic, with statistics suggesting up to 400 inmates are injected daily with the heroin substitute. The atmosphere was claustrophobic, oppressive, exacerbated by chronic overcrowding. Slopping out, an unspeakably degrading practice, not to mention a fundamental breach of human rights, was abolished only in 2004. That was not so many years after a rooftop protest by prisoners wearing balaclavas, who had rioted and overpowered guards in B Hall, a stand-off broadcast around the world. They blamed it on the brutality behind bars. As one governor eloquently put it, 'This is not just a prison. This is Barlinnie.'

Its uncompromising reputation meant I was well aware I'd have to stand up for myself from the outset. Predators prey on the weak and there are plenty of both kinds in Barlinnie, with no means of escape until your time is up. Staying out of harm's way would be easier said than done, especially given the prevalence in D Hall of prisoners with mental health issues, a drug habit or both. There were remand prisoners, murderers, waiting for sentencing.

Also my profile made me a target. Or as one newspaper put it, the Scottish Prison Service's 'most famous customer since Rudolf Hess'. God almighty, some comparison that! Adolf Hitler's former deputy! For some boys inside, Barlinnie bizarrely represented a kind of Easy Street compared to life on the streets of the Gorbals, Govan or Possilpark. Many became institutionalised. At least here there was the provision of three daily meals, a roof overhead, education and even pay for the work you did in the prison. It must be truly miserable for them on the outside to prefer Barlinnie, I thought.

The authorities seemed powerless to control the widespread drug use at Barlinnie in spite of the doggy boxes, random searches and other punitive measures. I read somewhere that Ross Kemp, who's been to war zones and met some particularly unsavoury characters in his various TV docs, was not at all prepared for what he experienced during a week's filming in Barlinnie in 2017. A third of inmates, he discovered, had tested positive for drugs. All I can say is that the majority of the other two-thirds must have dodged the drug testers.

Drug use was at epidemic levels and it was ingenious how the drugs got peddled around. Barlinnie's a big old Victorian prison and between the wall and the heating pipe that runs from one cell to the next there's a gap, right? That was used to shift drugs, phonecards and messages, too.

Contraband was put in a 'stiffy', an illegal letter they passed from cell to cell. You get a long piece of paper, put your drugs in it, mainly hash or heroin, and somebody bangs on the pipe – 'Dunc, pass it along'. I panicked the first time. I thought I was getting stitched up, that the door would open, I'd get caught, and get more time inside.

A couple of taps on the pipe signalled that a stiffy was coming your way, all the goods rolled up inside it. The paper would get pushed along and pulled through on the other side until it reached its destination, all around the block, on its own little smugglers' route. This was how they moved the drugs around Barlinnie. I couldn't move that stiffy along quickly enough.

Passmen, basically prisoners with privileges, were tasked with undertaking various jobs, some of which included responsibility for cleaning the streets around the prison – Lethamhill Road, Smithycroft Road, Lee Avenue. So they'd be outside, under supervision of course, but some of the most industrious of these passmen were actually some of the biggest traffickers in Barlinnie, dumping the rubbish they collected into bins which had drugs placed in them by their mates. The drop-off could be as straightforward as that.

Prison contraband was big business. I don't know how many times I saw a boy come into Barlinnie and drink out of a bottle of shampoo, absolutely down it in order to make himself puke up the gear he'd swallowed before he came in. Or came back in, as was often the case. I saw it. 'Dunc, I'm not stupid,' one of the inmates said to me as he drank a full bottle of shampoo, and threw up his gear. They'd also swallow the drugs then shit them out into a toilet roll. I witnessed that too.

Barlinnie was overrun with these drug mules. They passed drugs from both ends of their bodies – absolutely vile when you think about it, but anything to feed the habit and the drugs culture that thrived inside. It was sick stuff seeing guys snort or inject. Cocaine, heroin, Class A drugs. They were using all the time. And they nicked methadone and other medications from the hospital unit, which could accommodate up to twenty prisoners at a time and had an area set aside for suicide supervision.

I actually got a job in the hospital unit after spending my first few days during work hours mopping up and cleaning around D Hall. That's where it got more dangerous for me because I was always being put under pressure by boys to supply them with needles and pills. The guards warned me, 'Duncan, you're in a privileged job here in the hospital and you'll have to be careful because some of them will want you to take out needles and steal other stuff. Don't fall into the trap.'

Some boys did, and I had to stand in line-ups whenever anything went missing – a regular occurrence. Guys stole things all the time so they could ingest, inhale and inject themselves and the guards had to be seen to treat me in the same way as everybody else. I made sure I kept my nose clean, literally.

On the second night I received a stiffy from another cell. Tap, tap. It was from a guy in C Hall and he wrote simply, 'Any problems, big man, we'll sort them out.' He signed off as John, and one of his crew, a boy called Chad, a big lump of a lad, made himself known to me a few days later in the prison gym. Chad had been in Barlinnie off and on from a young age and he reiterated the message from John: 'Any problems, we'll sort.'

I accepted their assurance in the spirit it was offered, but if someone stuck a knife in me, what would be the point? But at least I knew if there was going to be bother, it wouldn't be big boys putting me under pressure. It would be a little smackhead connected to nobody.

I'd spent enough time in bars back in Stirling to know there was always the potential for trouble around a pool table. Really stupidly, I ended up in the recreation area one day when, sure enough, this little guy started shouting his mouth off about his mates. All of them were so-called hard men in Stirling.

'Son, you're talkin' shite,' I said. 'My mates are the top boys in Stirling.'

I knew every hard case in Stirling and they weren't his mates. They were mine. In fact, they were family, lads like my cousin Tam Begley, and Stephen Dennehy, my minder. Men who never took prisoners.

My dad's advice was always 'Get your retaliation in first', which I followed on the football pitch my entire career. Of course, he didn't mean for me to get sent off every week. As life went on, I would reflect on that. 'Mr Ferguson, who threw the first punch?' Invariably, me. But that's how I was brought up. My old man used to say to me, 'Hit them first, son, get the first one in.' When I was younger, that was my mantra: throw the first punch. Mum always said to Dad, 'Stop telling him those things, you're going to get him in trouble.' And sometimes I did get into trouble because it's always the last man standing, not the man lying on the floor, who gets done. My dad was old school, he could handle himself and got stuck in first. That's what I lived by. Whenever I felt threatened I threw the first punch. Be a doer, give them a reducer, hit first and ask questions after.

And now this wee skaghead, Stewart, was mouthing off in my face. The guard alongside, whom I got to know quite well, made it plain the boy was fair game if I chose to chin him. The guard looked straight at me, stood to one side and turned away very deliberately.

Do it, Dunc, put one on him.

I wasn't the only one thinking I should belt him one as a small crowd congregated around the pool table. But the consequences – possibly six more months in Barlinnie, I calculated – outweighed the benefits. So I walked away. Nice and slowly. How things might have been different had I walked away more often.

Stewart was a remand prisoner and a total gobshite. He grassed people up, so before he came in he shot a big hole in his leg to get himself into the hospital wing. He didn't want to end up in A Hall, the worst hall, with all the gangsters and drug dealers, that's for sure. They'd have sliced him into tiny strips.

I can make light of it now but there was no doubt in my mind at the time: had I not stood up to Stewart and faced him down, the consequences could have been more grim than the mere questioning of my manhood, which is what he did. Any display of weakness in those circumstances and you can become a potential victim.

Another time, I had problems from a different fella. We had a small television in the hospital unit. It was Saturday and we were watching *Grandstand*. Suddenly, a guy called Jake got up, walked over to the TV and said, 'We're not watching the football again, Ferguson.'

Casually, he switched channels to a programme about farming. But it could have been Stephen Hawking on cosmology or fucking *Columbo* or *Miss Marple*. My blood was up, my heart pounding. I knew he wasn't taking the piss. He was trying to be the hard case, the bully. And so everyone's eyes were locked on me.

'Ferguson, we're not watching the football.'

I stood up, walked over to the TV and turned to face everyone, Jake included. 'Who in here wants to watch the football?'

To a man they said, 'Aye, I want to watch the football.' All bar Jake.

I switched channels back to *Grandstand* and looked directly at him. 'We're watching the football, boy. That's the fucking end of it. The football's staying on. Do you have a problem with that?' He never answered me back.

He saw my eyes fixed on his, no compromise in any bone in my body. No weakness. Jake swallowed it.

And that was the moment for me. You just couldn't betray any weakness inside Barlinnie. Being weak could get you slaughtered.

THE BARLINNIE LETTERS

I didn't take a step back. Jake could have been carrying something too, a knife maybe, a razor perhaps. He was a slasher and, had he smelt blood, he'd have gone for the jugular, a boy like him. They all had Mars bars in that room, every last one of them bar me. I sat back down and we watched the football. And no one else tried it on with me inside Barlinnie.

The actor Eric Cullen, Wee Burney out of *Rab C. Nesbitt*, spent fifteen days in Barlinnie pending appeal, not long before my own spell. Cullen characterised his experience as an 'indescribable hell' even though he was said to have received special treatment, being confined to a cell in the hospital wing. In his case, this was probably a sensible move by the prison authorities. But it was perceived as Cullen's celebrity saving him from something more punishing, so that wasn't repeated. Partly for that reason, there was nothing I was to be spared from.

D Hall houses prisoners with mental health issues, not quite so ill that they could be sectioned but not a million miles off, some of them. My job in the hospital wing brought me into contact with guys who were clearly struggling and in some cases highly volatile and dangerous. But the job came with considerable perks. You had use of the shower and food was brought to your work station. So from that point on, I ate my meals there.

Part of my job was to serve the hospital inmates their meals. There was one, a paedophile who murdered a wee lassie having subjected her brutally to serial rape. I'm a father now to three kids, Evie, Ross and Cameron, and the thought of what he did and how he seemed to be comfortable with it, utterly unrepentant and unashamed, chills me to my marrow. I was as shocked, sick and maddened by it then as I am thirty years later when reflecting on my proximity to this despicable man. In my eyes, he's not a man at all. I felt justified and even good about spitting in his food before I served it to him. I kicked and banged on his door too, frustrated at not being able to inflict more suitable retribution. There were other paedophiles and murderers, but he stood out for me as an embodiment of evil. Hell will come for him with a vengeance one day, that I firmly believe.

Many in Barlinnie lived with the possibility of daily attack motivated by the nature of their crimes, sex offenders mostly. A former policeman convicted of fraud, I recall, was under protection too.

Then there were those under close observation, considered suicide risks. One such boy had been a youth team player at Rangers. It was sad. He'd been released, as happens in football, and his life degenerated from there. Hard drugs entered his life in a serious way from the time that football no longer played a part. He tried to hang himself more than once. Deep welts in his neck bore angry evidence of those unsuccessful attempts. His whole demeanour spoke of a fragile young man whose confidence was shot, whose direction and sense of purpose had deserted him. Genuinely, I felt sorry for the boy.

When the guards asked me to go and talk to him I didn't hesitate. I'm not a trained Samaritan, mind, so I'm not sure what I said to him would be considered textbook material – in fact, I'm quite sure it wouldn't – but, hopefully, I was able to help the boy a little. I'd sit in his cell and listen. What can you say when all a man talks about is drugs? The night before, he'd tried to hang himself.

It's easy to fall on tough times. Sometimes it's impossible to see a way back. I've often wondered what happened to the boy when he got out. I had family who loved me and I was returning to them and to friends I could rely on and a football club that stood by me. Sadly, he was a lost soul.

I worked along with a wee boy called Craig and one or two others keeping the hospital wing clean and tidy. Craig was in for arson. The way he told it he'd just been robbing a shed, that was all, nicking some golf clubs, some golf balls. Before he knew it he'd lit a match and the shed went up in smoke. And next to the shed was a house. And so on. But Craig was all right. I got on with him.

For my job I washed the cells down, too. If someone was sick, slashed themselves or got slashed by others, it was down to me to clean up the mess. The blood, the puke, the piss, the shit, the lot. I got to being quite handy with a mop.

I didn't get particularly close to anyone in Barlinnie. A heightened state of wariness works against building close relationships inside but I was friendly with all the guards. To me, the guards were good people doing their job and my sister was a prison warder in Stirling. They knew I wasn't a threat. I'd talk football with them, as I did with everybody. One guard from Coatbridge on the hospital wing took out his guitar and we started up a wee session, singing Irish songs. Yes, Irish songs. He was a Celtic fan, a funny guy actually, and so there I was with a prison officer in uniform strumming his guitar, singing Irish songs. Him Celtic, me Rangers. And I'm singing along with him and we have a group around us all doing the same. At moments like that I briefly forgot where I was. It was brilliant.

I didn't see it as us and them with the guards. I'd always say 'Excuse me, sir' if I wanted their attention. I was polite to them always. I didn't see them as the enemy. Other inmates would have done because that was their life. It wasn't my life. If a prisoner attacked a guard and I was there, I'd stick up for the guard. I'd certainly stand in the guard's corner against prisoners if I had to. No hesitation. I'm just glad I never had to intervene in those circumstances.

The forty-four days I was there felt like forty-four weeks, those first few days in particular and the last few days as well. Time passes slowly in prison. It's true what they say. I tried to keep myself busy but I was sitting around a lot and the truth is it's hell. Pure hell.

I made it my business to get to the gym, and the guards allowed me to do training sessions on my own. They were happy to keep me away from the other inmates as much as possible as they didn't want anything to happen to me. That wouldn't have been in their interests.

But once the other boys found out that I was going to the gym, separate from the main PE activities available to everyone, they wanted to go to the gym too. The guards had to hold firm.

In my cell I'd do press-ups and sit-ups. Because I was due to go straight back to Everton from prison, maintaining a degree of sharpness and fitness was something I wanted to achieve and this gave me a goal. It helped kill time, too. Everton never fined me and I was fighting fit when I came out. People were going in the Priory, spending tens of thousands of pounds and not coming out in as good shape as I did from Barlinnie.

Tick tock, tick tock. God almighty, you've never seen the hands of a clock move so slow. I thought about the pigeons I kept back home, and how I released them to fly free and they'd return. I never called home. Phone calls weren't really my thing.

What got me through the long, lonely nights in Barlinnie was that I must have received 10,000 letters. Incredible. I killed time reading them all. Fans wishing me well and, yes, some expressing rather different sentiments. Yes, some urged me to rot in prison. Most lifted my spirits. A young boy called Wayne Rooney wrote. He must have been only nine or ten. I wrote him back, without a clue who this passionate football fan would turn out to become. (Apparently Wayne still has the letter today.) The letters kept me going, they really did. It was incredible to be thought of by people.

Some sent me books – books about pigeons, books about football, books about breaking out of prison. They sent me a blow-up sex doll, which got confiscated. Honestly. Women sent me pictures that left absolutely nothing to the imagination.

Guys from Northern Ireland wrote, from the Maze prison, loyalist prisoners, friends of Rangers players, telling me that 'if anybody touches you in there, Big 'Un, we'll sort them out'.

It's always nice to have friends, even friends you never knew you had, or people you might never socialise with in normal life. The word was sent out about me and maybe that's why I never had too many incidents inside Barlinnie. The guards began to monitor my mail, and withheld some, but they told me that Michael Stone, a notorious figure even by the standards of the Northern Ireland Troubles, had written to me. Stone was locked up for lobbing grenades and firing pistol shots into the crowd at the funerals of three IRA men shot by the SAS in Gibraltar.

'Have you any idea who's writing to you?' they asked.

'No, I don't.'

'All the notorious UVF.' Those letters raised quite a few eyebrows, not least mine when they told me. These lads who were writing wanting to protect me. They considered me some kind of emblem of Rangers and Protestant loyalism. In my mind I was never that kind of figure at all. I supported Rangers as a kid and played for them, but I cannae sing 'The Sash'. I don't know the words. I was never sectarian in my thoughts. Never.

The letters I treasured most were from Evertonians like Wayne. They were all from the heart. An open letter I wrote in response remains as true today as it did thirty years ago in capturing my feelings for the fans of Everton Football Club as well as some of my feelings generally at that time. It's very important to me so I'll give it to you in full here.

> I have been overwhelmed by the fantastic support I have received from Everton fans everywhere. I can tell you that it has helped to keep my spirits up through this most difficult period in my life. The amount of mail I have received and

continue to receive is enormous. I spend a tremendous amount of time reading your letters. Obviously, I am limited on the number of replies I can send out at the moment. But my family have been collecting the letters and taking them away for safe-keeping.

I'm going to reply personally to every supporter who has taken the time and trouble to write to me. Those messages have been coming in by the sackful and it is going to be a major job dealing with them. But it is something I want to do.

I kept a big box of the letters, and the Everton secretary Sue Palmer went through them all. I was determined to reply to these fans, as I continued in my open letter:

I feel it is very important to tell people just how much those messages have helped to lift my spirits. I would also like to thank the club for being so supportive. To be honest, I really didn't realise just how much I would miss Everton and the fans. I have been made to feel very much at home on Merseyside since I moved down from Scotland.

Many friends have been wanting to show their support in a personal way by coming to Barlinnie. But in truth, it's really not the kind of place that I want to see people. For the time being, I'm just happy to receive those letters which keep me in touch with Merseyside. I was pleased to see my manager Joe Royle, Club Chairman Peter Johnson and Director Clifford Finch recently. They were able to pass on some messages from my team-mates as well as bring me up to date with everything that is happening at the club.

Looking back now, I still can't believe the top brass of Everton came to see me at Barlinnie. It was really nice of them, brave as

THE BARLINNIE LETTERS

well. They came into the waiting room at Barlinnie, and it's like fucking Beirut in there. It's a total war zone – people bringing drugs, and misery and menace in the air.

'It's like a scene out of the Wild West,' Joe said. 'But you'll be used to that, Dunc,' he added with a wink. Typical Joe.

Still, it must have been unsettling for them. 'Fucking hell, Dunc, you're in with all these?' Yes. Welcome to hell. Joe, the chairman and Clifford Finch were the only people who came to Barlinnie, them and my solicitor Blair Morgan and my best pal George. George blagged his way in as a solicitor. Gave me a Mars bar! (Not a scar, a real one.) I was made up. But they were the only five people who visited me. I didn't want people to see me in those circumstances.

Having that support from the high-ups at Everton and the fans meant the world. Knowing that one of their most important players was in the nick, they were concerned about my welfare and how I was bearing up psychologically.

Mind you, when it was time for Joe, Peter and Clifford to go they didn't linger, they hurried away. Not even visitors felt safe in Barlinnie. But before leaving, all three reassured me that the club would stick by me and that my team-mates, fans and everyone at Everton were all thinking of me.

In my open letter to Evertonians, I made sure I sent a message that was I thinking of them, too:

In my own way, I have been trying to keep in touch. I've got a radio and I wait anxiously to hear our results.

I was actually able to tune into the Feyenoord game in Holland [on 2 November, European Cup Winners' Cup second round, second leg; Everton lost 1–0 and went out 1–0 on aggregate]. The lads played well and I was disappointed for them and our travelling supporters that we didn't get the result we deserved. I would have given anything to have been out there helping the lads.

I didn't realise just how much I would miss football. Obviously, I have no special privileges up here, but I am trying to keep as fit as I possibly can under the circumstances. I am able to exercise for up to an hour a day and I put as much into it as is possible.

I have been keen to express my thoughts to the thousands of people on Merseyside and elsewhere in the country who have been urging me to keep my head up. I can assure you I am doing just that. I owe it to the Evertonians who are right behind me.

Can I once again thank you all for your continued support. I can't wait to pull on that blue shirt again and repay everybody the only way I know how . . . on the football field.

I felt better having written that letter.*

The night before my release on 23 November, I tapped on the pipe and pushed along a rolled-up piece of newspaper to Danny in the cell next to mine. He'd been all right with me and so I put the money I'd been paid from my job in the hospital wing – £9 a week – into the package of contraband.

The package included a small amount of hash which an inmate had dropped in a cup of coffee I was about to pour for myself a few days previously, with one of the guards stood there

---

* Even today, thirty years later, from time to time I'll visit an Everton supporter in their home and they'll say to me, 'I've still got that letter.' And that means a lot. As for Michael Stone – and for obvious reasons I wouldn't wish him to take any offence – I don't believe I responded to his letter.

watching me. I removed the hash very quickly out of the cup and stuck it in my pocket. I poured my coffee as if nothing had happened. And all the while I was hoping to God the guard hadn't seen. I was left with this small amount of hash and I thought Danny should be the beneficiary. I told him there was a big box containing confectionery, batteries, fags, tobacco and a Walkman stereo that I was leaving under my bed and he should make sure to collect it from my cell in the morning. He thought it was Christmas, the lad. Me? I was just relieved to get rid of the hash.

My suit and possessions were brought to my cell and I was processed that night so that I'd be able to make a sharp getaway before dawn. This, I would learn, was customary practice for any high-profile inmate. That's when I robbed my prison shirt. I must be one of the few inmates from Barlinnie to have a souvenir. I still have it. Everton sent a driver and a limo, a classic burgundy Daimler, to take me back to Merseyside. It had tinted windows and black curtains to prevent photographers from capturing images of me as I departed through the gates and it was parked inside the prison overnight.

By the time the driver picked me up, four Everton fans who'd set off on their journey from Liverpool at 2 a.m. were at the gates: Alan Hawkins, Ken Wright, Lee Mulholland and his dad, Tony Mulholland. 'He should never have been in there,' they told the media pack assembled at the gates. 'He should have got community service like Eric Cantona, shouldn't he?'* I saw those Evertonians and I really wanted to go over to shake their hands

---

* Earlier that year, on 25 January, at an away match against Crystal Palace, Cantona had kicked and punched Palace fan Matthew Simmons who was shouting at him after the Frenchman had been sent off. After appeal he was ordered to do 120 days of community service, which he spent teaching kids football at Manchester United's training ground.

and thank them for trekking all that way to be there. But the priority for me was to escape the media melee. Some photographers gave chase at high speed on motorbikes as I was driven away and we didn't shake them off until just after Penrith when I told the driver to hang a left to take us off the M6 at the Shap summit. It was a dark and misty morning, lending an eerie intensity to the journey, but it was a happy day, an emotional one for me.

Big Joe Royle was asked that afternoon at Goodison about my whereabouts but he refused to say, so it was reported I was 'in hiding'. Incredibly, I managed to make my way to the training ground at Bellefield the next morning entirely unnoticed. That would be unthinkable today given the 24/7 news cycle and social media. Inside Bellefield, I had a full English cooked by the kitchen staff and it was beautiful.

After breakfast I stepped outside to breathe in the fresh air and I stood there in peace and quiet, in the comfort of my own clothes. There was a clear blue sky above the green grass of Bellefield – the grass and the mud of Bellefield to be precise, but still a heaven after Barlinnie. I can see it and feel it now if I close my eyes. One of the most peaceful moments of my life. It was the freedom of space, a very special feeling.

Six weeks of hell I'd endured. Slashings and Mars bars, slopping out and shit and piss and blood and cleaning it all up and the violence and the paedophiles and the murderers and the dangers that were ever present. And me a Premiership footballer. Was prison really the only option for me? And Stewart, that gobshite. God knows how but I'd managed to survive it all. Now I was home again. I was free again.

I really didn't expect the welcome I got. I saw the *Echo* front page – 'Hero's Return'. Ten thousand turned up for Everton's reserve game against Newcastle United at Goodison on 7 December. My God, this Everton family, I love them. Some wore

'Duncan Is Innocent' T-shirts. I had to repay them, starting then, with two goals – only a reserves game but it mattered hugely to show my gratitude for their support. And they were decent strikes in a 5–0 win.

I couldn't believe how many came to that reserves game. Everton even laid on pipers for me! Music to my ears, but the sweetest music was the sound of the fans singing my name. The night was freezing cold, but it was a night of warmth. I felt loved. Everton fans loved me and I loved them. That's all that mattered. And I was free.

2

THE TARGETMAN TARGETED

Let's rewind a bit. Not all the way back to the beginning. Not yet. (We'll get to my childhood and my career in football soon enough.) But back to my late teens and early twenties. Because to understand why I ended up in Barlinnie, you have to understand some of my 'troubles' growing up. I won't glorify it, I'm not proud of it. I was young and daft.

At the time I regarded these 'troubles' as misdemeanours really. Normal split lips and black eyes blown out of all proportion because I was a young footballer. But looking back now, I have to accept all responsibility for my actions. I was a stupid, daft laddie at the time. Sometimes you really can't put an old head on young shoulders. And yes, this juvenile behaviour was the basis of a 'reputation' that undeniably played a part in my sentencing to prison. Rightly or wrongly. Despite the deep sense of injustice I still feel to this day about being banged up.

So let's go back to when I was just nineteen. I'd only recently made my professional football debut for Dundee United's first team, a few months before. I was young, I was healthy, I was living the proverbial dream of doing what I'd always wanted to do. I was still spending quite a lot of time where I grew up in Stirling, just an hour away from the football club where I played. I was getting to be a bit of a face about town now. I was earning a few quid, I was enjoying myself. I was also an easy target for jealous, pissed-up people.

It all began with these boys from Fallin, a village just east of Stirling. They'd come up to Bannockburn School, where I had attended, and to nightclubs in Stirling. They would often stand outside just looking to pick fights. One evening, I was walking down the road from my house to go to the local pub, the Anchor, and a wee disco they had in the room above the bar. The lads from Fallin were in there. Wisely, I didn't stay long. But walking back up the road, two of the Fallin boys followed me, shouting, 'There's fucking Ferguson.'

I was a wee bit drunk and I was thinking, 'What am I going to do here?' I started walking away from them, away from my house. But they followed me. They got closer so I started doing a wee jog.

'Come on, lads, just leave it out,' I shouted back to them.

I wasn't scared, I was six foot four now,* I was a professional athlete. I just wanted to go home. By starting to jog I was really trying to separate the two of them. My strategy was I'd fight them one at a time, not both together. So I was edging away and they were starting to jog too, and sure enough, one of them was getting a bit further ahead of the other.

'I don't want any trouble, lads,' I shouted again.

One of the lads was now 30 to 40 yards behind his pal, so I made my move. I turned and waited, and hit the closest one – bang, he was down.

His slowcoach mate finally caught up and picked up his friend, before scampering off.

I headed home. But I knew I'd see them again.

A couple of weekends later, late one night, I was in the taxi rank at Stirling train station, which was packed with people going

---

* We'll get to my height later on. I was a late bloomer when it came to my size.

home after a night on the town. The Fallin lads were there while I was queuing for a cab. And this time, they had some more friends. There were five of them, all mouthing off and singing, 'Who the fuck does he think he is?'

During my teens I drifted through a lot of things because I was quiet, almost shy, but, like now, when somebody pushes a button and gives it to me, the alarm bells start going off in my head.

One of the Fallin boys came closer to me, jumped into my face, and I felt intimidated. I hit him. His friends piled on me. We wrestled across cars, heads down, fists flailing. I hit anything that was moving. Unfortunately and unknown to me, the police were now on the scene and were getting in my way. I didn't know who I was fighting, and unintentionally headbutted one policeman and kicked another in the balls. We were all scrapping and rolling around and gradually working our way down the street, like a chaotic rugby scrum. We ended up 50 yards from where the fight first broke out – me and six policemen trying to hold me down. The guys from Fallin who caused the trouble in the first place also got lifted. The police eventually got control and bundled me into the back of a Black Maria.

It was only then, once everything had calmed down, that I noticed there was blood on the face of one of the policemen. He had a chipped tooth. I knew one of his sisters. I was mortified. I knew it was serious.

'I'm really sorry, I didn't mean that,' I said.

I was told by the officers that I was going to Stirling police station. There was no discussion, and seemingly no issue with me having hit the Fallin lads. The problem was all about me having headbutted a policeman – and I didn't even realise then that I had.

Eventually, the police were fine with me, and stuck up for me in court. I was fined £100 for headbutting the policeman and £25 for a breach of the peace. If it happened today, you'd probably get six months in jail, and quite right too. But in my defence back then, I was provoked.

Me and that bloody Stirling taxi rank kept costing me. On 22 August 1992, trouble found me there again. The day at Tannadice hadn't panned out too well as I got sent off for my only time as a Dundee United player. It was a red card I didn't believe I deserved for supposedly headbutting the St Johnstone defender John Inglis. There was no contact, none at all, and Jim McLean, my manager, defended me to the hilt. Inglis made a meal of it.

I was seeing a girl at the time, it was her eighteenth birthday and that evening, even though I wasn't in the best of moods after the game, we'd gone out for a bite to eat. Drink was consumed as well and – guess what? – we were stood at the taxi rank when this lad started gobbing about my red card in the game and slaughtering my girlfriend with abuse as well. He called her a 'slut' and a 'slapper'. I recognised him, and I recognised trouble incoming. Two months before, this guy had confronted me in a local pub. He'd come up and initially asked for an autograph.

'Yes, no problem,' I'd said.

'Ah don't be stupid, I don't want a fucking autograph off you.'

'Oh, you're a funny fucker.'

'Yes, man, what are you going to do?' he'd said.

'Get yourself outside and we'll sort it,' I said. He wasn't too keen.

He'd run around all his mates, shouting, 'Let's go!' None of his mates would go outside. They knew what I'd do. So his bottle went. He swallowed it.

Two months later I was in that bloody taxi rank and you know what's coming. Now he was coming over with his mates and he was shouting the odds, getting closer, slaughtering me and calling her for everything.

'Your girlfriend's a fucking slut, Ferguson.'

'What did you call her?'

'A slut.'

The guy was on crutches. He tried to hit me with his crutch. Naturally, the way it was reported the next day was that I had set upon a disabled person. No mention was made that this so-called disabled person had started wielding his crutch. I was caught in a position where I either had to do something or get my head lopped off. I defended myself and her honour. He came at me so I flattened him. Bang. Right hand. I flattened his mate as well. There was CCTV, the police saw me, and it looked like I was beating the guy up. He was the aggressor, of course. In court he held his hands up and acknowledged he had set out to 'insult, goad and provoke' me and that he had also referred to my girlfriend as a 'trollop'. No self-respecting man in those circumstances could simply turn the other cheek. The fine this time was £200. That bloody taxi rank in Stirling was burning a serious hole in my pocket.

Seven months later, I found myself scrapping again. I'd just played for Scotland against Germany on 24 March 1993, and I felt on top of the world – on top of the then world champions actually.* Karl-Heinz Rummenigge, Bayern Munich's vice-president, was watching me at Ibrox that night as they were considering bidding for me.

We got beat 1–0 but it was an unbelievable atmosphere. I had a great game if I say so myself, I felt I'd arrived, and three days later I was still celebrating. Somebody had the bright idea to go to the Rock Bar in the middle of Menzieshill in Dundee. It's an old boozer in the middle of an estate that's rough as anything. It's not The Ivy. The Rock was the kind of establishment you frequent only when it's not your first or second drink of the day.

---

* We'll get to the game later. And the greatest overhead kick that never was . . .

THE TARGETMAN TARGETED

Years later, some guy on the internet posted about his experience in the Rock: 'Went in to see if it was as bad as we thought it would be. It was. Never, ever again.' He wasn't wrong. But back then I'd already had a couple. 'I'm up for it,' I said. Because, you know, I was young.

We ended up in there all day and I started talking to some bird, the only bird in there, apart from some little old grannies. I was buying them all drinks. This wee blonde was getting better-looking as the night (actually the day) went on. I didn't notice but the Rock got busier and busier because everybody knew me, and I was in their estate now, and I'd just beaten up the world champions for Scotland. I didn't know this bird was married. Suddenly, the door slams and I hear 'Ferguson, Ferguson'. As I turn towards the voice, this boy's just come down at me, bang, landing a punch right on my nose. I've got no bone in my nose, no cartilage, so he burst my nose. Blood pumped out everywhere. As I hit the ground, I quickly took a knee and uncoiled, leaping up and returning fire, defending myself as anyone would. Four or five of his mates waded in and the fight continued out on the street. That's when I think I broke my toe. I'd had a few drinks and never felt it. This lad was angry I was chatting up his wife – who's now his ex-wife by the way.

She followed me as I walked into town. I was covered in blood, and she tagged along as I went to the Ascott Bar. I was in some nightclub when the booze wore off and I collapsed. I was on the stage, and God almighty, I don't know what happened. My Dundee United team-mate Darren Jackson and all the boys were there, all laughing at me.

I could hold my drink, I was always the last man standing, that was the problem. Anyway, I was dancing around, and my teammates ended up taking me to hospital for my first real injury. The lads enjoyed pushing me around the corridors in a wheelchair.

Sadly, the big toe on my left foot is still bent to this day. I don't think I was ever quite the same again as a player. I still believe some of my many injury problems stemmed from that broken toe. It never set right. That was stupidity from me, that was me at the Rock. It even sounds tough, doesn't it? The Rock. It's not there now, they've knocked it down. My fight in the Rock certainly ended Bayern Munich's interest in me. Too injured for them.

All of these scraps culminated in an infamous incident in Anstruther, a quiet and pretty fishing village on the Fife coast where I'd gone for a Young Player of the Year event which was run by the East Neuk Dundee United Supporters' Club. I was twenty-one, away from home living in digs and, like a big, daft softie, I was too easily led astray.

The guy who organised the event was a massive Dundee United fan and, with some of the players at the club such as Eddie Conville who was my best pal up there at the time, we decided to sample the delights of Anstruther. I'd been presented with a silver tankard as the Supporters' Club Young Player of the Season and I was subsequently stepping into bars asking the barmaids to fill it up for me.

We ended up in the Royal Hotel. I was at the bar getting the drinks in, having a chat with the girl serving me, paying for the drinks as always. As I turned round I could see a lad called Frank, who was with us, in a confrontation with another boy at the counter. Absolutely strangling him, he was. What had happened was that a group of boys had been giving us grief because I was being linked with a move to Rangers.

'When's fucking Big Dunc going to Rangers?'

I went in to separate them. 'Leave it out, Frank,' I said. 'I'm here for a night out. I don't want trouble.'

As I split them up, I noticed this big guy at the bar sitting on a stool. 'I'll show you trouble.'

THE TARGETMAN TARGETED

'Look, we don't want any trouble,' I said. I'll never forget saying that to this very day: 'We don't want any trouble.'

But this big fella said, 'Well, I'll fucking give you—'

He never got the word out of his mouth. As he made to get up from his stool, I sensed what was coming and didn't wait. Boom. The fella slid off his stool and all hell broke loose in the bar. It was like the Wild West. I didn't know at the time but this lad had two brothers in there and they waded in. They were local fishermen, tough men. It all kicked off, tables getting knocked over, chairs flying around – it was a big melee.

Eventually I got us outside on the street but I realised my mates Frank and Eddie were still in there. The doors were locked. I put my foot through the window to get back in; the window shattered, and I hit the chairs in front of me. Crazy, what I'd done. I shouted at Eddie and Frank: 'Let's get the fuck out of here!' Retreat was the only sensible option, believe me. We managed to get out.

Nursing our wounds, we made our way back to Frank's house. At 4 a.m., the police banged on the door.

'Is Duncan Ferguson here?' asked one of the officers.

I was there all right. Laid out on the sofa, rotten, stinking drunk, buck naked aside from a pink hat someone had given me earlier that was still on my head. I had lipstick on, an earring and a silk glove. And nothing else. It was a strange night. At some point I'd got into fancy dress. I still don't know when. Or why, come to think of it. I also had the Supporters' Club Young Player of the Season tankard by my side, a little battered from the brawl.

Frank showed them in. The police took one look at me and said, 'We'll come back later.' Which they did.

The people in the bar phoned the papers right away, making a few quid out of it.

At Cupar Sheriff Court I was asked by Sheriff Charles Smith to write down how much I was drinking a week. A lot. He advised me to attend alcohol counselling. I didn't. I was also placed on probation for a year.

'I have considered very seriously a prison sentence in this matter. But I have discovered I can deal with the matter other than imposing a custodial sentence,' the sheriff said. 'There is the option of a fine. You are well paid. But it seems to me that might give the impression that you can pay or buy your way out of trouble. That will not do.

'You must get into no further trouble and give details of any change of address or your job. You will get counselling that will help you to grow up. This kind of behaviour is not expected from someone in your position. It is difficult to be a role model but there are young people who perhaps hero worship you. You are not giving them that image.'

By the time of this court appearance I was already a Rangers player, Britain's most expensive footballer, and this was a chastening experience. That was my last offence off the pitch. My defence counsel, John Baird, emphasised it was a very difficult time for me. I'd been taken to the very brink and been considerably frightened as a result of my actions. It was true. Things had got out of control. 'What this young man really wants is to put these matters behind him,' Baird said. 'He only wants to make news on the back pages of the newspapers, not the front pages.' The judge put me on probation.

What I look back on now is the anguish and stress I must have put my mum and dad through during these police incidents, the charges, the assaults. I regret what I put them through. I now know as a parent how worrying it is when the phone goes late at night. Recently I told them, 'Look, what happened, I must have put you through hell.'

'Well, you did, didn't you?' my dad said. 'If the phone was ringing or when the door was knocking, we didn't know who it was going to be or who was going to be there. Would it be the police again?"

I'm sickened now by the thought of how much grief I gave my parents; I'm not proud of those two, three years of my life. All those incidents accumulated and were on my record, so by twenty-one I had a significant and ominous rap sheet. I resolved at the time not to get myself on the wrong side of the law again after those shenanigans in Anstruther. Some people might not have fancied my chances of staying out of trouble. But no one, me most of all, would have thought my ultimate downfall would be an incident on a football pitch.

3

IFS AND BUTTS

I'll take you back to what really happened on 16 April 1994, against Raith Rovers. I've never opened up properly on this before.

And here's the rub. Nobody knows this, not even the Rovers defender John McStay. But I had a motive with McStay.

Over a year before the incident, when I was twenty and still at Dundee United, I went to a Scottish FA Young Player of the Year awards dinner in Glasgow. I was invited by the late, great Walter Smith, the legendary Rangers manager, and my agent at the time, Dennis Roach, because Walter was tapping me up to go to Rangers. As well as Walter and his assistant manager Archie Knox, there were other officials and bigwigs from Rangers and Glasgow at the table. Among these was a well-known Glasgow businessman, James Mortimer, pulling on a big cigar. He looked like Al Capone.

It was early in the evening when I remember going over to the bar. I wasn't drinking, as I had the car.

'Dunc, get me half a lager,' James shouted over to me.

'OK, James,' I shouted back. I turned to the barman. 'Excuse me, half a lager and a fresh orange juice, please.'

As I said this, two fellas at the end of the bar looked at me.

'Oh, it's James now, is it?' one of them said sarcastically. I'm almost sure it was John McStay.

I was only young but I was fearless. And I was sober and could hear every word. I put my orange juice down, went towards them and challenged them. The one lad said, 'It's all right, Dunc, he's drunk.'

'OK, no problem.' I let the moment pass and headed back to my table. But that jibe stayed with me. He'd mouthed off at me. I never forgot. I'm 99 per cent sure one of them was John McStay. But to this day, I'm not completely sure.

Looking back on it now, maybe if that incident hadn't been in the back of my mind I'd never have confronted McStay on the pitch in April 1994, on the spur of the moment, in the manner I did. Maybe Barlinnie would never have happened had I cleared it up and established the truth of that night long ago. 'John, was it you at the bar that night in Glasgow? Because our clash at Ibrox probably only happened because of those two fellas who were drunk and said something real sarky about me being on first-name terms with James Mortimer. I may be wrong if it wasn't you. Enlighten me . . .'

But we'll never know; 16 April 1994 happened. I had been at Rangers nine months by that point after my move from Dundee United. As we'll explore later in the book, I hadn't had a prolific start at the club. When that home game came round I hadn't scored in a match for Rangers for 700 minutes. I was getting restless to end the drought, and I'm sure the manager and the fans were too. Raith Rovers would eventually get relegated that season and we dominated them that game. But with the awards do encounter still fresh in my mind, I was fired up against McStay. And the clash came.

All it amounted to, really, was a wee bit of a tussle for the ball just after half an hour's play. There were arms out, mine and McStay's, we were grabbing at each other, and then he squared up and moved towards me. I reciprocated and put my head into his face. I lunged at him, yes, and connected, yes, but there was no force in it. His teeth weren't rattled, he had no black eyes, no swelling or claret visible beyond a nick on his upper lip. It wasn't a headbutt. I just lowered my head towards his. That was all. I never went forward with any power. Let's be honest, if I had gone forward with any power McStay would have got caught a bad one. Maybe McStay would say differently. He went down holding his face, and why wouldn't he? There was contact, minimal contact. Referee Kenny Clark took no action. If he had done, there's a possibility I'd never have gone through this. Me not getting a yellow card was unquestionably a major contributing factor to how events spiralled out of control. The fact I was allowed to stay on the pitch helped stoke the controversy and the outrage – as well as the calls for retribution.

That afternoon I finally managed to break my duck for Rangers and scored in the second half in a 4–0 win. McStay played on too. Afterwards I don't believe that he went out of his way to say I'd butted him. In fact, I have a lot of sympathy for the position in which he found himself. He simply tried to defend himself from accusations of having taken a dive or having gone down like a sack of spuds, which he didn't do.

The press grabbed him after the game. 'You're a cheat. Rangers people are saying you fucking dived.'

McStay went, 'I never dived. Ferguson connected with me.'

That was it then – boom. All the headlines were 'Ferguson headbutted me'. The boy didn't want to say anything, but the press pushed, got the headline and got me done. McStay didn't want to charge me. McStay didn't want to go up in court. He got railroaded into that. He didn't make a formal complaint to the police either. I doubt it even crossed his mind. He just didn't want his team-mates and people in the game to think that he'd cheated.

IFS AND BUTTS

I was raging with the press. Bear in mind there were 42,545 witnesses in the stands and 200 police, and nobody complained. Normally with an assault it goes the other way, there's a complaint and there's witnesses. With mine, it came from the top down. They stitched me up. In Glasgow, I'm convinced the press had a campaign to push this as far as they could. There was an appetite for that headline. Because I had a few assaults against me at a young age, and because I was a big name up there, having gone for a record transfer to Rangers, it was a big story. Everyone knew I was on probation. Everyone knew my next brush with the law would mean me going inside. The attitude was, 'Fuck him, put him in Barlinnie, the big fella, who does he think he is? Been in a few assaults, running a bit wild.' There was an appetite to get me banged up. I'm sure of it.

About a week after the game I was told by Rangers that the police wanted to question me about an assault, and this came as a complete shock. The Procurator Fiscal in Glasgow, the esteemed Sheriff Andrew Normand – essentially the public prosecutor – must have seen the headlines, watched the incident, and thought this famous footballer has broken his probation, I could put him in prison here. Normand sent police to Kilmarnock, where Raith played the following week. He wanted to get McStay to testify that I, as the court would hear, 'did lunge at him, seize hold of his clothing, butt him on the head and knock him to the ground, to his injury'.

Quite why Sheriff Andrew Normand deemed an incident on a football pitch, which did not even register a caution on the day, to be a matter to be pursued judicially remains a mystery. Let's be frank, as Zinedine Zidane made clear years later after he put the head on the Italy defender Marco Materazzi in the 2006 World Cup final in full view of a global TV audience of almost a billion people, 'Things happen on the football pitch. It's happened to me many times.' Zidane never received a criminal charge.

Media hysteria played a part. Maybe someone with a grudge as well as an appreciation of the shaky ground on which I stood lobbied for the Procurator Fiscal's intervention. Whatever the cause or motivation, Normand acted with a great deal of zeal.

I have no doubt that the Scottish FA played the part of judge and jury when they swiftly issued me with a twelve-game ban. Compounding their error, they found me guilty on the strength of a report by referee supervisor Mike Delaney, despite referee Kenny Clark not having issued a card over the incident. It was wrong and also deeply prejudicial. The SFA said the ban would not come into effect until after the judicial system passed sentence. For me, that was premature and prejudicial. I've never forgiven the SFA. A whole year went by before we went to trial at Glasgow Sheriff Court, by which time I was an Everton player. I was just a young man.

What the justice system didn't take into account, or even understand, is that we were engaged in an activity on the pitch at Ibrox which is inherently physical. Physicality and aggression are embedded in our national game. Look, I'm not proud of the incident with John McStay. But football's rough and it's tough and it has inglorious moments.

Craig Levein once floored his own Hearts team-mate, Graeme Hogg, during a pre-season 'friendly' against Raith Rovers. And the footage of four players being sent off in a Junior Cup final between Glenafton and Largs for exchanging punches and headbutts – along with the Levein incident – formed part of my defence. It was shown by my lawyers when the trial finally got under way before Sheriff Sandy Eccles in Glasgow Sheriff Court on 9 May 1995.

This didn't do much good, however, with Sheriff Eccles ruling both examples irrelevant because they 'took place in play and immediately from continuing play, unlike the present case'. His

IFS AND BUTTS

view was that play had stopped when Kenny Clark awarded a foul against me, so the encounter with McStay could not be considered accidental but was a deliberate action with intent to hurt.

Several of McStay's team-mates at Raith Rovers stated under oath that it was a clear headbutt. This was wrong. I didn't like it. I hadn't asked any of my Rangers team-mates to stand in the dock to say it clearly wasn't. I know Ally McCoist for one would have said precisely that because that's what he believes to this day. In fact, McStay himself was deeply uncomfortable, insisting under oath that what took place was 'just a clash of heads'. Thank you! Case closed, surely. It was accidental. 'We were going to square up to each other,' McStay said, 'and we just clashed.' I felt very positive about the outcome after that. If only McStay had stuck to his story and stayed strong in the dock. He came under pressure to say it was a headbutt. He buckled.

Then Sheriff Eccles reminded McStay about the dangers of prevarication. 'Do you know what prevarication is?' asked the sheriff before helpfully explaining, 'It is avoiding an answer in court. It is a contempt of court and is a serious offence. Bear that in mind.' Sheriff Eccles also reminded McStay about the consequences of perjury. The Procurator Fiscal Depute, Alasdair Youngson, read from McStay's statement to the police when he was originally questioned.

'The game was fairly uneventful until midway through the first half,' McStay had said. 'At this point I got involved in a tussle for the ball with Duncan Ferguson of Rangers. There was a pull on me by Duncan Ferguson and then a bit of arm-wrestling and tussling. I heard the referee blow the whistle and realised he had decided to stop the game. A small gap emerged between Duncan Ferguson and me. Before I could do anything further Duncan Ferguson, who by this time was in front of me, suddenly lunged at me and headbutted me on the mouth.

'He never said anything as he butted me. I fell to the ground clutching my head. The blow was a fair old blow and I felt severe pain in my lip. As I lay on the ground, I felt my mouth and saw it was bleeding. I was completely shocked by what Duncan Ferguson did.'

Youngson then asked: 'Were you describing to that police officer an accident or a deliberate action?'

'I have already said – a clash,' McStay responded.

'What is your evidence today?' Youngson enquired.

'We clashed on the field,' said McStay.

He was shown footage of the incident and asked to describe what he saw.

'A game of football,' he said, 'a tussle for the ball and a clash of heads.'

Asked if he now considered it accidental, he added: 'I don't know if it was accidental. It's hard to say. Contact was made.' I felt for McStay. He was under pressure. His testimony was hardly the most incriminating ever heard in court from a victim.

One of the linesmen was very odd. Christ, he was funny when he gave his evidence. They played the footage and asked him if he could see the headbutt. 'No, I cannae,' he said. Finally, with his nose only a few centimetres from the TV after he was asked to take a closer look, he acknowledged reluctantly, 'Maybe it does look like there's contact.'

My own testimony brought some laughter around the courtroom too, when the Procurator Fiscal Depute asked if I considered myself to be famous for heading the ball.

'I consider myself to be famous,' I replied, 'but not for heading the ball.' I then described what happened. 'There had been a tangle for the football. Then the two of us squared up to each other, eyeballed each other. I stepped forward and I clashed with Mr McStay. Mr McStay fell to the ground. I didn't strike him in the face. The referee spoke to us about tangling arms and told us to get on with the game. Neither of us got cautioned or anything.'

My defence counsel, John Baird, argued that it was artificial to suggest that a break in the game represented a complete suspension of matters in the sporting context, and the criminal law then applied. Me and McStay were both fired up. We're competitive. It's our job. 'Violent conduct in the context of sport can't be justified as a criminal assault,' Baird declared. 'Of course players get aggressive. They are supposed to be aggressive. It is a contact sport played at a professional level and it would be nonsense to say that seizing hold of a player's shirt or lunging at another player constitutes an assault.'

Sheriff Eccles disagreed and determined that the action was 'not accidental but deliberate'. He acknowledged the incident needed to be viewed in the context of a highly charged atmosphere 'in a game which involves a considerable amount of body contact and aggression'. But it had happened, he ruled, after play had stopped 'and the accused in his evidence admitted play had ceased'. For Sheriff Eccles, this was the point at which the criminal law applied and I was a guilty man. I was to be 'imprisoned in the public interest'. He told me, 'This is not the first time you have been convicted of an incidence of violence and I am taking into account your previous convictions. Such behaviour cannot be tolerated.'

I was stunned.

Just days later, on 20 May, I played in the FA Cup final for Everton. As I walked out of Wembley afterwards, a couple of Scottish journalists asked if they could have a few words. I had two in particular. 'Fuck you,' I said, and walked on. I felt animosity towards the press because they'd fuelled the appetite to send me to Barlinnie. They'd pushed McStay to say it was a headbutt. I celebrated with Everton and then returned to Glasgow for sentencing on 25 May. Three months. I couldn't believe it.

I was fed up. 'I'll do it now – let's do the sentence right now,' I told my barrister, Donald Findlay QC.

'You cannot do that,' Findlay replied. 'This is an injustice, Duncan. It is barbaric what they've done to you.'

'Look, it's summer, I'll get it done, I'll be out in six or seven weeks.'

'You cannae, you've got to go to appeal.'

So, advised by Findlay, I appealed.

For the appeal on 11 October, John Mitchell QC took up my case because Findlay wasn't able to act for me. It was held before Lord Hope, the Lord Justice General of Scotland, who presided alongside Lord Allanbridge and Lord Osborne. I wasn't appealing the conviction, just the sentence. My QC appealed to the court to consider the option of a community service order: 'This young man has prospects of being a very successful and responsible member of his profession. The destructive effect of a custodial sentence would be difficult to overstate.'

I could hear the young judge, Lord Hope, saying to Allanbridge and Osborne, 'He's not done community service. He's only a young man.' I was sitting at the front of the bench. I heard his words. 'He's got a career. Do we have to put him in prison?'

'He broke probation,' one of them said.

I looked at Lord Hope and prayed that he lived up to his name. He seemed the only fair one there. He looked like he felt it was a travesty, but it was the law. I was asked whether I understood community service. I felt Lord Hope was pushing the other two to say, 'Come on, let's give him community service.'

'He was on probation,' I could hear the two of them insisting.

Lord Hope agreed that Sheriff Eccles had overstated the case when he described my record as appalling. But the most important factor about my record, he said, was that the incident involving McStay happened while I was on probation for another assault. 'For a person who has been dealt with leniently in that way to commit an offence of the same kind while on probation is a serious matter and has to be weighed up very carefully by the court in considering whether a further non-custodial disposal would be appropriate,' Lord Hope said. 'We have reached the view that we would not be justified in interfering with the sentence. In our opinion, in all the circumstances, a sentence of three months' imprisonment which was intended to be an effective punishment and a deterrent to others cannot be described as excessive. We have no alternative in this tragic case but to refuse the appeal.'

A 'tragic case'. Lord Hope was saying he felt it was unjust. Community service is what I should have been given. I'd expected the worst because I was on probation.

'Witch-hunt', Joe Royle called it. As I was led away, I knew Joe would stand up for me. I heard his words later, and will never forget his support for me. 'We can't really believe, in a society that seems dedicated to keeping people out of prison, that we are putting away a young man who is in a good job and is no danger to society,' Joe told the papers.

Joe knew me. Joe knew this punishment was unjust.

'Anyone who knows him will tell you he is a very pleasant young man,' Joe said. 'He is no bad lad at all. He has been guilty sometimes of stupidity, but mostly immaturity. We all see events on football pitches every week and they are a lot worse than what Duncan now finds himself imprisoned with hardened criminals for.'

And so I was taken off to prison, seething at how wrong it was, denied my freedom for forty-four nightmarish days.

*

As the years have gone on, many people, including the press, have softened to what happened to me and have been more in my favour. 'Actually, you know what, it's a bit of an injustice, that,' someone from the media told me nearly a decade later. It's never happened again, a footballer going to jail for an incident on the pitch. And you know why? Because they changed the rules, didn't they? And rightly so.

Many years later, I bumped into James Mortimer at Gleneagles with Alex McLeish – 'Big Eck', the Scottish manager who would also steer Rangers to much success. I said to Mortimer, 'Do you know why I went to prison?'

'No.'

'Because of you.'

'What do you mean, because of me?!'

'Because this boy McStay mouthed off at me in the bar when I bought you that drink.'

Mortimer was in total shock.

The clash follows me to this day. I still have to get a visa to go to America because of Barlinnie. But McStay's been the innocent guy in all this. I gather he had a hard time of it for years after our 'clash', getting called a grass. John, if you read this, I want you to know you're not a grass. I know you were pushed into it. If you've suffered because of the incident, I'm sorry. Very soon McStay wasn't playing the game at a high level any more. He retreated from the game altogether, it seemed, which is a shame. I've never spoken to him since that day. I suppose we're forever linked by the events of 16 April 1994.

4

THE END OF THE AFFAIR

After emerging from Barlinnie at the end of November 1995, I returned to competitive football on 11 December, at Goodison Park, back where I belonged. I came on after an hour against West Ham and was almost stopped in my tracks by the wave of emotion that swamped me, embraced me, overwhelmed me. Everton fans were amazing, just as they had been four days earlier at that reserves game. When I regained my composure, I found myself attacking a goal defended by Julian Dicks, not at left-back as usual. I was fighting fit, having been in the Barlinnie Spa. Dicks was in goal because Ludek Miklosko had been sent off. He still saved a header from me.

Although I was back, I still had to fight the Scottish FA, which on 13 May 1994 had so undermined my case by presumptuously imposing that twelve-game ban and continuing to push for it. Rather than rally round and support a young player during the most challenging time in his life, the SFA twisted the knife. I wanted nothing more to do with the SFA. Nothing. I was bitter.

My appeal against the ban was heard while I was still in prison, on 8 November 1995. Donald Findlay QC, back in my corner, went to town on the supposed custodians of Scottish football. They should have waited. 'The SFA were advised from a number of sources of the position this young man found himself in and they declined to consider a postponement of this matter until a future date,' Findlay said. 'I think they were wrong. I think they have acted unfairly and contrary to the player's wider interest, remembering the fact that he is an accused person.'

The SFA rejected my appeal against the ban, meaning that eleven of the twelve games would have to be served after I was released from Barlinnie (I'd sat out one game as a Rangers player before the ban was put on hold pending the court hearing). In my mind, it was vindictive. It should have been backdated to my entry to Barlinnie. I was unavailable for selection for eight games while incarcerated. Because of the SFA, I was punished twice for the same offence. Where was the justice in that? 'You have to say he has suffered enough,' Peter Johnson told the SFA tribunal. 'Having visited Barlinnie for two hours, six weeks in there is quite a sentence.'

Ultimately, at the Court of Session in Edinburgh, Lord Prosser ruled that a judicial review into the twelve-match ban should take place. The remaining seven matches of the ban were then wiped out on 19 January 1996 by Lord Macfadyen, acknowledged as the most respected judge in Scotland. Macfadyen determined that the SFA had acted outside of their powers.

Everton were taking on Arsenal in the Premiership the very next day, and I was free to play. I had won my case against the SFA. I never served that ban.

5

REMEMBERING BANNOCKBURN

Let's go back further in time. The fight for freedom has always been in my life. Bannockburn was the backdrop to my youth. William Wallace and Robert the Bruce, towering figures in Scottish history, are celebrated in monuments on the 1314 battlefield that dominated the landscape where I was born and grew up. I heard and read all the stories of the heroic deeds of Wallace and Robert and their fight for freedom. As children, we learned of the Wars of Scottish Independence, the Battle of Stirling Bridge and the Battle of Bannockburn while the old men recited the poem by Robbie Burns:

> *Scots, who have with Wallace bled;*
> *Scots, whom Bruce has often led;*
> *Welcome to your gory bed;*
> *Or to victory . . . Lay the proud usurpers low;*
> *Tyrants fall in every foe;*
> *Liberty is in every blow, Let us do or die!*

Burns' last line always stayed with me: 'Let us do or die!' Powerful words that struck a chord. There was always a bit of a battle going on in my life.

My dad, also Duncan, sacrificed everything in his own life to make a better life for his family – my mother Iris, my sisters Iris and Audrey, and me. Dad came from St Ninians, a suburb of Stirling, and my mum from the Raploch, which was renowned as one of the worst areas in Scotland. My mum met my dad at a nightclub, dancing. Dad was working on lorries that tarred the roads at the time, and Mum, a really sweet, gentle woman and a hard worker herself, was a cleaner at one of the local schools. She refused to give up her job when I went to Rangers. We lived in the tenements to start with, in a two-bedroom flat on Graystale Road in St Ninians. Me and my two sisters shared one bedroom and Mum and Dad the other. There were about eight flats in each block. Our flat was 27c and we had all the amenities of a built-up area – nothing grand, mind – and then acres of countryside to go and run around in. Cow fields, farmland, woodland. It was a wee boy's dream. Out in the open air, playing with the other kids, not a care in the world, a really safe environment. There was no one getting robbed, no fighting, and we never had any trouble. We were jumping over hay bales, running around – the fancy term now is 'sports science'.

My closest mates growing up were Callum and David. We got up to all kinds of mischief, mostly harmless. Mostly. Callum, who was in my class, lived on a farm. We used to mess around there, when we were only kids, five, six or seven; we weren't running riot then. One day, me and Callum were watching the sheep, and one was jumping on another trying to hump it. I had no idea what they were doing.

'What's going on here?' I laughed. 'Look at this! Look at this!'

'Well, look at this!' a voice behind us said.

I turned round and saw that one of the other lads around us had lit a bale in the barn. All the time back then we collected wood and built bonfires, but not inside. This day, this lad decided to set light to some hay. Boom! The wind caught hold of the fire and it ripped through the hayshed, destroying it. It went up in seconds, like *The Towering Inferno*. I bolted, off across the fields, getting away from it. I panicked and never went back for hours. I heard the fire engine sirens racing to the barn. The barn was next door to a farmhouse, which was just about saved. The blaze and smoke could be seen for miles.

Our tenement backed on to the farmer's field and my dad saw the smoke, jumped over the fence and sprinted towards the barn. 'Where's the kids?' he was shouting. He got a terrible fright and, of course, I got a terrible telling off when I eventually returned home five hours later, shame-faced. I was petrified. And the farmer, he got a new barn. A metal one. When I go back, the barn is still there. I still look at where the tenements were. I think of the journey I've been on, becoming the British transfer record breaker. I wonder when a Scottish player will break the British transfer record next.

There was no real trouble when we were kids. The one time the police came to our flat in the tenements was when my friend Darren got hit by a car as we ran across the road carrying home some chestnuts. Darren dropped some of his as we crossed near a junction, hesitated to pick them up and couldn't get out of the way of a car. Darren got a good whack and rolled down the road 20, 30 feet, but he was that shocked when he got up that he started to run away. The driver got out of his car, caught up with Darren and said, 'You need to be careful, lad, and you need to come with me to the police station.' We were only six, seven, maybe eight years old, two frightened little boys. Very sensibly, the man was making sure that Darren was all right. The police took both of us home to the tenements. All the neighbours were looking out as I arrived back and was taken out of the police car by the policeman. Back then, we were frightened of the police.

When the police left, my dad looked me hard in the eye, not a trace of sympathy, and said, 'I never want to see a police car come to this door again.' He knew I'd done nothing wrong but he was making a point. If only I'd listened to my dad.

The tenements eventually came down, and we moved into a council estate called McLean Court, the new-builds, which was nice. I got a wee room on my own, Audrey and Iris shared. We had a wee garden. We lived on a cul-de-sac colloquially known as Legoland because of the shape of the houses. Nearby was a grass pitch packed with kids kicking a ball about. To begin with, loads of us would all be on the grass playing 'Wembley', a one-goal, free-for-all game, and I loved it. I'd play in the street until it was dark or until my mum shouted me in. I'd get a 'piece and jam', essentially a jam sandwich, or if I was really lucky I'd get some of that yellow stuff, lemon curd, and then I'd run back out and play on. I'd carry on playing until Mum shouted me in again, this time for my tea. Nobody on our estate really ate properly. I certainly can't remember sitting down to big meals, it was usually just a piece and jam and a bit more for tea.

Ours was a warm, loving upbringing in a close-knit, working-class community where that deep sense of pride in our roots and heritage was firmly embedded. It was safe and secure.

Directly behind my first school, Borestone Primary, stood the Robert the Bruce monument at the site of Bannockburn battlefield. In the distance were more fields and hills. It was natural to imagine myself in heroic circumstances, getting involved in wee mock battles. Our imaginations ran wild. We used to run to school through the blocks of flats, building up our stamina without even knowing it. As kids, we ran around all the time. Everywhere.

When we moved to Legoland, Borestone was 3 or 4 miles away, so I went to another primary school, Braehead.

I was shy as a kid. I was never a big mixer or talker. I'm still not. I never had many friends, still don't. I still see myself as shy. Nobody really knows me.

REMEMBERING BANNOCKBURN

In more recent years, when I was working in the academy at Everton, I looked at the kids and thought how different they were from me, and my upbringing. Kids are more educated now. I was running about the estate, doing daft things. As I said earlier, we'd spend our time searching around for cigarette packets, opening them up in the hope there was a fag still in them. Refuelling for me was the odd bottle of cider – Woodpecker for a nicker. Although it continued into my teens, it began as early as aged ten, eleven, twelve: I'd occasionally be asking the older boys to go into the shops to buy me the booze. Cider – filthy stuff, horrible, made me ill, but it was a rite of passage. I've never drunk it since.

Eventually, when I was thirteen, Dad moved us into a bigger house he bought, still in St Ninians. It's still our family home. Back then, as now, the Bannockburn Visitor Centre was situated only 100 yards away and Dad often looked out the window at all the tourists arriving in cars or on buses. He would smile at us and say, 'These people haven't come to look at artefacts going back to Robert the Bruce or William Wallace or seven-hundred-year-old wars and battlefields, Christ, no – they've come to see the Fergusons!' And we'd always laugh.

As I got older and became known as a footballer, Dad's joke actually came true. A decade later tourists knew where we lived because of Dad's car. I remember one particular day well – Saturday, 25 February 1995. Everton were playing Manchester United and it was Mum and Dad's wedding anniversary. I got a present for them, a blue Granada Scorpio: black interior, automatic, fantastic, the bollocks. But we needed a good plate. We heard that FERG1E was up for auction. I had to have it. The story was, or so we were led to believe, that it was Sarah Ferguson's number plate, right? We were told that Sarah Ferguson sold it before she married into the Royal Family. Maybe the royals didn't encourage them for security reasons. Or they were just a bit too flash. So me and one of my friends, George, went into his office in Liverpool, he got on the phone and bid for FERG1E. We got it for £12,000 – a lot of money, cost more than the car.

So on the Saturday morning I parked the car up, got Mum and Dad, and said, 'I've got something to show you.' They came down and saw the car, a beautiful thing, with the FERG1E number plate. 'Just so the people know where to go when they come to the Visitor Centre,' I added to Dad, and winked. 'Happy anniversary.' We went to the game, we beat Man United 1–0, I got the goal, took my shirt off and whirled it round, and afterwards we all went into Mathew Street in Liverpool to celebrate at a lovely Italian restaurant. It was all of us having a big party. It was a great day.

My mum and dad have still got the FERG1E number plate, just on a different car, a BMW, and it still sits in front of the same house.

For my dad in those times to have worked his way up on oil rigs, to later do jobs including tiling bathrooms, and to have saved the money to secure that kind of property, all the while raising three young kids, took some doing. Dad also grafted so we could afford holidays – nothing fancy but always good family time. We stayed in a caravan in Arbroath and Nairn or at Haggerston Castle holiday park, Berwick-upon-Tweed, if we were lucky. Never abroad – we never had that sort of money. Berwick was good, no problem, just playing cards, as normal kids did back then, playing, and of course running around.

I ran all the time – round the tenements, round the estate, through the woods. I ran in the Boys' Brigade, and I ran at Bannockburn School: I was school champion for 800m and for 1500m, I was the cross-country champion, and I finished seventh in my only county race. Every other little bugger took shortcuts and cheated. When I was at school, at lunchtime, the moment I heard the bell I was off like a shot, running the couple of miles home, and Mum would make me a nice wee bit of lunch if she was there. Then I'd run back. When I later went to play for Dundee United, I'd be at the front in the cross-country training at sixteen. I had a good engine and was thin, really thin. I basically lived on a piece and jam for my first sixteen years. Mum and Dad would go crazy, I never ate anything else.

I boxed a wee bit when I was thirteen, sparred down at Bannockburn Boxing Club. I was addicted to the training but the coaches threw us right in the ring back then, getting a bit of fresh meat in there! The first guy they put me in against was quite good. He had all the gear, gum shields and shorts, and I beat him up. The coaches went, 'Oh, we like him.'

A week later I got put with a better boy, who'd been doing more training. You know those old, heavy leather gloves? I got thumbed in the eye and that was it, enough for me.

'I better stick to football,' I thought.

The world I grew up in pushed me down the road to being a footballer. I worked hard. I delivered newspapers. I picked potatoes for a few quid. I washed dishes at the Hollybank Inn. I delivered milk. I was up at dawn, getting the milk, whatever the weather, even when it was freezing cold. My dad stopped me doing it in the end, to keep me fit and fresh for football.

I look at the lives of young kids today, with their Xboxes and smartphones and Facebook and Snapchat. Sadly, if I'd had an Xbox then, I probably wouldn't have played football. I played on the streets, played against older kids on the concrete, and it toughened me up. Kids nowadays have lost that aggression. They're not getting chased as much by the police! Some kids can't even cross the road now because their parents don't let them on the streets as they might get stabbed. I ran free. I was always outside.

I wanted to be a professional footballer from a young age because I loved the game. I remember watching World Cups on TV, as far back as 1978 – about the only TV I watched. Scotland were in Argentina and everybody in the flats was glued to the games. Mostly I was in the streets, practising with the ball against a wall under the street-lights. I could hear the noise and the atmosphere in people's homes as wee Archie Gemmill scored his goal against Holland and I said to myself that I wanted to get to that level. I wanted to play for Scotland.

Raploch was the area of Stirling that Billy Bremner hailed from, a legend of football and very supportive of me when I began to make my way in the game. A few other players came from that Raploch estate. John McLaughlin, Everton. David Goodwillie, Scotland briefly. All good players. I was determined to be the best I could. I always had that belief.

Football runs in the family. My mum's brother was Big Willy Cunningham, goalkeeper for Dundee with the biggest hands you could ever imagine. Craig Brown knew him. He told me, 'See, Dunc, I used to play with your uncle, Big Willy Cunningham.' Craig stood up for Willy because he was deaf and wouldn't let anyone take the piss out of him.

Every kid in our area played because we had nothing else, really. I was called 'Wee Dunc' then before I grew in my teens and I was getting lumps kicked out of me, but I wasn't bothered. The fifteen-year-old lads are like men when you're five, six, seven, eight, but I took the knocks and the tumbles, and the graft I put into it helped me develop. I practised by myself, heading the ball against the wall and doing keepy-uppies to improve my touch. I had a good touch because I developed it playing on concrete and red ash too – hard surfaces. In my opinion, academy players today play on surfaces that are too good, too early on. We played on different surfaces and this helped develop a better touch in a young footballer. For me, my game was never coached. On the streets, you play instinctively and you play anywhere. You can't tell what position a kid will flourish in until he develops.

I was a goalkeeper at first because when you're young you can't play out against the big boys. I got stuck in goal at four, five, six and got balls smashed at me. Eventually, the next wee guy came along to get balls smashed at him, and I went out. My first organised football was in the Boys' Brigade and then the school team before I progressed to a local team to play Saturdays and Sundays.

I was nine years old undergoing a trial for Cowie Colts Under-12s and one of the coaches asked in the dressing room, 'Who here's a left-back? We need a left-back.' I was so keen that my hand went up immediately even though I didn't know what a left-back was or what role he had in the team. And so I began as a left-back, before moving into positions higher up the left-hand side and finally into the centre-forward spot.

Almost always stood on the sidelines was my dad. He drove me to games and fuelled my dream with his endless encouragement. He filled me with an unbreakable conviction that I'd make it as a professional footballer. Let us do or die!

6

CHASING MY GOALS

'Football record. 1982–83. Cowie Colts. Age 10, Age 11. Leading goalscorer. Duncan Ferguson.'

In my dad's neatest handwriting in a little blue hardback notebook, with various versions of what looks like my autograph scrawled across the front cover, are some of the bare facts from my early years in organised football and other sports. Gold medals that year for the school seven-a-side team and in penalty kicks, as well as gold in the 400m at the County Sports Championship. A silver medal in the School Cross-Country in 1983, with that seventh-place finish in the County Sports Cross-Country recorded too. Out of a field of 120 – not bad, given how many took shortcuts. Gold medals also for darts and table tennis in youth club tournaments – I was a good table tennis player – and the Players' Player and Leading Goalscorer trophies in 1984 for ICI Caley. I'd hope so too, as that season I scored more than a hundred goals. Then for my next team Carse Thistle, in 1984–85, another Leading Goalscorer trophy. Only seventy-eight goals that season, mind. Medals for table tennis and swimming. Training with Hearts and Dundee United, and I was asked by Hibernian to go for trials. In the East Fife League I played for Central Boys and there were enquiries from Rangers and Manchester United.

And all the while my dad was writing it down in that little notebook, which gave way to an A4-sized notebook as the years

CHASING MY GOALS

went on. All in neat tables, with ruled lines and perfect handwriting. County Cup, 1985. Carse v. Forth Valley, 3–1, 'Dunc 3 goals'. BP Boys' Club in the Scottish Central Boys' FA Knockout Cup final, 6–2, 'Dunc one goal, Higgie one goal, Smith three goals'. The back page of the *Stirling Observer* carried the headline 'Carse Sweep the Board' accompanied by a photo of the proud winners. That night we were also presented with the League Championship Shield. Winning was in my blood.

In the Challenge Cup, Carse beat my old team, ICI Caley, 9–0 – 'Dunc two goals . . . and Boney'. Alex Bone was a talented striker who went on to play for St Mirren, Stirling Albion and Ayr United and was once banned for five games by the Scottish FA for receiving three red cards. In the same game. And people think I was a hothead! When we won the Under-14 Scottish Cup in Edinburgh, Boney was in that team, as a forward.

I almost didn't play in the final. I missed the bus from Stirling. I walked down the Bannockburn Road to the roundabout at St Ninians Toll where we usually got picked up. We used to think we were all gangsters, YST, Young St Ninians Toll, standing on the St Ninians roundabout, the chip shop across the road, waiting for the bus, striking a pose as if we were from our favourite film, *The Warriors*. As I walked down, I saw the bus leaving. 'I'm half an hour early, what's going on?' I'd got the wrong time. I cried my eyes out – I thought I'd missed the Scottish Cup final. I ran to my nana's, she lived 50 yards from St Ninians Toll, and she got one of my uncles to drive me to Tynecastle, Hearts' ground. We battered the road all the way there and almost got done for speeding. I got into the dressing room at Tynecastle and the boys were all changed. But I played and we won.

My dad noted down every game of Carse's league-winning season in 1984–85. The day we beat Rancel 15–0. 'Dunc five goals.' Raploch 12–0. 'Dunc six goals.' In the whole of the 1984–85 season with Carse, I scored forty goals in fourteen league games. The records are there for every other competition we played in, too. The Scottish Cup, Matheson Cup, Steven Rae Cup, County Cup. A dad's devotion to his lad, eh? No wonder the Carse Thistle manager, Dick Taylor, once said, 'Duncan always wanted to be a footballer. He was a good trainer. And his dad was more interested than a lot of the other dads. He was very keen on his son's career.' My dad had stopped drinking by then and my football gave him a focus. He said to me it was a good distraction.

No matter about all the coaching, practice makes the player. For me, that meant playing three games on a weekend: Boys' Brigade followed by Cowie Colts (and later ICI Caley and Carse Thistle) every Sunday, having played for the school on Saturday. On full-size pitches. Now young players don't play eleven-against-eleven until they're fourteen, but we were thrown in at the deep end. I was a late developer and a lot of people in football didn't fancy me, which was incredible looking back at my record. I wasn't quick, I wasn't particularly strong, and it was only as the years went by that I grew bigger and filled out. That time I was touted to go to Rangers when they made their enquiries, I wasn't considered big enough. Ironic, isn't it? And that was the only reason. Back then I really was Wee Dunc. Big Dunc was my dad.

It was the same, too, with Scotland Schoolboys. I owe a lot to my PE teacher at Bannockburn, Mr Halcrow, a good guy and a big supporter of mine. Mr Halcrow was on the Scottish Schoolboys selection panel, and on 6 November 1987 we went down to the Inverclyde National Sports Training Centre at Largs for trials. I got through to the last twenty-eight but was then overlooked. Politics seemed rife at every level of the game in Scotland even then. We always felt it was more difficult to be selected against the Glasgow clubs. There seemed to be a bias against us. Halcrow, and a scout for Dundee United who had also worked for Celtic, Graham Livingstone, fought my corner tooth and nail and got me back in. On 19 December I was informed I'd been selected for Scotland Under-16s Schoolboys, the first ever to come out of Bannockburn High School.

Not that I was spending much time there. 'Football's everything to me,' I'd say to my mum because I wasn't going in to Bannockburn High very often. I wanted Mum to understand that I had the belief in myself about what I was going to do. I was going to make her proud and I was going to make it in football.

I trained with Hearts and other clubs too, which is how players got signed, but the local scout only recommended his favourite players from his own grassroots team. The boys who were running Carse Thistle were Ian Mason and Dick Taylor. Mason was a scout for Hearts and he'd signed all the Under-13s on registration forms, known as 'S forms', except me. All of us were told there was Hearts training but I wasn't sure when it would start. Me and my dad were driving along Bannockburn Road one day, and Ian was walking along. My dad stopped the car and went over to Ian.

'What's happening with the training at Hearts?'

'Oh, I forgot to tell you, we started two weeks ago.'

Ian deemed me not good enough to be signed on S forms for Hearts or I would have been at Hearts. So we got a cob-on, fell out with Ian, and didn't go to Hearts even when they showed interest.

When the Carse Thistle lads went to Hearts, the manager Alex MacDonald asked, 'Where's the laddie Ferguson?'

The coaches said, 'Oh we never signed him.'

Alex phoned the house and spoke to my dad. 'What's going on, Dunc? We want your lad here at Hearts.'

'No, Ian Mason never told him when the training was, doesn't rate him, so we've gone to Dundee United.' And we had – Dundee

United training at Stirling University. And the players that went to Hearts all got released.

I played for Carse Thistle in a tournament in Edinburgh, and Graham Livingstone was there, scouting for Dundee United, and he spotted me.

Livingstone supported me a lot and he really rated me. He was the one who got me in to Dundee United really. Graham was the one who pushed me. George Skelton, a scout, probably got me originally but I played for Hamilton Thistle boys and Graham ran that team and that was a feeder club to Dundee United.

The scouts there were Skelton and Kenny Cameron, a coach at Dundee United and a striker with the club back in the day. I trained with Dundee United for two years, every other Thursday night, on the red ash university pitches at Stirling University. No one ever said I'd be kept on. None of the scouts. Nobody.

They didn't fancy me, right? That's what I thought. I was sure I was getting released from Dundee United. The club were preparing the scholarships, known as YTSs, for other players and I never got asked. They held a trial game, probably a last selection game, at Stirling University on a Tuesday night – winter time, freezing.

You know, I've heard and read different versions of what happened that night. So here's what really happened. Walter Smith, the great manager, came along. Walter was embedded in Dundee United back then, a club legend. He was Jim McLean's assistant and now he was coming to watch this trial.

Before kick-off Walter asked the two scouts, Skelton and Cameron, 'Who are we looking at? Who do we like to come up to Dundee United in the summer?' They named everyone bar me. I know all this because Walter told me directly years after the fact when he became my manager at Rangers. 'I spotted you right away,' Walter told me. 'You're on the left wing, thin, big baggy shirt on, you looked like a strong wind would have blown you away. You were struggling to run, big, long, gangly legs like big daddy long legs, all over the place.' But Walter could see something. 'You were trying to head it, you were aggressive and you were making good runs.'

Walter watched the first fifteen minutes and that's when he said to Skelton and Cameron, 'Who's the big skinny kid struggling to run on the left-hand side?'

And they went, 'It's the laddie Ferguson, we're releasing him tonight.'

Walter went, 'OK.' He turned his back on them and watched the remainder of the half on his own.

I was out of position, a lanky puppet at the time, but Walter knew I'd fill out and I'd be a player then. Walter had the vision because he's a football man. Fifteen minutes was all it took to convince him.

Walter told me he came back at half-time and said to Skelton and Cameron, 'I don't know what you're doing with the rest of them, that's up to yous, but see that big skinny kid? You get him signed right now.'

Walter had only seen me for a half. They had watched me for two years up there, training with them. They liked everybody else bar me. But Walter knew – yes, he knew.

I scored a good volley. After the game, my dad said, 'You had a cracker there, you had a blinder, big man, son you had a—'

'Dad,' I interrupted, 'that was Walter Smith – you know, Jim McLean's assistant?'

'Son, you were brilliant.' My dad always believed in me. All dads think their sons are the best, but he said to me, 'You will make it, you've got it, you mark my words.'

So I went into the Stirling University dressing room, and all the rugby boys were now getting ready. Steam was rising, and not just inside. When I came out, my dad was screaming at those two guys, Skelton and Cameron. The two of them were against the wall and my dad was over the top of them in his big sheepskin jacket with its furry lapel like Del Boy used to wear in *Only Fools and Horses*.

'It took a proper football man to spot him. One half of a game and he's spotted him and yous two couldn't see it. I told you from day one he's going to make it, and by the way, he's not signing for yous ever.'

Well, I was pulling my dad away, shouting, 'Dad, Dad, what are you doing?' They were sliding down the wall, getting smaller and smaller.

'Come on, son, let's go.'

And he got me in his old Princess car – big brown thing, big suede seats – and we're driving out of Stirling University and I'm crying, I'm upset. 'Dad, Dad, what's happened?'

'They've offered you a scholarship, son. They've offered you a YTS, at Dundee United. Walter's obviously spotted you, he's told them to sign you. But you're not signing. I've told you you're going to make it, we'll go somewhere else.' I was desperate to get signed.

I didn't know what to think but I trusted my dad.

Jim McLean started phoning the house, trying to convince us Tannadice was the right place for me. Walter Smith had told him all about me. He spoke to my dad. McLean was a Masonic member, my dad was too, so they started chatting and coming to an agreement, and Dad felt Dundee United was a good place for me. McLean asked me to go up to Fir Park one night to take in Dundee United Reserves against Motherwell Reserves, watch the game and have a chat. McLean's brother Tommy was Motherwell's manager and we used his office at half-time. McLean and my dad shook hands in their own secret way and were close to getting the deal done.

CHASING MY GOALS

McLean made his case once again. 'We want to sign him on a YTS, Duncan.' McLean then pulled out an envelope, handed it to my dad and put the contract on the desk. 'Sign that, there you go, that's for yous. There's £400 in that envelope, son.'

'What is that?' my dad asked, a little disdainfully. He pulled out his wallet, opened it, and there was more than £400 there. He was grafting on the rigs at this time. 'I'm not interested in that, Jim, I'm only interested in you looking after my lad. End of. We'll think about it and we'll make a decision, and after the game we'll come back down and tell you.'

Tommy's office was in use after the final whistle, so we stood in the corridor with Jim McLean. We had to sign the contract on the floor. So I took the contract from McLean, knelt down in the corridor and signed it on the floor.

'That's the best player you'll ever sign,' my dad told McLean.

'I've heard it all before from parents,' McLean replied.

'Well, I'm telling you now, you've just signed your best ever player.' I was embarrassed.

But my dad was not far wrong. Five years later I broke the British transfer record. I never got a penny for it and I never saw any of my YTS money either. Carse Thistle made a few quid. They wanted money from Dundee United before I signed. They got £5,000 eventually and a bag of balls.

With my dad away working at sea on the rigs I was bending my mum's ear: 'I don't have to go to school, Mum. I've got a YTS at Dundee United, I'm going to be a football player.' So when all my friends were heading off to Bannockburn, I spent time practising with my ball getting ready to go up to Dundee United.

Mr Halcrow called the house.

'Look, Duncan, you're in the Scottish Schoolboys, could you not come into school? That's part of the condition.'

'I know, sir, but I want to practise. I'm going to Dundee United.'

'Well, look, just come to the school, sit in the back of the class and just get on with it.'

So that's what I did, sat at the back in Geography or History, saying nothing, and in Maths the only thing I counted was the days before I went to Dundee United. I struggled at school. Arithmetic, bottom of the class. I couldn't work out the numbers. History, top. I loved it – the First World War, the trenches, I was great at that. I got three O levels and one was History. B+. I was bright but I'm not a great speller and not good with numbers. I was never in trouble at school.

I was soon in Dundee United's very good youth team with Christian Dailly, who went on to play sixty-seven times for Scotland, and Gary Bollan, who would later become my coaching assistant after my playing days. We won the youth league two years in a row but I wasn't fancied, I was always behind the rest. I developed late. In fact, I never even had a hair on my bollocks until I was seventeen, eighteen. I was bald down there, which caused me a lot of problems in school. I'd get bullied for having no pubes. I'd go into the showers at Bannockburn or Tannadice and they'd all be singing 'Baldy, Baldy'. Nowadays kids wear underpants in the showers to protect their privacy but there was no hiding place then either at school or at Tannadice.

It was horrible. I ended up fighting people because they sang 'Baldy, Baldy'. One lad in particular at Bannockburn was a smart arse, a constant irritant. I mentioned it to my dad that there was a lad mouthing off and, to be honest, he was getting to me.

'It's not like you, Dunc, to allow it to get to this stage. What's his name?' my dad asked.

'Carruthers.'

'Carruthers? I know his dad. His dad's a bum and his boy will be a bum too. Next time he opens his mouth to you, let him have it. You're getting bullied, son, and you're trying to laugh it off, but don't. Don't ever let him or anyone else get away with it.'

So the next morning I was prepared. Sure enough Carruthers was in front of me as we were walking up a set of stairs inside the school. 'All right, Baldy,' Carruthers said as he turned round. He wasn't being friendly. Out came the lazy leg to trip me up and then he tried to kick me. And that was it. I grabbed hold of his foot, dragged him down the stairs and got on top of him. I was ending it there and then, and he completely bottled it, just like any bully once you face up to them.

'Don't ever call me Baldy again.'

Some kids have loads of hair down there, like big bushes. I never had. My head was fine, just nothing downstairs, nothing, so I'd never been with a girl. I was paranoid. I kissed a few girls but I didn't want them to put their hands down my pants. Now it's all on trend isn't it? Shaving yourself and having no hair down there. Maybe I was just ahead of my time! But seriously, it was a big thing for me, it really upset me.

I guess I never had the hormones, or at least I got them late. I was paper thin, and only when I filled out and got some hairs, got stronger, boom, I went from being at the back of the sprinting group to being right at the front within months. I went from being the slowest player in the team to the quickest. Maybe Walter Smith was right all along – I was a late developer. The second year in that Dundee United youth side, bang, away I went. I scored four times against Aberdeen with the reserves.

There were some good young players coming through, not only me and Christian. Ray McKinnon and Billy McKinlay were in there. Andy McLaren, a winger, went on to a good career at Dundee United, and won a Scotland cap. Gary Bollan went on to play for Rangers. John O'Neil, a midfielder, also won a Scotland cap. I used to sit next to Kevin Gallacher in the dressing room, four or five years older, a good winger who went on to win the Premiership at Blackburn Rovers in 1995. I enjoyed their company. But then, in 1990, I came into the realm of Dundee United's manager.

7

TYRANNY AT TANNADICE

Jim McLean was a total tyrant. He ran Dundee United with an iron fist. He was chairman, manager and bully. He intimidated players, even senior players, pinned them up against the wall, shouted at them so much they cried their eyes out. He'd fine them so much money they couldn't pay their mortgages and their wives would come up to the ground and plead for the money back.

Jim McLean was not a very nice person to me and certainly to many at the club. With hindsight I know I wasn't easy to control, I made a lot of mistakes and did a lot of stupid things. Jim was right with a lot of the things he did with me, but it was wrong putting other people almost on the breadline by taking their wages. These players had families and mortgages. I didn't. I lived with my mum and dad. My dad was earning good money and I didn't care about money. I still don't. McLean could fine me as much as he wanted.

Jim was a good coach, and I could see what he was trying to do. He wanted to keep me hungry. My first YTS deal was £38 a week plus £8 for digs.

Jim's staff could be as mean as him at times. Every week we got called into the coaches' room to collect our £8 digs money.

'Do you think you've trained well this week, Ferguson?' a coach would ask.

'Yes, I trained well.'

'No, you fucking no' trained well, so you're not getting your digs money.'

I was always arguing with them. I stopped queuing for it, fuck it, so I was short of the £8 in the end. This went on every week. I ended up sleeping one night in the car park of the Stobie Bar in Dundee because I couldn't pay for my digs. I slept in a wee Ford Escort owned by Mark Perry, one of my team-mates. Mark was another victim of Dundee United's tight-fistedness. We were both in the first team and every fifteen minutes we were turning the key in the ignition to keep ourselves warm through the night. He was absolutely ruthless, wee Jim.

Wee Jim didn't pay you a lot but he gave big bonuses. When I made my debut in November 1990 and we beat Rangers I got a special £600 bonus. Fantastic! Jim cottoned on that money was a motivator but he'd also withhold the bonus at times. It didn't take long before I just felt I was getting crap wages. Shocking. In a few years' time I would be playing against world stars like Ruud Gullit, Ronald Koeman, Frank Rijkaard and Marco van Basten at Euro 92 and I would still be on buttons. But I never had anything anyway as Jim kept taking it off me. He kept fining me. He kept trying to break me.

Way before my debut, I stood up to Jim McLean.

His coaches, Skelton and Cameron, were screaming at me in training at Stirling University one day. I was fourteen, fifteen. Why the Dundee United people didn't like me was because my mum and dad had got me a Denmark shirt, the 1986 World Cup one, lovely two-tone pinstriped top, beautiful. I went out to training in it and trained well.

'Stop showing off you, Ferguson, stop showing off with your fancy shirt,' one of the coaches said.

'Who are you talking to?' I was all defensive. 'My mum and dad got me this shirt. Shut your mouth. I'm made up with this shirt.'

I was the same with wee Jim, I stuck up for myself. I went to McLean's office and banged on the door. Nobody dared do that. I did. I marched in.

'I've had enough. This is not for me, release me out my contract.'

I mean, imagine Jim McLean sitting there going, 'What the hell is this guy doing here, his veins popping out of his face?' Every young lad was desperate to be a footballer.

Things got smoothed over. For a while.

We were always in confrontation. It was my fault. I was my own worst enemy. I was never a cheeky kid. Maybe I was just a rebel and fearless. And I'd get bored with mundane stuff. In my early days at Dundee United I helped with the kit, sorted out the strips, got them cleaned and laid them out for training. The numbers were all done with black felt markers and sometimes, while waiting for the dryer to finish the job, I'd break the boredom by putting random numbers on the kit, mixing them up. So the first team would pick up their kit and no. 8 was no. 18 and so on. Of course, such daft things got back to Jim and he'd fine me a tenner at a time when I was only on £38 a week.

There was another incident, a Youth Cup game, and we were in the dressing room, and Jim was pointing at me and shouting.

'You get your finger out of my face right now!' I yelled at him.

Jim pulled his finger down, and said, 'I blame your dad. It's the way you've been brought up.'

I jumped up. 'You little fucker!' I screamed at him. I was going to down my manager. He mentioned my dad again and I flipped, I flew at him, and everybody got between us. I was going to batter Jim McLean.

I was emotional, shaking, and ran outside. My dad was in the road, waiting for me, and saw I still had my kit on.

'You had a great game, son. Hey, what's up? Tell me.'

'I've had another run-in with McLean, I've had a problem in there.'

'In what way?'

'The manager again. He's mentioned your name again, Dad.'

'What do you mean he's mentioned my name – again?'

'He did it before and I didn't want to tell you.'

'All right, son. Go up and get changed.'

'Just leave it, eh, Dad?'

My dad wouldn't leave it, would he? He waited for McLean and he was going to wipe the floor with him. I went back in and the next thing I heard was this commotion. Wee Jim came out of the stadium, and he had a couple of security guards with him, and my dad went for him. 'You wee fucker!' I heard my dad shout. 'Don't you ever mention my name.' Dad was a hard case, who was stood on the door as a bouncer at eighteen at a time when the bars in Stirling were like the Wild West. He could handle himself. My dad would have wiped the floor with him.

Paul Sturrock, a coach and club legend, said once I wasn't starting one youth game against Brechin, and my dad growled, 'He'd better play.' Sturrock didn't want to leave me out. McLean left me out. Coaches just followed his orders. He was the boss. Sturrock was a good guy and a good coach but he was another one bullied by McLean. All the staff and players were bullied by McLean. I blame them for the bad atmosphere at Dundee United because they never stood up to McLean, but I get it: they had wives, kids, houses, mortgages, and I never did. I didn't have those overheads.

Like Paul Sturrock, the other coaches Maurice Malpas, David Narey and Paul Hegarty were former Scotland internationals, all fantastic players, but they were all petrified of Jim. He'd leave them shaking in their boots. The effect was that young players walked away completely disenchanted. Even my mate John Clark, who scored in the 1987 UEFA Cup final and got told by

Jim after the game 'that wasn't fuckin' good enough, cleared out at one point to work on his father's fishing boat in the Firth of Forth before he came back.

'Everyone was treated the same,' Maurice Malpas said of Jim McLean. 'Everyone was battered with the same brush.' 'Tyrannical', 'Visionary', 'Despot', 'Tactical genius', 'Absolute bampot' – Jim had all this and more said about him over the years. If you want to get a sense of him, YouTube his name along with the name of John Barnes (no, not that John Barnes, but a BBC Scotland reporter) and the interview that plays out could be straight from WWE. Except it was real. So was Jim's fury. And so was the punch he threw at Barnes.

Even if he angered me on many occasions, deep down I had tremendous respect for Jim. His drive and determination led Dundee United to glory that is scarcely believable now: overcoming the Old Firm and an Aberdeen side managed by Alex Ferguson to win the Scottish title in 1982–83; reaching the semi-finals of the European Cup in 1984 when they lost 3–2 on aggregate to Roma only after a Roma director offered a £50,000 bribe to the referee; contesting the 1987 UEFA Cup final. Dundee United had so many great players, like David Narey, who scored that amazing goal for Scotland against Brazil at the 1982 World Cup – top player, idolised up there. They were all good guys, Big Narey, Paul Hegarty and Paul Sturrock. It's incredible, and Jim was an incredible man. Not only was compromise not part of his vocabulary, it wasn't in his nature. Jim was a Larkhall man – small but fiery.

'The game means too much to me, but unfortunately it doesn't mean as much to him,' McLean wrote in the *Daily Record* once. He had a column and just seemed to write about me. What he said was untrue. McLean was being unfair. The game means everything to me, then and now. That's why I played it my whole life, that's why I scored 126 goals in 423 games, that's why I got stuck in and was aggressive on a football pitch, that's why I've worked so hard in my coaching, that's why I'm in management now. I didn't love the game? People talk rubbish at times, don't they?

Jim and I always seemed to be fighting, but Jim was in a permanent state of war, not just with me but with the world, it felt like. That didn't mean I didn't like him. A lot of the time he was right but I wanted to stick up for myself, especially when I felt wronged. If I wasn't happy about something, I said so, instead of rolling over like a lot of the other players.

'If I sent your wages home to your house, you wouldn't even turn up for training or games,' Jim said to me.

'If you sent my wages home to my house, I don't think I'd survive the shock,' I replied.

He kept fining me. I once ended up with a weekly wage packet of minus £10. That's right, I owed the club £10. I showed everyone the wage slip. They just laughed. I got fined for daft wee things all the time, like leaving my socks lying on the dressing-room floor. Like me and a few other apprentices driving the first-team players' cars as well as Jim's up the road to the nearest car wash, when we were meant to be washing them ourselves. We didn't have a driving licence between us at the time. Then there was the time when we took a few pots of paint, put lighted matches in them and, yes, blew a vast hole in the toilets we were meant to be decorating. Damn near blasted away a whole block of Tannadice. Next thing, fire engines are coming down Tannadice Road. I could just imagine McLean going, 'What's that Ferguson done now?' And there was the day I climbed in the kit van, turned the ignition, kept the handbrake on, floored the accelerator, dumped the clutch and the black smoke from the spinning wheels engulfed Tannadice Road – just as Jim emerged in my near-side wing mirror. His arms were flailing like a drowning man as he waded through the dark clouds, coughing, spluttering, apoplectic with rage, his big red face with veins sticking out – I'd see that face many times – trying to damn me to hell, but he couldn't get the words out. McLean never did see the funny side of that. And I got another fine.

One time he fined me for turning up late. In fairness, the team meeting had already started when I walked in.

'Turn up when you want, why don't you?' Jim said. 'Why are you late?'

'Why do you think I'm late?' I retorted. 'The crappy wee car I drive because of the crappy wages you pay me broke down up the road. Again. I wouldn't be late if I could afford to run a proper car.'

I had a clapped-out Capri, a gold one – fantastic, but it kept breaking down, the engine smoking, the radiator steaming. It kept spinning in the snow too. Anybody who's had a Capri will know, any time the roads are slidey with snow, the back end just goes. I weighed it down with bricks in the boot but it kept sliding so I eventually got rid of the Capri.

Jim challenged me. I was covered in oil from my broken-down Capri but I walked across the room to put on my training gear. Jim was massively affronted. He immediately set his feet as Mike Tyson would ahead of the first bell of a heavyweight title fight. He looked like he was ready to rumble there and then before he calmed himself. Getting a whack in the Dundee United dressing room would have been no novel thing. Players punched one another to keep themselves in line, though no one set upon me.

Dundee United had some good lads coming through at the time with me, Ray McKinnon, John Clark, Eddie Conville and Christian Dailly. Michael O'Neill was there too. A lot of the local boys ended up being released or getting sacked, but that was Jim for you. Some contributed to their own demise. We were out all the time, never resting, young lads in digs going wild, drinking, chasing girls. We'd go to midfielder Grant Johnson's flat and then on to the Tally Ho pub in Dundee on a Tuesday night – student night, karaoke night. All the boys. Great times but also crazy times. We were young, what else were we going to do? Staying in or resting never crossed our minds.

Jim was on the telephone to the landladies every night at 10 p.m. to check we were in our rooms. We'd prime our landladies before we went out. 'Tell Jim I've popped out to the chippy and I'll be back in ten minutes.' Jim would go, 'Tell him to call me back in ten minutes then.' There was no fooling Jim McLean.

He'd phone my parents' house to check on me – another of the many reasons why my dad got upset with McLean. Jim would shout down the phone at my mum and she'd be crying her eyes out. That's what McLean would do, he had no qualms shouting at women and that's one of the reasons why I didn't like him. My dad would be away on the rigs and my mum would phone him and say, 'The manager's been on the phone again and Duncan's not in the digs.' That's when my dad started going for McLean, phoning him up: 'Don't you ever phone this house again and upset my wife because I'll be up there and be seeing you.'

Jim was interested in only one thing, he would say, the success of Dundee United Football Club, and over the years he'd seen and heard and dealt with everything. Well, almost everything. The escapades of a few of us floppy-haired, pesky lads were not going to divert him much, however hard we tried.

Some of it was crazy, like police knocking on the door of my digs to question me about a hit-and-run which witnesses said my car was involved in several hours earlier. Hit-and-run? My car?

'I can assure you, officer, it can't have been my car. I've been in all evening.'

'I can assure you, Mr Ferguson, it was your car. The bump on the front would suggest as much, too.'

The bump? Then I pieced it together. A couple of the lads I

shared digs with had gone to McDonald's, taken my car, unfortunately knocked down a young lady on her bike on their way back and, in their wisdom, never said a word to anyone. It was me who ended up in the police station, but they ended up being sacked by Jim when the truth came out. Thankfully, the young lady recovered.

Another time the word went out that I was going to get shot. Yes, shot! Given that the man putting it about went by the name of 'Shotgun' Higgins, this was a threat not to be taken lightly. Shotgun headed up a small firm in Dundee. We were on a bad taste social night out in the run-up to Christmas. We were dressed up for it in the worst gear you could imagine. The mood was merry, to put it mildly. Ray McKinnon, a good-looking fella who could pull the women, must have said the wrong thing to somebody because before I realised what was going on a bar was getting wrecked. Ray, who couldn't fight his way through candyfloss, was in the thick of the melee. I waded in only to protect him. He needed protecting. We ended out in the street, where I flattened a couple of guys who'd gone after Ray and there was blood everywhere. Anyway, these guys were part of Shotgun's firm. The word went round Dundee that there was a guy hanging about Perth Road who had battered two or three of Shotgun's fellas. They knew it was a Dundee United player but they thought it was Billy Thomson, our goalkeeper. But of course it wasn't, it was another 6ft 4in player who was only a kid – me. I was a marked man for having saved my team-mate. I said I'd meet with Shotgun to sort things. Thankfully, he declined.

I didn't understand all the consequences at the time. I was a teenager, totally naive. I only started drinking seriously when I went to Dundee United. Going out after games on a Saturday was just what we did, rather than go back to our digs. Tuesday, the same.

The police were at Tannadice every other week, which must

have been sending McLean round the bend. It was wrong what I did, crazy. There were boys getting drug-tested, boys stealing money, it was all going off. At times it was surreal. One day McLean locked the stadium down. His staff were all running around going, 'Right, nobody move.' Next thing we were all rounded up – players, staff, groundsmen, office people, brickies, joiners, everybody. We were all lined up in the boardroom.

'I have you now!' Jim announced.

What in the name of God was going on? No one knew.

'There was £3 in a Tupperware box for the fridge and it's gone,' Jim continued.

It had been going on for some time, money not being put in the honesty box for bottles of Coke and Mars bars.

'I have the serial numbers,' Jim went on. 'Someone's been stealing. All of you, empty your pockets now!'

Jim had written down all the serial numbers on the notes before putting them on the fridge. A sting operation! You couldn't make it up! He ordered everyone to strip down to their underpants. He went first.

'Just to show you that I've not got them,' Jim said as he stripped down to his wee white Ys. He stood there with his big hairy chest and back in the middle of the boardroom.

Young lads, senior players, we were all stripping off. Even the lads out of the local prison that Jim had over doing manual labour around Tannadice got strip-searched. That was McLean for you: he'd got the boys out of prison to come and clean up the terraces and do all the manual labouring. So they too had to strip down to their Ys to prove they had none of McLean's precious pound notes. Once everyone was stripped off, McLean's coaches went down to the dressing room to look for the notes. It wasn't me, I never lifted them. It was some of the younger lads who took the pounds, only because they needed the bus money to get home. So they were lifting up their clothes, emptying their pockets, and the pounds were dropping on the floor followed by wee bits of hash. In the end they all got caught, and one or two got released.

That was Jim McLean for you. He was a control freak and, in an era before the 1995 Bosman ruling empowered players, insisted that everyone at Dundee United sign this terrible contract system of four-plus-four. A player would sign a four-year contract after which a four-year option could be exercised, but it was a club option. So it was essentially an eight-year contract. And they could keep you on £160 a week. Who wanted that ball and chain?

I was the last guy McLean tried to make sign a four-plus-four. I wasn't budging. No way. Not when the basic wage at Dundee United was around the meagre £160-a-week mark. Established first-team players, Scotland internationals, for goodness' sake, struggled to pay the bills. No wonder some ended up in tears or fishing to catch some dinner.

'I'm not signing it, and that's the end of it,' I told McLean. So he put me in the 'bomb squad'. Jim had me labouring, trying to get me to crack. I spent months on end with a labourer called Shuggy, all the way up to Christmas one year, working down trenches and toiling around Tannadice. In rain, hail and snow, Shuggy and me in our yellow hats and high-vis overalls. Once I'd done my hard labour at Tannadice, Jim had me training on my own at five or six o'clock in the evening. Even though I was in the first team, Jim was trying to break me. He had me cleaning toilets, cutting the grass, painting the stadium and sweeping the terraces – the best job going, because if I was lucky I found a lost fiver or a tenner. I built extensions and dug holes, lots of holes, even trenches for renovations going on at Tannadice or the AstroTurf pitch they built at the training ground, Gussie Park. I was so busy with this work that I even got a hard hat initialled 'DF' on the front so no one else swiped it in between jobs. Seemed like I spent half my time at Dundee United down a hole digging, or with a brush or mop in my hands. The groundsmen, joiners and brickies, I knew some of them better than I knew my own team-mates.

One day, McLean again sent me out to do some more manual labouring. 'Paint the outside wall of the gym,' he ordered. So I put my DF hard hat on and set to work on the wall with the bucket of whitewash. It didn't take long to write JIM MCLEAN'S A CUNT. All the players and coaches were walking in and they all saw it. Not another good move by me.

'There's no point in me fighting you is there?' McLean eventually said.

'Have you just learned that?'

McLean didn't know what to do with me. He didn't understand me. The core of my nature is I want to get on with people. I've always been big-hearted. I went to Dunkeld, a big hotel, with Dundee United, and some of us were down on the riverbank fishing in the Tay. 'Do you want something to eat?' I asked the other players. They were ravenous. 'Can I get some sandwiches for the players?' I asked the coaches. I was only eighteen. They said, 'Yeah,' so I got ten steak sandwiches from the hotel. It cleaned me out, but my heart felt full. It was a lovely steak. Good pre-match meal that! I'd take some of the players to the amusement arcade. I'd go to McDonald's next door and pay for burgers and fries for them all.

Look, as I've said, I admit I made mistakes which riled McLean. I wasn't Snow White. I did daft things. One time I was out in Stirling with a mate who had this blue Mark II Escort. Fantastic car! Wish I had one now, they're a right few quid. He had all the fancy seats, the quick-shift gearbox and the loud exhaust. I worshipped the car. I had this lovely Italian suede jacket, smelling beautiful, cost a few quid – £300 – but it was immaculate. The first night I had it on we headed to this bar in Stirling, and my mate said, 'God! Your jacket!'

TYRANNY AT TANNADICE

'Yeah, nice isn't it?'

'I love that jacket, can I get it?'

'Oh, I like your car,' I told him, so we swapped.

The car was worth only £400 and I soon wrote it off. I came over the brow of a hill in Dundee and a car smacked right into the back of me. The back end nearly ended up in the back seat. I sold it to Cowdenbeath Racewell, the stock car track, for £50. I got a few quid insurance. I was ahead. You live and learn. Well, try to.

Those months I spent with Shuggy working down holes and skivvying around Tannadice ended when I said to him one day, 'See ya, Shuggy. That's it, I'm off.' It was snowing, it was miserable and I thought, 'What the hell am I doing?' I downed tools, hoisted myself out of the hole we were digging and walked away, jumped in my car and disappeared. I didn't return to Tannadice for weeks, one of many of us who did that, who walked out. Most of the boys did that in the end. Many never returned at all to Jim's boot camp.

There's nothing wrong with manual labour, but I hadn't joined Dundee United to be a labourer. Of course, I was fined on my return and that was nothing new. Jim was unforgiving, unyielding, because I wouldn't sign the contract. He wouldn't play me. It affected me with Scotland, too. I only played three times for Scotland Under-21s. I never played for Scotland Under-18s. My dad said McLean was hiding me until I signed the contract.

Then the agent Dennis Roach came on the scene. He had a big reputation having negotiated deals for Johan Cruyff, Trevor Francis, Glenn Hoddle, Mark Hughes, Tony Adams and others. Roach knew some reporters at the *Daily Record* and asked them who the next good young player in Scotland would be. I was the best up-and-coming young player coming through at this time. I'd put myself in that bracket. Dennis phoned and came up to see me. He offered my mum a couple of grand. He then said to me, 'Look, sign the four-plus-four contract with the club, don't be worrying, I'll get you out of it.' So I signed.

The contract with Dundee United was shocking. They gave me two or three grand for signing it, a shocking fee. The basic terms were £160 a week plus an additional £72 a week for making the first-team pool. On appearances of 50 per cent or more with the first team, it rose to £232 per week. The minimum first-team draw bonus was £50 and the minimum first-team win bonus £100, and of course that big win bonus if we won at the Old Firm. I didn't care. I signed the contract to get out of the club. So Jim McLean could get a fee for me. After I signed, McLean believed in me enough to hand me my full debut against the champions, Rangers, on 10 November 1990.

On the bus going down to Ibrox, I was quite calm.

'Are you all right, big man, everything fine?' our midfielder Billy McKinlay asked.

'Yes, all good, ready.'

'Good, just relax and enjoy it.'

The players knew I was coming strong, they knew I was ready to step in.

Ibrox! What a place! I replaced Christian Dailly after an hour, and ran out into this wall of sound. I couldn't shout at my teammates, there was no chance of them hearing me! I felt truly alive, almost electrified by the atmosphere. I got the ball and just dribbled by two or three players. Within eleven minutes we'd taken the lead when my flicked-on header set up Darren Jackson. Ally McCoist equalised with ten minutes remaining but we cut through along our right flank four minutes later, Alex Cleland sent in a cross, and Jackson met it just ahead of me at the far post to net the winner. It's so vivid in my memory, it could have been yesterday.

For my dad, a staunch Rangers supporter, it was his 'proudest moment', he wrote in one of the scrapbooks he kept, surpassed only in his estimation by my selection for Scotland Schoolboys. I was a big skinny kid, and my dad was sitting with the other parents at Ibrox.

'Who's this coming on?' they said.

My dad was instantly up, standing there, telling them, 'That's my laddie coming on there, you watch this.' My dad showing once again that he always believed in me.

'You are going to make it, believe me,' he told me time and again. He saw the aggression in me. I loved my debut, knowing that dad was watching.

'You should have been in that first team long ago,' Dad said. 'McLean hid you until he had you tied up in that contract. He knew you were coming.'

Dad was even more overjoyed to hear Richard Gough, the great Rangers captain and centre-half, comment that I'd turned the game.

Inevitably, wee Jim's take was different. 'Duncan tends to be lazy and doesn't like discipline,' he told a newspaper reporter. 'He is a really good finisher and his control is very good for the size of him, but he needs to do more work.' Thanks, Jim. But I'd forgotten listening to him by then. McLean certainly got the disciplinary bit right, but I don't know about the rest of it.

A fortnight later we played Aberdeen in a clash of the New Firm at Tannadice. Between them, the respective managers, wee Jim and Alex Smith, had forty years' experience, and after a 3–2 rollercoaster that went Aberdeen's way they both agreed it was the best game they'd ever been involved in. Even in defeat, Jim was satisfied. 'I'm happier with the situation at Tannadice than I've been for several seasons,' he said. 'I can now see light at the end of the tunnel.'

Yes, the light from an express train coming in the other direction. Me and Jim McLean were on a collision course. Another one.

The week after Aberdeen, Jim decided to fine me a month's wages for being ten minutes late one morning. I was livid. We had a blazing row and I told him I was quitting the club. I was injured and had gone home to stay with my parents in St Ninians. The terms of my contract contained a clause consistent with every other player contract at the club: I had to be resident in the Dundee area while employed by Dundee United. Basically the club ordered me to live within 14 miles of Tannadice. Well, I was resident in Dundee. All I'd done was drive down the road to stay the night with my parents in my own family home. I was ten minutes late on the treatment table the next morning because I overslept. Hands up, my fault. But was that worthy of being fined a month's wages? I was seething.

'You can stick your fine,' I told Jim, slamming his office door on the way out.

When it hit the newspapers, Jim appeared a lot more relaxed about it than I was. 'He has been guilty of numerous breaches of club rules,' Jim explained. 'The punishments will still be here waiting for him when he returns. He'll find out, as others have, that if he wants to play football it will only be for Dundee United. Walking out may seem the easy way, but they always come back.' I suppose the eight-year contracts took care of that.

I cooled down over ten days at home in Stirling and, as Jim predicted, I came back. The fine was reduced from a month to two weeks but I had to issue a public apology. Most of what I 'said' were Jim's words, not mine.

'I have been very stupid,' I said in the statement written by Jim for me. 'It was a crazy thing to do and I'm so sorry it has happened. The young players at Tannadice are not allowed to go home during the week. But I broke that rule by travelling to my home in Bannockburn on the Tuesday night after the Aberdeen game. I slept in the next morning and did not get to Tannadice until 9.10 a.m. when I should have been there at nine o'clock for treatment on an injury I was carrying. The boss found out and was not happy. He told me I was being fined four weeks' wages for breaking club rules and I just blew my top. I couldn't believe what had happened to me and walked out in a fury.

'Then I suddenly realised what a terrible mistake I had made. I knew immediately I was totally in the wrong and that I'd made a big mistake. There I was sitting at home after walking out on one of the top clubs in the country. I felt such a fool. I had been given a great chance in life by breaking into the United first team. All of a sudden it seemed I had thrown it all away by one reckless act. Having watched players like Alex Cleland, Brian Welsh and Christian Dailly getting into the top team and staying there, it made me more determined to get my chance. Now this rash decision has threatened to ruin my hopes.'

It went on a bit. Jim had clearly enjoyed writing my statement, and rubbing my nose in it.

'I want to be part of the set-up at Tannadice because there are exciting times ahead for Dundee United. I sincerely apologise for my actions and I just hope I can now return and fight my way back into contention. It was a crazy thing to do and I want to try to make up for it.'

As ever, Jim had the last word: 'Duncan walked out two weeks ago but he has contacted me to apologise and will be back at training tomorrow.'

Football, eh? No matter what happens, it's always about tomorrow and the next game.

My reason for bringing that incident up now is this: fining me one month's wages for being ten minutes late was disproportionate in the extreme. The punishment didn't fit the crime – a theme of my life – and, on top of all the other petty fines (some more justified than others), that's why I reacted the way I did. It was an accumulation.

I felt I'd make it regardless of Jim McLean. I had that belief in myself. I was only eighteen but confident. A bit gallus, as we say in Scotland, bold as well as brave. You have to be. Otherwise you'll never make it.

I'd played only two reserve games since recovering from an Achilles injury when, at the end of January 1991, Jim threw me into a Scottish Cup replay against East Fife – my first game with the first team since my walkout and only my second start for Dundee United. It went into extra-time at Tannadice before our Yugoslav defender Miodrag Krivokapić drove forward, picked me out with a perfect pass and I lifted the ball first-time over Ray Charles – no, not that Ray Charles – into the end known as The Shed. My first goal for Dundee United, the decisive goal in a 2–1 win.

'Duncan Ferguson was tremendous for us,' said Jim McLean. I almost fainted! All was forgiven. Well, for the time being. Jim's Jim.

My first goal in the Scottish Premier Division came a month later and was again decisive in a 1–0 win over Dunfermline. Jim was more like himself afterwards. 'Ferguson is not working hard enough,' he lamented. 'He wasn't able to do much training this week because of a groin strain but that's no excuse. He must do better.'

Dundee United were still doing well enough for Jim to slap what the tabloids called a 'not-for-sale sign' on our young talent – the likes of Christian Dailly, Ray McKinnon, John O'Neil ('Wee Del Boy' we called him) and me. One of the clubs interested in me back then was Everton. 'I know English clubs are beginning to take a look at some of our new faces,' he said, adding that the club would not consider any offers for 'the youngsters who are the key to our future'. And all are essentially on eight-year contracts, he might have added.

Even after relenting and signing that deal, I still struggled for money.

Still, I've got to be honest and admit that in many ways Dundee United was a great place for a young player to develop, provided you were a strong enough character. And I was. I was getting games and developing quickly. A 3–1 victory in a Dundee derby extended our run in the Scottish Cup, Ray McKinnon, Darren Jackson and myself on target. I headed in John O'Neil's cross. We'd been practising all week to lay the ball off and spin to the back post. McLean coached me to link up play. No doubt about it, McLean was a fantastic coach and I learned a lot from him.

But a groin injury I picked up against Aberdeen forced my withdrawal from the Scotland Under-21 squad to play Bulgaria at Rugby Park and also left me doubtful for the cup semi-final against St Johnstone on 6 April 1991. On the eve of the game at Dunfermline's East End Park, Jim ensured that, if I recovered in time, I knew what he expected of me.

He was always talking to the press about me. The man was obsessed. On he went. 'He's got a good first touch, can beat a man and is an excellent finisher. But he lacks what everyone should have in every walk of life – determination to succeed. Fear of failure still motivates me to this day. But today's youth have the wrong attitude. Duncan has a wonderful opportunity. He is exceptionally talented but he must apply himself far more.'

In calmer moments, I understood what Jim was saying. Looking back, I can see how I tested the patience of managers like him. Football was easy for me. I worked harder than anybody to get where I got to. But my worry was whether I was going to grow and fill out. Was I going to have the pace to play at the top level? Once

I knew I was a player, I never again viewed the game as difficult. Whether I retained the eye of the tiger every day for every game at that time of my career, I'm not sure. Jim may have been right.

So going into that semi-final I vowed to deliver, and thankfully I did, setting up John Clark for a goal in the first half before scoring the second in extra-time in a 2–1 win. 'Just what the boy was needing to boost his confidence,' Jim said after reaching his sixth Scottish Cup final as a manager. I was happy for Jim, although Hampden Park represented something of a hoodoo for him, Dundee United having lost on all five of those previous occasions at the national stadium. Unfortunately it became a sixth straight defeat as on 18 May we lost 4–3 after extra-time in a classic cup final to a Motherwell side managed by Jim's brother, Tommy.

The 'Family Final', as it was dubbed, ended prematurely for me at half-time when I was substituted, suffering from double vision having sustained a knock to the head. Perhaps this was just as well. At the end of the game four of our players – John Clark, Darren Jackson, Freddy van der Hoorn and Jimmy McInally – received red cards after confronting the ref in the tunnel. David Syme had failed to spot a foul on our goalkeeper for the decisive goal. Jimmy, stricken by blisters on his feet, was carrying his boots off the pitch when one of them just happened to bounce off Syme's head. For once, when trouble flared I was far removed from the action.

Our opening game of the new 1991–92 season ended the same way as our final game of the previous season, in a 4–3 defeat against Celtic at Tannadice. Packie Bonner produced a world-class save to deny John O'Neil an injury-time equaliser. 'I must say I like the look of young Duncan Ferguson,' said Billy McNeill, Celtic's European Cup-winning captain. 'He carries threat because of his presence in the area and his courage and determination will bring him and Dundee United goals.' Only Charlie Nicholas and Tommy Coyne at

Celtic and Mo Johnston and Ally McCoist at Rangers scored more goals by the end of October. The winner in a 3–2 defeat of Rangers on 29 October did me no harm in front of Walter Smith, who was not at all enamoured about the way his team let slip a 2–1 lead.

I continued to do well on the pitch for the rest of the season, and into the next one, but I always felt McLean on my back. In January 1993, Jim fined me £100 for dissent and made me train with the youth team. I complained to the Scottish Football League. My agent Dennis Roach went on TV and said that I would not be 'intimidated or bullied', that Dundee United weren't giving me enough money, and the only places I could eat were cheap fast food restaurants. I took Dundee United to an SFL tribunal over another fine, this time for two weeks' wages. The reasons for the fine were detailed to me by the club as follows:

1. Not staying in digs overnight on Wednesday 17th November [1992] as required.
2. Disobeying instructions during training session by the physiotherapist because you couldn't be bothered training (walk or jog), and
3. A more serious offence of being involved in a fight on Friday 21st November 1992 in Anstruther and subsequently being charged by the police for assault. This is not the first time that you have been charged by the police. With your latest incident you have publicly tarnished the name of the Club and embarrassed not only the Club but also the players and officials. This incident is regarded very seriously by the Board.

Now, I could argue the merits or otherwise of those specific points, which I did via the appeals process. But my appeal was never likely to go any way other than it did. I knew immediately.

A lad called Chic Charnley, a midfielder and a bit of a character, was up there before me; when his case finished, the Dundee United representative on the adjudication panel just changed sides and did the case for Dundee United against me. I was never going to get a fair hearing – story of my life.

When I addressed the tribunal, I explained, 'Look, they keep fining me. All my money, and I've got no money.'

'You must have deserved it,' they replied. Absolutely zero sympathy.

In the end I knew I had to leave. I couldn't work with Jim any longer. I know what Jim thought of me. I heard what he said. 'Duncan Ferguson didn't want to make the sacrifices necessary. He could have been a top player.' Could have been? What the hell does that even mean? What sacrifices? I scored thirty-five times in eighty-eight games for Dundee United, then got my £4 million transfer to Rangers, and I got nothing from the move but Jim made a few quid from it – £150,000 I heard. I was one of the most talented players in the country at the time, I went on to have a fantastic career, and if it hadn't been for injuries things could have been even better.

And as for Jim . . . If you speak to anybody at Dundee United they'll tell you my relationship with Jim McLean basically exhausted him. I'm not proud of that. I got his iron grip off the club because he couldn't handle me. I stood up to him. He stepped down as manager shortly after I left, probably exhausted.

Jim McLean almost never gave me credit for anything that happened at Dundee United. The club was a part of my life that went quickly. I never even thought about Dundee United when I was down south later in my career. It was like it never happened. I've never even looked back on any of my goals at Dundee United. When I go back up all these people start remembering all these stories like they happened yesterday. To me they're gone. It's only really now and then that I think about them.

Jim McLean was a great coach who taught me a lot but he was not a very nice man to me. But I caused him a lot of grief. It couldn't have been great for him. I'm embarrassed looking back. If I had my time again would I do it different? Bloody right, I would. I should have been in my house drinking water. Of course, I felt for Jim and his family as dementia gradually claimed him. They asked me to go to his funeral in 2020. I didn't feel it was appropriate.

8

PIGEONS, FERRETS AND OTHER CREATURES

People who know about my difficult relationship with Jim McLean try to square that with the image of me as a country man who loves creatures, especially pigeons. People are fascinated by my love for these birds. I'd hope they are clever enough to see why. I care for them. I love setting them free to fly, and then that great moment that lifts my heart when I see them returning to me. It's about love, freedom and loyalty. At heart I'm a family man and returning home is always special, no matter how short a time I've been away. And when I've caught up with family, I go and check on my pigeons. I have such a strong connection with them. I like being with them. They're calming.

People relax in different ways. I'm not a great music lover, certainly not modern music. I listen to Smooth FM. Believe it or not, I love old romantic songs. I like the storytelling I suppose, and there's a story to most of these old songs. 'Hotel California' – Eagles good but pigeons better! I relax by holding my pigeons and spending time with them. That works for me more than anything. When I was a kid, I caught my own pigeons, setting a trap with a crate, using bread for bait and a stick to prop up the crate with a piece of string attached, which I'd pull on when the pigeons took the bait. Bingo.

PIGEONS, FERRETS AND OTHER CREATURES

Pigeon fancying is more than a hobby, as I've heard it called. It's a passion for me, a very peaceful way to spend time away from the pressures of football. I can completely lose myself in that world. I was twelve when one of my mates got some pigeons to race. I liked the colours and the styles and patterns. I liked looking after them as well as the breeding and training. Before long I had my own pigeon loft at the back of the house. It was there that a lifetime's fascination was born. The loft was the size of a wee rabbit hutch stuck on the end of the shed. I bought two pigeons for a pound each, and put them in there.

My dad saw that I loved the pigeons so he started motivating me as I headed off for games with Carse Thistle. 'If you score a hat-trick today, son, I will make that pigeon loft a wee bit bigger.' I scored five. So he knocked a hole through into the shed, built a cage inside the shed, and the pigeons came out of the rabbit hutch into there. My motivation for scoring soon became extensions to the pigeon loft. In the end the whole shed was a pigeon loft. Dad also gave me a pound a goal at Carse Thistle. With that money I bought more pigeons.

Dad was into the pigeons when he was young and all of a sudden me taking an active interest reinvigorated his own and we formed a partnership, D. Ferguson & Son of Bannockburn Club, with a team of pigeons that we owned, bred and raced. We took it seriously. The lofts were always kept immaculately, as were the birds, and we gave them names like Wullie Wallace, Bannockburn Boy, Castle View Boy, Mr F, The Pecker, Evie's Boy, The Slatey. We had one called Pegleg; it broke its legs but we fixed them. They won club and federation competitions and the Stafford Open and the Lauriston Open. We were winning on a regular basis and ours wasn't the best loft position in the federation either. The 'loft position' is the position within the area, and you're better to be on the east because of more west winds. Hard work and devotion to the wellbeing and contentment of our pigeons showed in the results. We had that passion for it. My dad was a good pigeon man.

Later in my career, as I grew older and made more money, I spent £20,000 on a beautiful state-of-the-art loft. The pigeons drop on a conveyor belt, I can press a button and the loft is cleaned for you, and there's underfloor heating, all mod cons. Lofts are expensive, pigeons are expensive. You wouldn't believe the money they're paying for a pigeon in China now. It's crazy. Armando, a pigeon owned by a breeder in Belgium, was bought for £1 million in 2019. There's a lot of money in pigeon-racing now abroad because the Chinese love betting. Queen Elizabeth II loved pigeons. There were royal lofts at Sandringham in Norfolk with about 260 pigeons. Mike Tyson had lofts. It appeals to different people. It's popular. Gerry Francis, the former footballer and manager, still flies them.

When I was playing, after a game on a Saturday if Dad wasn't at the game, I'd be on the phone as soon as I could: 'How did the race go, Dad?'

My dad would always be modest: 'Och, no' bad. How did the game go, son?'

One terrible Friday night we lost some of our best birds in a fire which broke out on a lorry transporting them to Linlithgow for a race. Dad was especially devastated. I don't think he left the loft for two days. We lost many birds that night, most of them winners. After the fire we concentrated on young birds and built up the team again. I reared the youngsters (squabs), about forty of them each season, so they learned to find the best line of flight for race days, which can make all the difference between winning and losing.

Along the way there were plenty of duds, too. When I went on tour with Scotland in 1993, I took a few quid off Ally McCoist at

PIGEONS, FERRETS AND OTHER CREATURES

cards on the flight home. I invested my winnings in a £450 pigeon which I called Coisty. Unfortunately it wasn't as good at finding the target as Ally and disappeared.

But the fascination has always remained. Occasionally you'll still see me take birds in the back of the car to an open field to release them for training in the afternoon. These birds don't belong to D. Ferguson & Son any more but, if they did, I know my dad would be stood by the loft, poised and ready to observe their return, counting every last one of them home.

As well as pigeons, I love animals, fishing, and a walk in the country. I'm a Scottish lad, aren't I? Growing up, I kept ferrets. I'd take them poaching. Put the ferret down the rabbit hole, put nets at the top of the hole and catch the rabbit. We never ate the rabbits, we'd sell them to the butcher for a pound. I had ferrets in a hutch at home, polecats too. I loved keeping them.

In fact, a ferret is the only thing I ever stole in my life. I was out poaching with a mate, and we put our ferret down the rabbit hole and never saw it again.

'I know there's a ferret round the corner,' my mate said. 'We'll go and steal it.'

I was lookout. I stayed in the corner of the garden and my mate went in and nicked the ferret. We put it in a wee cage and hid it in my back garden.

Back then few people had ferrets, and there was a knock at the door. It was a policeman. My dad was away working on the rigs, and I just started crying my eyes out. I was only ten. 'The ferret's in the back garden, they'll be here for the ferret,' I cried to my mum. It could have been anybody's ferret but I blabbed. 'I'm sorry, I'm sorry.' The police got the ferret's owner to come down and take his ferret back. There were only ten ferrets in the community so it was easy to identify.

When my dad came back home, he tore into me: 'Don't ever steal again in your life.' I just stood there and shook and I never ever did. 'I was only the lookout, Dad.'

'I don't want to see the police at this door again.' It didn't quite work out that way, but a ferret was the only thing I ever lifted.

My dad went poaching and brought home rabbits which my mum cooked for dinner. He bought me a fishing rod, and I'd take myself off to the Iron Falls, which was on the Bannock Burn. Scottish brown trout, salmon and rainbow trout were all in there. I'd always catch the brown trout, float fishing, with worms I dug from the surrounding farmland or river banks. I really loved the fishing. There is something deeply relaxing about catching fish. I could spend all day still by the burn.

Maybe it was the feeling of isolation that appealed to me. I'm not a loner, that's not true, but I'm happy in my own company. I could go fishing, ferreting or walking the dog and be the most content boy alive. I had a dog, too, a black Labrador called Laddie, a great dog, lovely character. We were still in the flats when Laddie arrived as a pup. He came out of a litter of puppies from the dog owned by the family next door. Not long after Laddie came along we moved from Graystale Road to McLean Court, and the number of times Laddie would run back to the flat, my God. I'd always go and get him.

Years later I got followed by a mongrel street dog, a cross between a sheepdog and a springer spaniel. I picked him up at Glasgow Central, fed him some Rolos, even my last one, and he followed me all the way back to Stirling on the train. I couldn't shake him, so he became part of the family too. Lucky, he was called. I should have called him Rolo.

I loved greyhounds. My dad's brother, Archie, was into greyhounds. We used to go to the track together and I started buying greyhounds. I named them after team-mates, like 'Tricky Trevor' after Trevor Steven at Rangers. Archie looked after them. Archie liked a wee bet and the greyhounds kept on disappearing.

I didn't fare much better with horses. When I was at Everton later in my career, I bought a horse off the trainer Micky Quinn, the former footballer. I was pally with Micky's brother Mark in Liverpool. We'd just been to Chester races on a day out – a very good day out – we'd had a drink and thought, 'That's a good idea, let's buy a horse.' As you do. I agreed to buy a horse off Micky, went down to his stables, they led the horse out, and to this day I remember my shock.

'Jesus, Micky, it's not very big, is it?'

'It's just a yearling, Dunc, it'll grow.'

It never grew. Micky said he got it from Mick Channon, the ex-player and highly respected trainer. I bet he never. He probably got it off Blackpool beach and said, 'Here you go, a horse.' I bought it for £24,000 plus £3,000 VAT. £27,000 it cost me. The wee jockey Franny Norton from Knowsley rode it for us. Franny's a good jockey but the horse wasn't any use.

By that point I had a family and we watched it on TV. We all gathered around the TV, and I told the kids, 'We've got a horse here.' They were very excited. I said to Micky, 'Get the horse in the front, the kids want to enjoy it in the front.' Franny put the horse in the stalls, and the next minute he came out like a bullet and Franny coaxed it into the lead. It was twenty lengths in front of everybody else, the kids were jumping up and down, but it inevitably got reeled in. It came last.

Micky always used to explain the horse to me. 'Dunc, he likes a mile, he likes half a mile, he likes two miles, he likes an inside track, he likes an outside track, he's got sore feet, he's got sore teeth.' Micky did everything he could for me to keep it in training. But it cost me money and the horse wasn't worth a carrot.

'Just sell it, Micky,' I told him.

Micky took it to the auction, then phoned and said, 'There's been a car crash on the motorway. There's nobody at the auctions, Dunc, there's no point selling the horse.'

'Sell the bloody horse. Just sell it.'

Later, he phoned back. 'Dunc, you'll never guess, I only got £1,200 for your horse.'

'I'm made up, Micky. Keep the £1,200, mate, and don't ever phone me again.' And I put the phone down.

It's the best thing I ever did, getting rid of that horse. It must have cost me £50,000 in the end, all in, over two years. You'll never guess the name of the horse . . . No Regrets!

9

SCOTLAND THE GRAVE

Regrets? I had a few with Scotland. My international career actually started well and nobody could have predicted I would end up with only seven caps. My performances in my first full season for Dundee United persuaded Andy Roxburgh, the Scotland manager, to call me up for a warm-up trip to North America two weeks prior to Euro 92.

Roxburgh had tracked my progress with the Under-21s where I liked the coach, Craig Brown. He once sent me home from an Under-21 camp because I wore cycling shorts under my kit. I did apologise. I played only three times. My favourite moment was when Craig called me in for the second leg of the European Under-21 Championship quarter-final on 24 March 1992 at Pittodrie. There were 22,500 there, and I tore Germany apart. That night we were terrific against the best young team in Europe. They had some good players, like Mehmet Scholl, Heiko Herrlich and Christian Wörns.

'We could not match their skill but they could not match us for heart and that was why we won,' Craig said. It was me, Gerry Creaney and Eoin Jess up front. We fell 2–0 behind but I just launched myself into their defence and set up Ray McKinnon to make it 2–1. We battered them in the second half and won 4–3. The skipper, Paul Lambert, put it down to my singing. 'Duncan grabbed the mike on the team coach the night before and he never put it down,' he said. 'He may not be the best singer in the world but he didn't half relax us.' Craig, a good man, was really kind about me afterwards. 'Duncan Ferguson terrorised the German defenders. He didn't score but he was such a presence. It made the Germans jittery.'

The consensus was that I played well in the game, and the call-up to the full Scotland squad was a source of deep pride for my family and me. But I wasn't at my best on my debut, coming on for Pat Nevin, at Mile High Stadium in Denver against the USA on 17 May. Afterwards, Roxburgh asked me, 'So, Duncan, what was wrong out there?'

I was honest. 'I can't get up for these friendly games,' I said. Not one of my proudest moments.

Of course, I was a proud Scotsman, very proud to make my debut. My dad was proud, my family were proud. But things were moving that quickly. To me it was just another step. I was going places, I was moving on, I was thinking 'I'm invincible here'. On that trip it was basically me following round the Rangers boys going from club to club, bar to bar. We were getting ready for Euro 92 by going out and training and having a great time at night.

I started against Canada, in Toronto on 20 May, and we won 3–1. 'Ferguson Shines on Tour for Scotland' ran the headline in *The Times*. I'll take that.

Before we flew out to Sweden for Euro 92, I struggled with a tooth abscess and was worn out having not slept much. But I managed to do enough to convince Roxburgh that I was worth my place.

For the Scotland national team over the years, rising above the ordinary has proved by and large to be a losing struggle. Occasionally we manage to galvanise ourselves, producing results which restore pride and a hint of promise. Reality soon reasserts itself and all the doubts, fears and paranoia come flooding back. It didn't take long at Euro 92. We got drawn in a group with world champions Germany, European champions the Netherlands and CIS, the Commonwealth of Independent States, created after the break-up of the Soviet Union. In Sweden, we honestly didn't need to be confronted by a Group of Death to remind ourselves of our mortality. History did the job well enough on its own.

But we headed out with all the usual Scottish excitement. I looked at the strikers I was in with: Ally McCoist, Brian McClair, Gordon Durie, Kevin Gallacher – serious players. I didn't expect to be a starter. Everything had happened very quickly. I came on in the final minutes of our opening game in Gothenburg on 12 June against a great Dutch team featuring Marco van Basten, Frank Rijkaard, Dennis Bergkamp, Ronald Koeman (with whom I would later have the pleasure of working alongside at Everton) and their captain, Ruud Gullit (with whom I would also have the pleasure of working). I bet Koeman and Gullit didn't have a clue about me then!

Looking back now, I can say Gullit was the greatest player I ever encountered. A superstar. He glided across the grass, a totally dominant presence, and embodied the very essence of 'Total Football', which he combined with an attacking player's killer edge. That I would one day years later batter down his door and demand we straighten things out was unimaginable when we crossed paths for those precious few minutes. Shortly after Bergkamp scored in the seventy-fifth minute, I came on for McClair, and saw Gullit close up. Wearing no. 10 and the armband, tall and athletic, my God, Ruud Gullit was a player, among the very best who ever graced the game. When he got the ball, it felt like the whole Scotland team just ran back to the 18-yard line. Nobody could get near Gullit because he was that good. Bergkamp's goal proved the difference that day inside the Ullevi Stadium, but Gullit left the lasting impression. That's when I realised what a top player looked like.

It was still fantastic coming on against the Dutch. I was delighted! To reiterate, I didn't think they even knew who I was. I was only a kid, the youngest player in the whole tournament at twenty years, five months and sixteen days. The closest player in age to me was Sweden's Patrik Andersson, four months older. At that time I was getting touted for big moves in my career so it was exciting times.

I was made up because the Dutch manager Rinus Michels pulled Rijkaard out of midfield to man-mark me. 'Get him, get him!' Michels kept shouting.

'I can't believe it, *he* knows who I am!' I was in shock.

Three days later, a 2–0 defeat against the Germans meant that our 3–0 victory over CIS on 18 June, also in Norrköping, was academic. I played no part in either game.

But I felt part of the squad, even if the squad felt divided by the Old Firm rivalry. Rangers sent five boys, Celtic three, and there was very little mixing between them. The Celtic boys went out separately, they would return to their wee rooms, and Rangers to theirs. I'd be in with the Rangers boys. We'd play cards, and the Celtic boys would do their thing. That's just the way it was then. We'd still be pally, we'd say hello and all that, but we never socialised with the Celtic boys, no. There was a divide. If I was playing cards out on that trip in Sweden, I'd play with Ally and any boys connected to Rangers like Stuart McCall. I'd be sitting with them and Goughie, David McPherson and Andy Goram. I'd be following them round. I got on well with Andy, he was a great goalkeeper. Only Neville Southall would I put ahead of him.

We went to Bern after the Euros. The Under-21s played on the Monday night, 7 September, and the seniors two nights later at the Wankdorf Stadium in a World Cup qualifier against Roy

SCOTLAND THE GRAVE

Hodgson's Switzerland. Both Scottish teams lost, and we drowned our sorrows in a Bern bar afterwards.

Coming out the bar, everybody was working out how to get back to the hotel. I kickstarted a moped and beat them all back. It ended up with the moped lying out on the street outside the hotel. Durranty was already up on the top balcony with bottles of beer, firing them through the gap in the stairs and listening to them smash. Crazy night.

By the time I found my room, some of the other boys were already back and busy. They'd poured beer all over my bed so it looked like a giant pee stain.

'Who's doing that, Jukey?' I asked Gordon 'Jukebox' Durie who I was rooming with.

'It must be Them,' Jukey said. He meant Ally McCoist and Ian Durrant, who were down the corridor in the gable end of the hotel.

Andy Goram came in and he and Jukey went out. I fell asleep in a chair. I was woken up by the sound of furniture moving. I went outside and Jukey and Andy were blocking all the doors with all these beds and wardrobes.

'What are you doing?' I asked.

'We're blocking Durranty and Ally in the room.'

So I started helping them. 'Yes, come on Andy, come on Jukey, let's get them done then.'

Gordon soon gave up and fell asleep. Andy Goram disappeared too. I got back to my furniture mobbing. I pushed a wicker chair towards Ally and Durranty's room. I had a cigar and matches and I was drunk and I lit the chair. It just went boosh – up in flames. It soon went out – but it could have sent the whole hotel up. I staggered back to my bed, jumped on it and fell asleep, ignoring the giant beer stain.

I woke up to somebody hoovering. Craig Brown was hoovering

my room! He was clearing up all the mess and moving the furniture back.

'You bastard,' he said.

'What?!'

'Yous nearly burnt the hotel down.'

As I'm getting up, Craig added, 'And look, you've pissed the fucking bed!'

'Jesus Christ!'

The night's events began to come into focus. Poor Andy Roxburgh. Poor Craig Brown. We were all summoned downstairs into this big room to face Andy and the music. Oh my God, I'd nearly burnt the whole place down!

I'm surprised I wasn't banned there and then from international duty. My next cap came against Germany again, on 24 March 1993, which I mentioned earlier in the book. A friendly at Ibrox, where there is never such a thing, against the Germans, which can never be a friendly. Germany had some great players like Lothar Matthäus, Jürgen Klinsmann, Karl-Heinz Riedle, Jürgen Kohler, Thomas Helmer and the rest. But I destroyed their centre-backs, Kohler, Helmer and Guido Buchwald. Phil Shaw, reporting for the *Independent*, wrote that 'for the paying customers, the performance of the 6ft 4in Ferguson, a lavishly gifted centre-forward for whom Dundee United have turned down £2.5 million from Rangers, stole the show'.

The game was effectively won and lost in the space of a couple of minutes in the first half. I brought the ball down on my chest, passed the ball to John Collins and moved into the penalty area. Tom Boyd swung in an arcing cross from the left with his right foot and the ball hung in the air. 'As Boyd's cross descended into the German area, Ferguson launched into a spectacular bicycle kick from eight yards,' Shaw continued. 'But German goalkeeper Andreas Köpke, showing equal agility, twisted acrobatically to turn the ball over.' Everyone talks about my overhead kick hitting the bar, but actually it's an incredible save by Köpke.

The moment passed, and somehow I knew it would be characterised as a metaphor for my career. On nights like that at Ibrox I had the potential to pull off the spectacular. It was in me, that touch of class which could prove decisive in a game. Or not, as was the case against the Germans, who scored almost immediately through Riedle. But the promise was there, particularly when the opposition were the world champions, the Old Firm, Manchester United or Liverpool. I always wanted to prove a point in the big games. When the chips were down I backed myself. I knew I could do it. For other games, maybe at a subconscious level that same drive and determination wasn't there all the time. That was possibly a weakness in my make-up.

I played against Greece in Athens on 18 December 1994 in a European Championship qualifier, but then I quit.

Regrets? Not at the time, not when I remembered what the Scottish FA had done to me. Even years later I was still not happy at the twelve-game ban the SFA gave me before the John McStay court case was heard. We got it reduced to five games on appeal but that wasn't the point. The SFA destroyed any chance I had of a fair trial. I fell out of love with Scotland. I felt bitter. I felt the Scottish press had done me in, everybody was doing me in the neck, so I chucked it in. Fuck them.

I was pig-headed. I felt it was an injustice what happened to me. I can never, ever forget those forty-four days in Barlinnie, horrific days surrounded by people who could cut me up or end my life.

When I finally won my battle against the SFA in January 1996, Craig Brown insisted I would be very much in the frame for his Euro 96 squad. 'I started with Duncan as a Scotland Under-21 player and he has never been anything other than a very good squad member,' said Craig, who'd succeeded Roxburgh. 'I've never had any problems with him and let's just hope his form and fitness continue because he is very much part of my plans.'

So, regrets? I occasionally think of what might have been if I'd gone to Euro 96 with Scotland, and played against England at Wembley. My dad forced me to go back after the Euros. 'You've got to go back and play for your country,' he said. So I played twice more, against Austria in Vienna on 31 August 1996 and a final appearance against Estonia on 11 February 1997, in Monte Carlo of all places. The 'one team in Tallinn' rematch. I kept on pulling out of squads. And that was it. I had only seven Scotland appearances. Nuts.

Craig still kept phoning me up. 'Duncan, you're not retiring in your mid-twenties. I'll just tell the press you're injured.' That was good of him. He protected me. He didn't want to tell the press and the Tartan Army that a 25-year-old fella had retired from playing for Scotland. He knew the abuse I'd get. Craig also hoped I'd change my mind. But I never did. They asked me every year. No. I was stubborn.

Regrets . . . Yes, now, here in 2025, yes I do regret my stubbornness. I deeply regret that after my performance against Germany – which prompted Karl-Heinz Rummenigge and Bayern Munich to try to prise me away from Tannadice – I played only three more times for Scotland. Seven caps for my country is at least ninety-three short of what I ought to have achieved given that I won my first cap in 1992 at twenty and was still being asked to play by Scotland managers in the mid-2000s. I wanted to play a hundred times for my country. I wanted to break the all-time appearance record of Sir Kenny Dalglish of 102 caps and score more goals than him, than Denis Law, than the lot of them. I was capable of it. I think I would easily have made a hundred caps, and I'm not saying that lightly: there was no Scottish striker better than me at that time, there was nobody going to take my position, I'd have been in every single squad for fourteen years. I feel I had the ability to break all records for Scotland.

The last time they tried to get me back was in September 2005. I was thirty-three and still playing well for Everton. Ally McCoist was Walter Smith's assistant then, and he called the house at 10 p.m. one night. 'Come back, big man. We're playing Italy, you'll play.' It was a World Cup qualifier, a massive game, at Hampden. Full house, full on, usually my kind of night. 'You're going to start the game, you're still the best striker we've got.'

'Ally, if I was going to come back it would be for you and for Walter, but I can't bring myself to do anything now.'

'Dunc, just come back. Play this one game.'

I couldn't. I was running out of contract at Everton. This one game would have likely led to me playing at the World Cup without a club. I would have been unattached.

Walter and Ally understood where I was coming from. They knew how angry I was at the SFA. But it's the biggest regret of my career, I can't emphasise that enough. I think I would have been the best striker we ever had. But we will never know. I fucked up.

'You should have played for Scotland again,' Sir Alex Ferguson told me when we met for a coffee in 2023. But he too understood my frustration with the SFA.

There were other factors, I'll admit, injuries mostly. The operations I underwent in my career would accumulate and step into double figures. My drinking was another impediment to producing consistently the level of performance of which I was capable.

Successive Scotland managers had called and tried to make me part of their plans. Berti Vogts made the trip to Goodison and I blanked him in the tunnel. I heard him say, 'I think ten years from now Duncan will look back and say, "I missed out."' He wasn't wrong. Vogts added that he could not understand why I could not forget, but in that case he didn't really understand me. Walter Smith gave Coisty a mission impossible. I love Coisty, and even he failed. But, yes, I've regrets. In 1998, I was on honeymoon on the beach in the Bahamas when I should have been playing in the World Cup against Brazil with Scotland.

10

TAPPING UP AND STEPPING UP

Scotland's Rangers contingent did not hide their admiration for me, and that helped my move from Dundee United in the summer of 1993. My team-mate Richard Gough was a big supporter. 'Look, you need to sign this guy,' Goughie told Walter Smith, the Rangers manager. Rangers eventually got fined £5,000 for tapping me up. It was rubbish, really, it was just Goughie saying in the paper that I was the best young player in Scotland. That wasn't tapping up. That was stating a fact. I knew Rangers were interested. Walter's assistant, Archie Knox, drove to Stirling and sat in laybys chatting to me. My dad talked to Walter and Archie. They were all big Rangers men.

It showed how paranoid Jim McLean was about Rangers that he sent one of Dundee United's most famous players, Paul Hegarty, to chaperone me to a game at Ibrox. I got invited by my agent, Dennis Roach, and Rangers to the Battle of Britain game when they played Leeds (then the champions of England) in the UEFA Champions League on 21 October 1992. McLean sanctioned the visit but he assigned Hegarty, back at the club coaching, to follow me everywhere. We stopped off at my parents' house in Stirling, got a cup of tea, and Paul was sitting at the end of the table saying to my dad, 'Mr Ferguson, I'm really sorry about this but Jim's told me I've got to follow your son everywhere. He's not to have a beer, if he goes to the toilet I've got to go with him, he's not to talk to anybody.'

This was Paul Hegarty! Dundee United legend, former captain, fifteen seasons' exceptional service, then a coach, always an ambassador.

Paul drove me to Ibrox, walked round with me, made sure I didn't talk to too many people and didn't have a beer, and then drove me back up the road. I saw Paul when I was up at Tannadice in 2023 – lovely man, great to see him, gave him a hug – but that's Jim McLean for you, that's how he treated his senior staff, as a minder. Anyway, I still got a good look around Ibrox and got to experience the amazing atmosphere again.

Ironically, Rangers could have had me for nothing only eight years earlier. While I was playing at Carse Thistle as an underdeveloped, uncoordinated thirteen-year-old, a Rangers scout came to have a look at me. I didn't impress. He reckoned I was too small.

'Maybe he'll fill out and we'll have another look,' the scout told my disappointed dad.

As I began doing well at Dundee United, Rangers and other clubs came calling again. Jim McLean wasn't the happiest around that time, brandishing newspapers in front of journalists and insisting angrily that their latest stories linking me to Rangers, English clubs or wherever were pure rubbish.

OK, so, for the record, Southampton, Sheffield United and Sheffield Wednesday fancied me. I met Glenn Hoddle at his home in London to discuss a transfer to Chelsea. A £2 million bid by Crystal Palace was flatly rejected by Dundee United. Kenny Dalglish came up from Blackburn to watch me a few times. He phoned the house. I spoke to him. My dad did too. Kenny's loved, isn't he? He was a Rangers fan as a kid. Blackburn's owner Jack Walker offered to build Dundee United a new stand. The club were desperate to finish a stand off. I imagine Jack had easy access to steel as he made his fortune there. Everton offered £600,000. I didn't know that at the time. McLean wouldn't tell me anything. The great Everton manager Howard Kendall revealed to me years later that he wanted me to partner Mo Johnston, whom he'd signed from Rangers. Howard told me, 'I'd phone up Jim and say, "I'm wanting the boy Ferguson." And Jim would say, "He's trouble. I'm fining him more than he's earning!"'

Were there other clubs chasing me? Yes. Aston Villa wanted me. I found out later that their manager, Ron Atkinson, turned up in disguise to watch me. How do you disguise such a distinctive figure as Big Ron?! He then approached Jim about signing me. Wee Jim was having none of it. I only learned this on holiday in Barbados in 1998. I'd just got married and was staying in the same hotel as Ron and his wife, Maggie. I'd never met Ron before. I was at the bar at 11 a.m. and spotted him sitting with Maggie on the beach. So I told the waiter, 'Take a bottle of champagne down to Mr Atkinson.' Off he went – bottle, two glasses, ice bucket. I just stood back and watched. Ron turned round, smiled, waved, came over and laughed as he explained how he'd tried to sign me incognito. Ron had apparently donned an old flat cap, dark glasses and a coat with the collar turned up to hide his face on his hush-hush scouting trip to Tannadice. I found the story hilarious. We spent the whole holiday together after that, had meals together, singsongs together. Ron's a terrific singer. Sending champagne to Ron Atkinson is always a good idea.

McLean kept saying Dundee United weren't interested in selling me, but they were. 'Right now we need money more than ever because we are constructing a new stand, but we also need Duncan ten times more than we need the cash,' McLean said with typical frankness. 'We will not tolerate any transfer conversations about Duncan Ferguson. The stories that he is supposed to be going to Southampton or Everton are nothing short of diabolical. And as far as the links to Rangers are concerned, having worked with Walter Smith for years I can assure you that he has never said a single word to me about Duncan.' No, Walter just said them to me.

If I had to leave, McLean wanted me to go to Leeds United, who were offering £3.5 million, a large figure at the time. Before I went south with my dad to talk to their manager, Howard Wilkinson, McLean phoned: 'Look, we're trying to finish this stand, and we need this transfer going through.'

We met Howard at a hotel on the outskirts of Leeds. The deal was good for me; it was certainly more than Rangers were offering.

'You're going to be one of the highest-paid players, if not the highest-paid player, in our club, at £3,000 a week,' Howard told me.

Three times the telephone rang for him in just under two hours. 'Has he signed yet?' It was wee Jim, desperate to complete a deal for me with the recent champions of England. He called the Elland Road offices too. I didn't mind the interruptions. Howard Wilkinson is a good fella, knows a lot about the game and brought great success to Leeds. But, my God, he can talk. I was sitting there, half-asleep.

Howard explained that he wanted me to replace Lee Chapman, who'd scored sixteen league goals in their title-winning 1991–92 season. Leeds were offering a lot of money, considering I was on about £160 a week at Dundee United – or less. After all the fines from McLean, I hardly had a penny in my pocket, never mind my bank. So Leeds was quite appealing. They also had a good team, Eric Cantona, Gordon Strachan, Gary Speed, Gary McAllister, David Batty and John Lukic among them. Howard wanted to build

TAPPING UP AND STEPPING UP

on this for what would be the inaugural season of the newly established Premiership, as it was before being rebranded as the Premier League.

Howard kept talking. I was just a young kid. Where's the money? What's going on?

'Do you want a nice steak sandwich, son?' Howard asked.

My dad was sitting there thinking, 'Do you think we've never had a steak sandwich?' My dad is a proud man. He got a bit upset by Howard. He felt it was patronising, as if these two Scots had never eaten well before. Don't they know where Aberdeen Angus comes from?!

Another call came through from Dundee, this time for Dennis Roach, my agent, who was with us.

'Has he signed yet?' asked McLean, sounding increasingly desperate, much to my delight.

'He's not signed yet, Mr McLean,' Dennis replied.

'Tell him to sign,' McLean said, and rang off.

As they wheeled in the exotic steak sandwiches, I asked Howard, 'Would you mind sticking the cricket on the TV?'

My dad looked at me as if I'd lost the plot.

'Oh, you like the cricket?' Howard said as he switched on the TV.

Now, I couldn't tell you a sticky wicket from a googly. I'm a Scotsman, for goodness' sake. I couldn't even tell you who was playing. Actually, I vaguely recall it being England–Australia, only because watching the cricket just at that minute was slightly less boring than listening to Howard. So I watched the cricket as the others talked, mainly going round in circles.

Howard even took me to see wee Gordon Strachan and his family at their home. He was eating his bananas, enjoying an Indian summer to his stellar career. Leeds suited him well and Gordon spoke well of the players there. 'Leeds are a great club,' he said to me. They are. But Leeds couldn't pull on my heart strings as Rangers did.

When I returned from Leeds, McLean pulled me into the boardroom at Tannadice and said, 'Look, Duncan, we're building this stand here, we can't afford to finish it off, you need to move.'

'I'm not moving to England, I'm moving to Rangers. That's the end of it.'

My heart was set on Rangers. My dad was a Rangers fan and I was raised a Rangers fan. They were the biggest club in Scotland at the time. For the previous seven seasons Rangers had virtually monopolised the Scottish domestic scene, and we're talking the pre-Premiership era in England. While it wasn't a question of whether Leeds would survive in the Scottish Premier Division, we hadn't exactly been peeking down at the old English First Division with a sense of envy or fear. The SPL was strong and, on the blue side of the Old Firm, Graeme Souness (until 1991) and then Walter Smith were backed heavily by the vision and hard cash of owner David Murray and a talented squad had been assembled, players such as Coisty, Goughie, Ian Durrant, Andy Goram, Stuart McCall, Gary Stevens, Trevor Steven and Mark Hateley. Their supremacy remained unchallenged.

McLean had good reason for preferring me to move to Leeds, not to a team he still regarded as a rival in Scotland. 'Who goes out of their way to make rivals stronger?' he argued.

And, of course, when I went down to Leeds, Rangers panicked.

'Have you signed for them?' Walter asked me.

'No, I want to come to you. I'm not going back to Dundee United for twelve months with Jim McLean.'

Rangers actually wanted to wait a year. Walter had McCoist and Hateley, his main strike force. I was always going to be behind them to begin with, I was only a kid. I wasn't ready for the move.

TAPPING UP AND STEPPING UP

'I don't want to stay a moment longer at Dundee United,' I told Walter.

'Look, we'll get you a flat in Dundee, we'll get you a car, we'll get you a few quid, we'll look after you. Just stay another twelve months there,' Walter said.

'No, I want to go. I can't do another twelve months up here,' I said. 'I need to leave. I need a fresh challenge. I don't want to go on at Dundee United.'

I got called again into the boardroom at Tannadice. McLean again tried to turn the screw.

'You'll be signing that contract Leeds have offered, won't you?' he said.

'To be honest, Jim, I think I'll hang around. I don't think Leeds is for me.'

I was blagging, making McLean believe that if they wanted the money then Rangers' cash was as good as Leeds'. I came back into training and spent pre-season at Tannadice. By that point, McLean was willing to do business with Rangers if that is what it took.

So he squeezed an extra £1million out of Rangers. Walter wanted me and he didn't want another team luring me away from under his nose if Rangers stalled. Walter told McLean they'd pay the £4 million.

'We're building a new stand here and we need the money from your sale to build it,' McLean told me again in yet another meeting in the boardroom.

'Maybe if you name the stand after me,' I said, 'but don't be sticking a clause in the contract that I have to come back and build it.'

Even McLean smiled at that. Rangers paid the extra money, a British transfer record fee of £4 million. Rangers paid too much for me but they were scared to lose me. The covered, two-tiered East Stand was built at Tannadice and opened a year later, and I tossed my 'DF' hard hat into a bin on the way out of Jim McLean's home of hard labour.

I knew McLean would be pleased to see the back of me. There'll hardly be a picture of me up in Dundee United, I bet. I was so desperate to escape him that I didn't even know how long I signed the contract for with Rangers.

When I went back to Dundee with Rangers as a player, I saw the fresh letters on the new stand they'd completed with the money they got for me. DUFC. They misspelled it. I paid for that – and also built it. It should be DUNC!

11

RANGERS DANGERS

Rangers wasn't a good move for me. I should never have gone. I went because I loved Rangers at the time, and my dad supported them. But I really needed to get out of Scotland. I should have gone to Leeds.

My first journey to Ibrox as a Rangers player on 15 July 1993 even began with an argument.

'We can't drive to Ibrox to sign for Rangers in that,' I said to my dad, pointing to his wee tiling van full of buckets and a ladder in the back. My dad had moved out of rigs and into tiling bathrooms. We were about to drive to this huge press conference for a British transfer record signing in a van. I couldn't believe it. I'd made an effort, I was smartly dressed. I always try to be clean shaven, looking right. Walter Smith set that tone. When you went into training, players had to have a collar and tie on. For training!

But a van? Dad!

'What's wrong with that?' my dad asked, as if I might be getting above my station.

'Your wee tiling van?'

'What's wrong with you? Are you embarrassed?'

'Too right I'm embarrassed,' I said. 'Look at that – you've even got all your tiles still in it. The two of us, we'll look like Del Boy and Rodney out of *Only Fools and Horses* if we turn up at Ibrox in that.'

So we climbed into my sister Audrey's wee Suzuki jeep to make the 30-mile trip. A large posse of camera crews and photographers were waiting outside the famous old stadium to capture my arrival. My dad didn't miss a beat. 'Should have come in the van,' he said, cool and deadpan. 'Look at all the free advertising we're missing out on here!'

Waiting inside Ibrox was Rangers chairman David Murray. My signing was a big statement of intent for him. Rangers had outbid the 1992 champions of England for the services of a young Scottish striker. Murray's ambitions for the 1993–94 season were clear: a sixth league title in a row, a third Scottish Cup final in a row, another Treble, which would make Rangers the first club in the history of Scottish football to defend all three domestic trophies. And a European Cup final appearance for the first time. Impossible as it may be for some to believe now given Rangers' travails and the decline of Scottish football overall, Rangers considered the European Cup to be the holy grail. I headed up the marble stairs to the Blue Room at Ibrox and was met with even more photographers.

I was honest with the press. 'At Rangers you must be successful and I feel this is an environment in which I will thrive,' I told them. 'My heart hasn't really been in it for the last four years at Dundee United. I didn't like the way players were being treated at the club and I'm not just speaking about myself. But it's all worth it now, I'm at Ibrox, and it's a big relief. Admittedly, it's an incredible price because I've only been playing first-team football for three years and I still feel like a rookie. But I've been waiting for this all my life, and if you can't play football at Ibrox you can't play anywhere.'

Formalities completed, I flew out of Glasgow with Walter via

RANGERS DANGERS

Heathrow and Pisa to join my new team-mates at Il Ciocco. There were big personalities, strong characters, everywhere you looked in that Rangers team and none of the front men were the slightest bit inclined to make way for the new kid on the block. Far from it. Dressing rooms can be raw and cruel, with rituals designed to probe and undermine as much as they may sometimes serve to galvanise. Shrinking violets need not apply, especially to a Rangers dressing room.

Mark Hateley's strike partnership with Ally McCoist had yielded more than 140 goals over the previous two seasons and Mark made it plain he didn't consider it was his job to roll out the bunting for me. 'As far as I'm concerned, it will be Coisty and me up front again next season,' Mark said bluntly. Mark was all right. He could have given me a hard time. He could have seen this young guy coming from Dundee United as a threat. But Mark was always good with me. He was a great player. He was thirty-two, probably coming to the end, and I was there to replace him, but Mark and Ally were the number one pairing and rightly so because they were the best players and a fantastic partnership. I was good but still developing.

I've heard some strange things about my attitude towards Mark which I want to clear up. I heard that I'd challenged him on the Rangers team bus and said I'd come to replace him. I'd never have had the bollocks to say that to a senior player. I heard that I cut up one of Mark's suits. Not true. Not my style. Anyway, Mark probably cut up my gear!

I also heard that at Rangers I'd try and wind up opposition defenders by telling them how much I was earning. Not true. I didn't really have a clue what I earned at Rangers. £2,000? £3,000? I don't know. I just know it was more than the £160 a week at Dundee United. Dennis Roach negotiated the deal with Walter Smith and David Murray. Conveniently kept me out of it.

'Do you need some money?' Ian Durrant said to me when I first came in.

'Why?'

'You've got no money, have you?'

'No.'

'There's my card. Go round the back of the Govan stand, out on the road, and there's a cash machine. Get yourself a few quid.'

I never forgot that. I also never forgot his balance, which I checked when I took £50 out. There was £10,000 in there! Durranty was loaded! Still, it was good of him to think of me. I never forgot that wee touch. Durranty was one of my favourite players. I remember him running a final with his socks rolled down, when Davie Cooper scored.

Davie was my idol at Rangers, left-footed like me, a dribbler. I liked the way Davie wore his shorts rolled up. I remember *that* free-kick against Aberdeen in the 1987 League Cup final at Hampden: he smashed it in the top corner past Jim Leighton. I just liked Davie Cooper, most people did. He was The Man. And this just shows you that they talk about legends but it doesn't matter how many goals they've scored, I just loved the way Davie played and the way he looked.

Ally and Durranty were my idols who became my friends. I sat next to Durranty in the changing rooms – under the portrait of the Queen. Ally was in the corner. He's special because he's so bubbly, so charismatic, a great talker. You can see why he's a natural for radio and TV. I idolised him. Ally would always give us fans hope – and entertainment. And he was always scoring goals, wasn't he? Rangers' record scorer with 355 goals. And he was good-looking and . . . everybody was attracted to Ally.

I roomed with him, which kept me busy. My main role was as Ally's secretary because the phone kept going. All I did was write down message after message. Before going out, Ally would say,

'Write all their names down, big man.' When Ally came back, he'd say, 'Right, big man, who's been on the phone?'

'Ally, who hasn't?! There's a long list!' So many were after tickets. Ally was popular with everyone.

People were always coming to the door. 'Ally, this blond guy came.' I didn't know who it was. It was the Simple Minds bass player, Derek Forbes, coming to get Rangers tickets off Ally. Ally was the king and I was one of his adoring subjects. I loved him. He would rebuff all the attention. I was single and I picked up all the broken hearts.

I was watching Ally and 'The Goalie', Andy Goram, fishing at Dunkeld on a Scotland trip. Ally was trying to work out how to cast and was messing about with the reel. He finally got round to casting, threw the lure about three feet, and, bang, hooked a salmon. That was Ally for you.

There were great players across that Rangers team. They'd only recently beaten Leeds in that Battle of Britain game. Brian Laudrup was a world-class player. He was fantastic for Rangers. He struggled a wee bit down south playing for Chelsea and stayed only eleven games. But he was great for us at Rangers. I remember my missus used to say to me, 'I like that Brian Laudrup. He's a good player.' I never knew she had that much interest in football.

Playing in an Old Firm game was nerve-racking. It's the biggest game in Scotland, isn't it? One of the biggest games in the world. I made my debut for Rangers in the Old Firm on 21 August 1993, at Parkhead. It was intimidating arriving at Celtic Park. I was the British transfer record signing, only young, and everybody outside that bus as we pulled up hated me. I wasn't too popular with Celtic fans. They knew I was a big Rangers man. 'He's tall, he's skinny, he's going to Barlinnie, Ferguson, Ferguson!' they would later sing. They'd as soon as slaughter you. It was frightening and exciting at the same time, the atmosphere incredible, a lot of hatred, a lot of rivalry as you'd expect, everything felt like it was happening at 100mph. It finished 0–0. I should have scored, but I wasn't 100 per cent fit. I talked positively in the press about how I'd settle, and show my Dundee United goalscoring knack. But it was a struggle.

I felt pressure being Britain's transfer record. Rangers probably paid a million too much. Leeds had originally offered only £3 million, or £3.2 million. The problem for me was that Walter only occasionally had the luxury of being able to bring me in. My Rangers dream descended into a nightmare, initially through injury: a hamstring injury when I first arrived, then a bruised foot, followed by a knee injury and then my hamstring went again. My body was paying heavily for that broken toe at the Rock in Menzieshill. I hardly played for Rangers. Twenty-two games in total, half of them starts, and only five goals. Just four months into my fifteen months at Rangers I was the forgotten man. The truth is I just wasn't ready for it. It was a year too soon.

I returned from injury to play in the mini Old Firm derby at Ibrox in January 1994. A post-war record 20,331 fans turned up to watch Rangers and Celtic's reserves on a Thursday mid-afternoon. The kick-off was put back fifteen minutes to get all the people in. Rangers opened up the Govan stand as well as the main one, and then the Copland Road stand. I got booked for an elbow, but did run on to David Hagen's through ball to score my first goal in a Rangers shirt in the 1–1 draw. That was particularly satisfying as the 2,500 Celtic fans brayed donkey noises at me. Asses.

But I couldn't break into the first team. Gordon Durie had signed from Spurs in November, and he, Hateley and Coisty were going about their goalscoring business in such a prolific manner I could do nothing to force my way back in. I never felt at home at Rangers. I was never really fit.

It was strange. I just couldn't immerse myself in this great club, even though I was a fan. I enjoyed it off the pitch. There was a drinking culture at Rangers and I just jumped into it. When I joined, Ally wondered whether I could keep up the pace as someone not used to the bright lights, the big city, big nights out. Rangers' culture was 'work hard, play hard'. I was of course used to drinking when I was a player at Dundee United, in digs, picking up bad habits. No one paid heed in those days to nutrition, diet, psychology, recovery and recuperation. I didn't know about amino acids and proteins, or the effect of alcohol consumption in the period following games and training. If I'd done a yoga class back then, I'd have left myself open to ridicule. Yes, yoga, and now players are all doing it and looking after themselves and making themselves athletes first. Recuperation for us at Rangers was the Tuesday Club. Maintaining your balance after ten pints of lager was our idea of pilates. Their players were top players, established players who'd won leagues. I was a kid. I should have been working, not drinking. I thought I'd made it before I had. I let down Walter Smith, another of my big regrets. Walter trusted me to come to Rangers. I never gave myself a chance to deliver and that hurts. Years later, I looked at how Wayne Rooney went to Manchester United at eighteen and how well he handled it. I didn't handle my move to Rangers well.

Rangers had great players, and legendary nights out. I was a very willing victim of this culture, falling into it with gusto, especially as I wasn't a regular on a Saturday. Early on I was a regular at Buzzy Wares on Buchanan Street in Glasgow, a Rangers stronghold, a favourite haunt. We'd go in there for lunch and a drink and that would be the start. I remember the whole team in there, tops off, muscles flexed, shoppers walking by and stopping to watch the spectacle through the windows as we held an arm-wrestling competition. Not too many beat me at the arm-wrestling. Those days were 'Over the Top' in more ways than one.

I soon found Glasgow life wasn't for me. Once you signed for

Rangers everything was different. I had a wee apartment but I was never in it. I went home to Mum and Dad's in Stirling. I wanted to be there, not Glasgow. I was a Stirling boy and wanted to stay around the area. The Glasgow scene wasn't me. Everyone knew me in Glasgow. I couldn't go anywhere unnoticed, and once again I became a target. The Old Firm tension was always there on the streets and in the bars and nightclubs. If I went out, I'd take three minders with me, but I soon didn't go out in Glasgow very often.

On one shocker of a night when I did go out, I was drunk, smoking Silk Cuts, and somebody passed me a joint. I took a drag.

Next day I was worried sick, and I had to go to Walter.

'Look, boss, I've done a stupid thing. I was drunk last night and somebody passed me a funny fag and I took a couple of drags. Just a quick draw on a joint.'

'Is that all you've done?'

'That's all I've done. I only done it because it was passed to us.'

I never took a drug after that. Drug-testing was beginning to come into football but you never really saw testers at games.

'Is that it, son, nothing else?'

'No, honestly, that's it.'

I was embarrassed. I should have been leading a better life. Walter knew everything that went on in the city.

'Be careful what you're doing. Stop putting it around so much. Start leading a cleaner life. You've not made it yet.'

And that was it.

Walter was a great man, loads of experience in football and in life. Down in the pubs in Glasgow, he was the man. He'd seen a lot. He even tried to set me up with Miss Scotland. She worked in chairman David Murray's office and Walter gave me her number. He tried to calm me down by setting me up with Miss Scotland! Yes, you know, 'This is the one, Dunc.' To marry! 'She's beautiful, you'll stick with this one. She'll sort you.' I didn't even phone her.

I increasingly felt I didn't fit in at the club I'd grown up loving. I went to a Rangers supporters' dance in Bridge of Allan and they all started singing 'The Sash', a traditional loyalist song. I didn't know the words. When I was on that stage, I was miming. Gary Stevens, our full-back, up from England, he sang every word. I was a local lad in the area, had family from the region, I was a Rangers boy, but I didn't know 'The Sash'. I wasn't even in the lodge, a Masonic thing where a tight-knit group would get together and make vows to each other and form a close band of brothers. When I went to Rangers, they invited me to go through one of their lodges, but I had lost interest. I'd already been blackballed from my dad's lodge in Stirling. I'd lost my family tradition. Even English boys had come up to Rangers and gone through the lodge – yes, no problem. They didn't have a clue but they still all got through.

I loved Rangers as a club, they're an institution. This was Rangers, don't forget, for whom Brian Laudrup turned down a move to Barcelona. 'Brian prefers to play Falkirk on a Tuesday night,' Walter would joke. And the fans were good to me. But, really, the move came too early in my career. I was twenty and just not ready for it. The pressure of being a big-money signing was too much for me, I struggled to cope, but I just never gave myself a chance. I was young and immature. Walter was right. I had to leave.

12

DOOMSDAY

'It could happen this afternoon against Raith Rovers.' So it says in the Rangers match-day programme from 16 April 1994 that rests presently between my fingers and my thumb. It will not surprise you to learn that the Rangers programme editor and contributors weren't referring to what did actually happen. Instead, they were hoping for a breakthrough for the player who was, ironically that week, 'In Profile'. I'd not scored for 700 minutes, and in the programme I remarked 'the fans are bound to get impatient but I'm feeling just as bad as them'.

It's strange to leaf through the pages of that programme now. I'm not a hoarder. I was never one to keep mementos or anything like that from my career. My dad kept all the memorabilia. Some old programmes and scrapbooks have been stored for years in a rectangular brown wicker basket in my attic, undisturbed for some time. Durie, Goram, Hateley are on the cover. Inside, I was quoted as saying, 'I can't wait to start scoring goals.'

I did score that day – my first in a top-flight game for Rangers – but by then I had already faced off with John McStay and everything from that day onwards changed for ever. Not that I realised this at the time, nor for some time afterwards.

'My mum and dad were here today from Stirling and they're absolutely delighted,' I said in my only interview after the game to *Rangers News*. 'My dad's been watching me play football since I was nine. It's him who's pushed me along and helped me from day one. If I'm playing, he'll come along, so I have to perform to keep in his good books. It was a great day for him. I hope I've made him very proud. He's a big Rangers man, so I hope this is the start of great things.'

Two weeks later I was back on the Ibrox pitch, warming up for another Old Firm encounter alongside a mascot wearing a bear costume, having fun as we knocked the ball about between us. Back and forth we passed the ball for several minutes before my furry friend approached and put the head on me. In the stands the fans laughed, and they cheered even louder when the bear removed his head and revealed himself to be the injured Andy Goram.

Looking back, it seems insensitive and naive, but it's what we thought at the time. The enormity of my encounter with John McStay eluded us. It would take weeks to comprehend fully. Far from it becoming the start of great things, it would sound the death knell for my career at Ibrox.

13

ESCAPE TO EVERTON

I had the spectre of a jail term hanging over me and little else to show for my fifteen months at Rangers. Walter Smith was brutally honest when he sat me down in his office and said, 'Dunc, it's best for you to get out of Scotland.' I cried my eyes out. It wasn't the first time I'd broken down in front of him. It was an emotional moment. Walter was fundamental to me first signing for Dundee United. And then with him at Rangers I believed I was at the best club in Britain. I was twenty-two and I thought the only way was down.

But where was I to go? Ossie Ardiles wanted to take me on loan to Tottenham, who were struggling in the Premiership. I didn't think London was a good move for me – for obvious reasons. 'I'd rather sit on the Rangers bench than play in the Tottenham first team,' I told Walter. Undeterred, Ossie came in again in September 1994. I turned him down a second time, a few weeks before Alan Sugar told Ossie he was fired – something he's become quite good at.

Then came a visit from Everton to Ibrox. On paper, Everton could hardly have been in a more contrasting position to Rangers. Champions of England in 1986–87, probably the best side in Europe in 1984–85, Everton had lost their way. They'd lost four of their first five games of the 1994–95 campaign and didn't have a single win after fourteen. Everton had never suffered a worse start to a season in their history stretching back to 1878. A great club was in crisis. The manager, Mike Walker, was up against it and was struggling. They needed players, so chairman Peter Johnson and director Clifford Finch came up to Rangers, trying to get Ian Durrant on loan.

'Look, we've got Duncan Ferguson here,' David Murray told them. 'Walter wants to get him out of Scotland. He's in a lot of trouble up here, we want to put him down the road. Would you be interested in taking him?'

Walter came to me and said, 'Look, Duncan, we want to put you into Everton. What do you think?'

'Yes, just do it,' I said straight away. I'd had enough. I thought, 'Do you know what? They play in blue, I'll go there.' I just fancied it. I didn't want to go to London. And I just thought, 'Well, Liverpool, Everton, come on, let's do it.'

'Is this the end of me at Rangers?' I asked Walter.

'No. It's a three-month loan, you'll be coming back. We want you to stay where you are, get yourself some game time, get out of the pressure that's happening up here. Everywhere you turn there's problems. Get down there, get yourself some minutes, and crack on.'

I desperately needed the change. And Everton urgently needed me. They idolised their big no. 9s, and I knew that. Everybody loved Andy Gray. He'd been at Dundee United. Graeme Sharp was loved as well, Sharpy scored a lot of goals. But particularly Andy Gray – the Everton fans absolutely worshipped him. Andy was one of the people. It was never about goal records, it was about him, his character, the way he played for the team, the way he represented the fans and the important goals he scored. I wanted to be loved like that. I said, 'You know what? They need me. I've found a home, and I'll give it a go.'

When I arrived at Goodison Park, it was love at first sight – the city, too. I immediately felt at home. Liverpool's a special place. It's the character of the city, the people, the feeling of community, the honesty and the humour.

'You're only going on loan for three months,' Walter reminded me. Rangers wanted to bring me back. 'Sorry, Walter,' I thought. I'd only been there a matter of weeks when I knew there would be no turning back. Once Everton is in your blood you do or die an Evertonian.

Before I arrived at Goodison, I'd looked at what the club meant to people. I saw what the legendary forward Dave Hickson said about the club after he retired in 1963: 'I would have broken every bone in my body for any other club I played for, but I would have died for Everton.' As Everton would quickly turn from a job to a passion for me, I understood what Hickson meant. The 'Cannonball Kid' became a good friend of mine. We'd go to Chester Races. He came to my wedding. He used to be on the lounges at Goodison.

And Howard, the great Howard Kendall, who became a good friend. 'With Manchester City it was a love affair, but with Everton it's a marriage,' he said when leaving Maine Road for a second stint at Goodison in 1990. I later spoke about that with Howard on many occasions. We always recalled Alan Ball's memorable line about the club too: 'Once Everton has touched you nothing will be the same.' Bally was so right. Everton would become the ten best years of my career. THE. BEST. YEARS. Everton would become the only team I ever felt I truly 'played' for. That's what happens when you play for Everton. You forget the rest. The rest mean nothing. Within a couple of weeks, I didn't want to go back to Glasgow. This wasn't a loan, this was love. In Liverpool I wasn't getting into trouble in the same way, people weren't targeting me. There were no doormen, no minders. In Scotland, I couldn't go to the shop, I couldn't go out anywhere without a minder. It was this small goldfish bowl and I was a name, who'd moved for big money, and I was a target. Even though at times I made myself a target. But in Liverpool I felt protected from the start. I found sanctuary in the city and in the people.

I was genuinely excited when I drove into Bellefield. Everton's training ground was nothing special – three showers, one toilet between the thirty of us, and only one communal bath. I met Mike Walker and chatted to him. I would play five games for him, and the Everton fans immediately seemed to take me into their hearts. I fought for the jersey. I fought for them. I liked the social side of Liverpool. I mixed with the fans in Mathew Street. I danced with them. I sang with them. I had many a night out with many of them. I always had time for them. I soon loved them and they seemed to love me too. I felt protected. I felt I was one of them. They could see me on the pitch getting stuck in for them.

Then Everton got rid of Mike Walker and brought in a man who was to change my life.

14

BY ROYLE COMMAND

Big Joe Royle came into the club on 10 November 1994. Eleven days later, my Everton career took off and almost crashed at the same time. We were fighting relegation, had one win in eighteen – eight points – were rock bottom in the table, our spirits were down, and just to make things worse, Liverpool were coming to Goodison Park on 21 November in Joe's first game. The pressure was on.

I was living in the Moat House Hotel, in the city centre, conveniently surrounded by nightclubs, which wasn't a good idea. I was in the hotel just living my life. On the Saturday, two days before the derby at Goodison, I went with a couple of mates for a nice Italian meal in Mathew Street. They were building the new bus station and part of the street was getting renovated. My mate George showed me how to cut through. I'd had a few glasses of red wine, and I shouldn't have driven, but I did – I was young and daft. I drove through the cut-through, into the Moat House car park. A light came on; the bizzies came in behind me and pulled me over.

I was thinking, 'Right, I've got a fifty-fifty chance here. He could be a Red [Liverpool]. Or he could be a Blue [Everton], and he could let me off.' As soon as he stepped out of the car, I realised he was a Red. He knew who I was, didn't he?

'Have you had a drink, Mr Ferguson?'
'I've had a drink.'
'Right, blow in the balloon.'

The limit was 35ml, and I blew 38ml, which surprised me because I'd had a few glasses of red. I thought it would be a bit higher.

I was taken to St Anne's police station where they put me in a holding cell. All around me it was chaos. They knew I was the Everton striker and the bizzies were all arguing with each other, screaming at each other, Blues against Reds. 'Why have you lifted him? Jesus Christ, he was in the car park. What's the problem?' Blues were saying to Reds. The hatch in my cell opened up and Blues started handing me pints of water, saying, 'Duncan, you're on the limit. We've got a doctor coming down to see you, to take your blood, because you're just on the limit, but maybe in another four or five hours you'll be clear.' The Blue boys in blue tried to help me. The doctor came down, took my blood, and I was still over the limit – just. They eventually let me out at ten the following morning. So I went back to the Moat House to try and get some kip. I was devastated to get lifted for drink-driving twenty-four hours before the Derby.

Later that day I had to go training. When I got to Bellefield, I said to Joe, 'Look, I've had a major problem here.'

'What's happened?'

'They stopped me drink-driving.'

'You're joking me, Duncan.'

'I came through the bus station. I wasn't that drunk.'

I felt terrible. I still do to this day. You shouldn't be drink-driving, should you? It's wrong.

'Can you play?' Joe asked.

'You're too right I can fucking play.'

Joe was thinking of pulling me out the derby. The press got wind. It was Joe's first game and he's thinking we're bottom and my star striker's been in the nick. I convinced him I was up for it.

'I want to play. I need to play.'

Joe could have dropped me. But he put me in right away, and that was good management, I thought, from Joe. 'Go on,' he said to me, 'go and get stuck in.'

And I did. I ran riot. I was feeling guilty, but I played well. Neil 'Razor' Ruddock, Liverpool's hard-man centre-half, kicked me early on, and that really fired me up. He then went through the back of me. I climbed to my feet and just glared at him. That woke me up. He prodded the bear.

'When you get angry, you become unplayable,' Joe said to me.

I went to war that Monday night for Joe, for me, for Everton. I absolutely battered Liverpool for our opening goal in the fifty-sixth minute. Andy Hinchcliffe delivered the perfect corner, as he often did, and I was too quick to meet it for Razor and John Scales – a towering header, bang. David James in the Liverpool goal had no chance. We'd worked on that set-piece. It was all about the delivery. Andy put it right on the money, all I needed was a touch for my first Everton goal. It was an incredible feeling to get that pressure off my back. Coming down to Everton, only on loan, that made me feel even more like I belonged. I ran over to the Gwladys Street end in the corner where the chapel was. Euphoria. I'd felt nervous, now I felt only excitement. I knew how special it was to the fans. I'd arrived. The rest is history, as they say. The Blue side of the city loved me for that moment. I was desperate to repay them.

Corners were where I would do a lot of my damage in front of goal at Everton. Razor would later say I was the best header of a ball he'd ever seen. Manchester United's Dion Dublin would also say I was a nightmare to mark at corners, because I ignored everyone and just focused on the area I was going to attack.

I had worked on my heading back in the day in the tenements. I'd head the ball off the entries and the walls again and again, building up my neck strength, accuracy and technique. I had a good leap and was aggressive in the air. I'd put my arms up for leverage and protection and make sure I got good, clean contact with the ball. I could hang in the air like a basketballer. I was the best at it. 'I want to head that ball.' That was my mantra. I don't think anybody could head the ball better. Not many could cope with me.

Eventually, thirty-six of my sixty-eight Premiership goals were headers. Up until a couple of years ago, my nine headed goals in one season in the Premiership (1997–98) was a record until Harry Kane beat it. And, let's face it, Harry played in a better team and got better service. I got a hat-trick of headers against Bolton in 1997. Only Solomon Rondon, for West Brom against Swansea in 2016, has done that in the Premier League.

Of course, these days I've heard about all the risks of heading. I've read the research linking heading to dementia. I'm a prime candidate, aren't I? I headed the ball more than anybody. People will laugh at this but I used to have a standing joke: 'You don't see many tall pensioners, do you?' If you're tall, you're in a bit of trouble, basically, you're not going to last. It's a joke, and people will always laugh when I come out with it, but then you think about it. All the time throughout my career, and even now, when I've been to old people's homes to meet fans, I never see a person that's six foot or over. Never! I know we shrink a bit as we get older but not that much. So, I spent a career heading the ball *and* I'm over six foot. My future's not good, I'm probably doomed. At least there's no history of dementia in my family. I've got good genes.

My dad's still going strong, and my mum's still there. There's hope for me yet.

Still, I wouldn't change anything for the headers, the goals and the mayhem I caused on the pitch during my career.

I was involved in the second goal, too, that November night against Liverpool. It was my challenge on James that set up Paul Rideout. I looked over at the ecstatic fans, saw and heard their love for me, and once again knew I belonged.

'Duncan became the legend before the player,' Joe Royle would famously say about me. I understood what he meant, that the fans had taken to me as a character, charging around like I did in that derby, but I would prove myself as a player too. In the years to come I always loved playing in the derby, and the fans loved to see that passion. The first eight times I locked horns with Liverpool we never lost. The fans *really* loved that. Eight times!

What did I do after my first derby win? I walked down to Kirkland's Wine Bar, then on to the Buzz on Lime Street, in a posse with my new friends like a wee firm. There were fifteen, maybe twenty of us who marched straight in and up on to the balcony. The whole place went mental. Punters were all jumping up on the stage, screaming, 'Duncan! Duncan!' Tops flew off as if it was a big rave. It was crazy. I had never seen anything like it. The incident with me and the police had really stuck with all the Scousers! I was a bit of a boy, wasn't I? A character. We'd just beaten Liverpool and I'd been in the police station twenty-four hours before. I was seen as one of the lads. 'You're a Scouser now! You're one of us!' they kept telling me. Of course, if we had got beat 2–0 and I was crap, then it would have been a different story, wouldn't it? But we were victorious.

'You'll never go back north. We'll never let you go.' Great times.

BY ROYLE COMMAND

I think from that game on I became a talisman for the Everton fans. I'd been lifted, I'd been in a few fights, but I was their striker, I was in their city, and I was going out all the time to the local bars on Mathew Street like the Retro. God, I loved that place – tiny but very thirsty. Retro knocked back more Cristal champagne than any other bar outside London. After hearing about the drink from some pals at Stringfellows in the West End of London, I got into the unlikely trade of ordering it with some mates for the bars in Liverpool. They'd sell it at £65 a bottle, and make a few quid mark-up. It wasn't a business for us. We'd just get the boys to order it in. And we'd drink it. And we'd get hundreds of people at places like the Retro. The bars would be heaving, full of my new Liverpool friends, and everyone was going through the new Cristal like it was water! The delivery boys brought cases in and said, 'I must be going to the wrong place!' Because the Retro was so small. No, we said, just put it in the corner there. Yes, all of it. We were spraying it everywhere.

Retro became the place to be, and Cristal the drink to have. The Liverpool striker Ian Rush used to stop by – he'd come in a few times at lunchtime for a drink. Quite a few Liverpool players like Rushie were Everton fans. Not many of the Everton players themselves mixed in the city. It was usually only really me. But I loved being in there, buying drinks, making friends. The Retro became a legendary place for me and for many in the city. So many people ended up going there. Even every crook and gangster. Many times the police came in and said to the owners, 'Look, we want to put cameras up in here, we want to put bugs in.' And, of course, the owners wouldn't do it. They didn't want to put people off. The gangsters drifted in because that's where the money was, that's where the Cristal was, that's where it was all happening. It was a vibrant place and was rammed. It was safe. There was never any trouble.

Everton apprentices like wee Franny Jeffers came down to the Retro, almost like a pilgrimage, for me to give them money. I'd be standing at the back, and they'd all come in and say, 'How are you, Duncan? Are you all right?'

'All right, son, what do you want to drink?' And I'd get them a drink. 'Here's a few quid. On you go.' I'd buy them a drink knowing full well they'd really come down to get a few quid.

In the end, I was giving them thousands. I should have been saying, 'Don't drink, son. Stay at home.'

I soon became so embedded in the city and the club that I was determined to make my loan deal permanent. After the Liverpool win, I played in the 1–0 defeat of Chelsea five days later. We battered them. I hit a post and hit one crossfield pass to Gary Ablett that showed my creative side. Then in early December we beat Leeds United at home, and I scored my second goal for the club – Hinchcliffe again, left-footed corner, inswinging, great delivery, and I just leapt and steered the ball in with my head. So easy. John Lukic, no chance. We were lifting clear of trouble, and I was playing a big part in the rescue operation. So Everton and Rangers got talking.

I got to know someone at Goodison who knew all the players' wages. I'd meet him in the toilet and he'd show me the players' contracts. Dennis Roach and I were in negotiations with Big Joe and Clifford Finch and they were saying to me, 'We're giving you £7,000 a week, you're going to be the highest-paid player in the club.' I was thinking, 'I'll find out about that.' So I said, 'I need to go to the toilet.' And this guy I was pally with would meet me in the toilets.

'They're offering me £7,000. They say that's top whack here.'

'Nah, there's more on that. I'm sure [Daniel] Amokachi's on more. Give me an hour to get hold of the contract and come back out.'

I went back into the meeting. 'Seven grand a week . . . I'm not sure. I need to talk about it with Dennis.'

So Dennis and I went outside.

'Duncan, it's good wages,' Dennis told me. Little did Dennis know.

'Yes, I know, but let's hold on a bit.'

I met my man, who had Amokachi's contract, and the first year was £7,000, then £8,000, then £9,000.

I went back to the meeting. 'No, no, I think I'll take £8,000, £9,000, then £10,000 a week.' I nailed it, and they gave me it in the end.

So at that time I was one of the highest-paid players in the country because I'd had the two biggest moves, to Rangers and Everton, in the space of eighteen months. I would eventually earn millions in my career, although at that point I was giving most of it away. When I wasn't giving handouts at the Retro, I was tipping the apprentices who did my boots. Suddenly all the kids wanted to do my boots at Everton because I was so generous. I'd give them £500 for a suit. 'Get yourself down to The Cricket, get them to make you up a suit and send me the bill,' I'd tell the boys who cleaned my boots. I had more boot boys than boots!

Anyway, my deal was made permanent on 11 December 1994. Rangers got £4.3 million so at least they made a few quid. Everton were happy – they got a targetman, which the club was famous for, a player prepared to give everything. Everton fans love someone who goes to war for them. All fans do, particularly the working class. I was a battler, wasn't I? I tried to be invincible. I was Big Dunc, who led Everton's line and smashed anybody I came across. And in the end, I played up to it a bit. It's not me really deep down, but I was aggressive on a football pitch. Hard. Even when I was battered by a centre-back I refused to go down, throughout my career. I cannot remember a physio coming on the pitch to me. I never dived either. I was an honest player. That's how my dad brought me up. I'm not a cheat, I played the game hard but fair, and fans related to that. 'Look at Ferguson, he's tough,' I heard them say.

I got hit plenty of times, I would soon have stitches and often blood everywhere. I'd go off the side of the pitch but I'd refuse to take treatment. I wasn't the only one. Loads of other players wouldn't get the physios on. Back then, it was embarrassing getting the physio to come on to you. Just look at it now, how football's changed. Players going down all the time, screaming. Physios on all the time. Too much.

On 25 February 1995, another Hinchcliffe corner, another powerful header from me, Manchester United's Peter Schmeichel the beaten keeper this time. I set off in celebration, ripping my shirt off, twirling it above my head and flexing my bicep. (Four years later, Ryan Giggs replicated this famous celebration in that FA Cup semi-final win over Arsenal – but I did it years before Giggsy! And with a much better physique!) After the game, I laughed when Everton got a letter from the FA condemning my 'excessive celebration'. Can't you celebrate a goal, especially the winner against the reigning champions? Aren't goals what the game is about? Excessive celebration? Killjoys! I was the first one to do that shirt-off celebration and then UEFA and the FA banned it and began booking players from 1995. Thankfully, it wasn't the last time I took my top off – and I don't mean dancing in the Retro!

Celebration or no celebration, that season Everton had real momentum. We went on an FA Cup run, beat Derby, Bristol City and Norwich, and the whole club lifted. They were magical times. The game on 12 March was a sweet one, the quarter-final against Newcastle. They had a great team – Paul Bracewell, Lee Clark,

Rob Lee, Keith Gillespie – and they were fancied to win. But my team-mate Dave Watson scored after I set it up, headed it down to him. That was a big moment for me. I got man of the match after we beat them 1–0. Night out!

The semi-final on 9 April, against Spurs at Elland Road, was another great day. I was injured so I went along with my mates. There was this great guy called Ray Parr, a massive Evertonian who owned No 9, a house across the road from Goodison where fans met for a good meal and a good drink before games. I slept at Ray's house before the Spurs game, then in the morning Ray drove me into Leeds, all the fans mobbing the car, shouting my name. It was special.

I was behind the goal, in a box with all my mates, having a day out. And all the fans around about were amazing, everyone singing my name. Everton absolutely battered Spurs 4–1, an incredible performance, one of the best Everton have ever put in. When people say 'Your name's on the cup', we had that feeling. You go on a roll, don't you? Tottenham were tipped to beat us in the semis; they had Jürgen Klinsmann, Teddy Sheringham, Darren Anderton and the rest playing for them, but we smashed them. Another night out! We had a party in Liverpool, all of us together again, down Mathew Street in an Italian restaurant, all the players in there, all partying again, ready to go to the final. Big Razor Ruddock came to the party, dancing around, jumping around. None of us were going to say to him 'You're not welcome, lad', were we? The size of him!

I sorted the nights out. Social organiser! I'd only been in Liverpool six months but I knew everybody. The two guys I first met down there, Tommy Griff and George Downing, are still my best pals. Massive Evertonians. I bumped into Tommy on my debut at Fratton Park on 5 October 1994, a 1–1 draw. Tommy was well respected, a big Blue and a fantastic character. Tommy sold anything – perfume, watches, jewellery, suits – and served them up to the players. Walter Smith was one of his customers. Walter phoned Tommy once and said, 'I need twenty tickets for Cream, can you get it sorted?' Tommy sourced the tickets for the nightclub through his contacts.

Think of *Only Fools and Horses*. Yes! You've got him! Tommy sold his famous fireworks to the players at Bellefield, including to Tommy Gravesen, who used to light them and fire them around the training ground. Three days after I met Tommy I met George when we played Southampton at The Dell. George was into property and has done extremely well for himself and become a very successful businessman. George was best man at my wedding. Tommy and George had mates who all became best pals of mine.

Joe started to hear about it, so Everton moved me out of the Moat House, out to Warrington somewhere. It probably seemed like a good move. That didn't stop me going back into town and going out. After I got a twelve-month ban for the drink-driving offence, one of the lads organised me a driver. I was in the town like the Pied Piper. It was great back then. Fantastic.

We saved the club from relegation. In our team we had the dogs of war in John Ebbrell, Barry Horne and Joe Parkinson, a midfield Joe Royle built that got fully stuck in. Some of them hadn't been playing under Mike Walker. Joe knew how to blend players together, put them in a team and get the best out of them. We were a tough, hard-working side that got the results Joe needed to keep us in the division, and to reach the FA Cup final at Wembley on 20 May 1995.

The squad made an official FA Cup song, and sang the chorus of 'All Together Now – for Everton'. I didn't get involved as I can't sing a note. It's a good song by The Farm, anyway. They rewrote the lyrics for us:

BY ROYLE COMMAND

Remember folks back in '66
We won the cup with Catterick;
Kendall's boys in '84;
Now big Joe Royle is coming back for more.

I talked to the guitarist from The Farm quite a bit, a big Evertonian, Keith Mullin. That was a catchy song.

Big Joe Royle had us heading south on the Thursday before the final. We trained at St Albans and stayed at the Sopwell House hotel with its many pictures of teams on the walls. It was inspiring. Then on the bus to Wembley. The cup final's mad. Everyone's obsessed by it – the history, the occasion, the shot at a trophy, Wembley itself. Ally McCoist had come down from Rangers and wanted tickets off me. I was actually in the dressing room getting ready and Ally was on the phone, demanding, 'Tickets, Dunc!' I had to go back out, through the tunnel, and personally hand the tickets over the top of punters to Ally. Anything for Ally.

Back in the dressing room, I listened to a truly inspiring team talk from Joe. This was Joe Royle at his best, focusing us, bonding us even more, and making us believe. 'Don't worry about the result or how you play,' Joe told us. 'I want you to enjoy it. Enjoy the moment.' He took all the pressure off us. 'Lads,' he continued, 'you've done brilliantly this season and the form you've shown in the league has been amazing. We're here now. So we may as well go and win it.' Brilliant. Then I banged on our theme song, 'Holding Out for a Hero' by Bonnie Tyler.

We lined up on the pitch, and Prince Charles came down the line. I like the royals. I sat under a portrait of his mother in the dressing room at Ibrox. I always made sure I got a good bow in. I nearly headbutted Charles in the chest! I made full sure I was telling him, 'I'm one of you lads!' That's why he smiled at me, if you watch the footage.

Everton were up against a great Manchester United team. Alex Ferguson's side beat everybody during that period, didn't they, really? Well, usually. They had Roy Keane, who was world class. He had aggression, ability, and everyone respected his ferocious work ethic. Keane was tough as anything, wasn't he? He actually said in one of his TV programmes that he 'used to stay away' from me. That surprised me. Believe you me, Roy, it would have been tough for us to square up to each other, because I had the same idea. Keane never shied from any tackle, never shied away from anything – any player, any team, any adversity. That's one of the reasons I admired him. A few years later, in that famous Champions League semi against Juventus in 1999, Keane was outstanding. Got booked, out the final, but made sure he still drove United there. To be the main man at such a big club as United for twelve years takes some doing. People talk about Keane being intimidating in the tunnel, but I never knew. I blanked everyone in the tunnel.

We had a decent side ourselves. Neville Southall was fantastic that day. Big Nev was coming to the end, thirty-six, but showed his experience, got himself in front of that ball, and made a double save from Paul Scholes. Nev was a great goalie. The best I ever played with, I'd say, was Andy Goram because when I played with him at Rangers he was at his peak. But Nev at his peak was world class, the best there's ever been. I liked Nev. Big Nev is an Everton cult hero, idolised at the club and I got on fantastically well with him. Nev had a lot of respect for me during that time as a player. He knew I was decent, he played with a lot of good players in his Everton time. He just saw that injuries inhibited me but he was a big supporter of mine.

I'll take you through the outfield players at Wembley that day. Right-back: Matt Jackson, good player who could get up and down the pitch. Centre-back: Dave 'Waggy' Watson, a great player, a great captain, brave and aggressive, said the right things, had respect, and had done it all in the game. People would follow him – and I was one of them. 'Waggy' was a warrior really, somebody you could trust in a battle. Again, like Nev, Waggy was coming to the end. Thirty-three. Loved at the club. I got on well with Waggy, still do, we keep in touch. He was an usher at my wedding. Alongside Waggy at centre-back: Dave Unsworth – strong player, left-footed, he marked Mark Hughes well that day. He had a good left foot and scored a lot of penalties for Everton. Very calm under pressure. Left-back: Gary Ablett. I was pally with Gary. I roomed with him before the cup final. He was a very good player, played for Liverpool as well as Everton, and a very versatile defender.

Right wing: Anders Limpar – a flair player, quick, could dribble by people. Left wing: Andy Hinchcliffe played further forward that game, had a good left foot. As I've mentioned already, I got a lot of my goals at Everton through him swinging in those corners. Central midfield: we had Barry Horne, one of the dogs of war, a hard player who battled away and got stuck in. Joe Parkinson, same again, tough. Joe and Barry did well against Roy Keane and Paul Ince that day, and smothered them. They were outstanding in the engine-room.

Striker: Graham Stuart, a good player who had a good career and scored goals. After thirty minutes at Wembley it was his shot that hit the bar, and our other striker Paul Rideout headed in the rebound. 1–0! Paul was a good player who scored a lot of important goals, none more so than the cup final winner. Our Bonnie Tyler.

Punters ask me about those players and whether they were good guys to hang out with at the time. Well, off the pitch I mostly didn't mix with them. I did my own thing. I was with my own mates in Liverpool. I wasn't in a group with them, other than during that cup run. I mostly hung around with my own crowd.

But they were all good lads at Everton, we all got on well. That was the secret of that squad's success.

We'd better finish the team overview with me. Well, I'd recently had a double hernia operation so I was on the bench for the final. I bent Joe's ear to get me in the squad for the final. I felt guilty that John Ebbrell missed out. He never even got on the bench because Joe took a gamble on me. Rideout came off quite early, on fifty-one minutes, so Big Joe put me in. I'd done well against United the previous game and Joe felt I could do a job, but I wasn't fit, and I shouldn't really have played.

I was up against Steve Bruce and Gary Pallister, proper, tough old-school defenders who respected me because of the game before. In fact, they had recommended me to Alex Ferguson. Bruce was coming to the end, a bit smaller, so Big Pallister used to mark me. He was good in the air, Pallister. I loved the challenge. I seemed to raise my game against United. On big occasions, against big players, I wanted to prove myself. I always raised my game against United and Liverpool.

The game finished 1–0. We had done it! I went up to receive my medal from Prince Charles. Another smile. I got one of those plastic blue noses the fans wore and put it on. Then it was off to the Everton party at the Royal Lancaster Hotel near Hyde Park. I'd booked four tables for my friends, while all the other players shared tables. I had forty people there, and we were uncontrollable. Bobby Davro, the comedian, was on stage, doing his stuff, and good luck to him because nobody heard him. We were making so much noise. We had ten round my main table. I got on top of the table, in my kilt, took my shirt off, and I was singing and dancing. Some of my mates got up too. Everybody was going by and shouting, 'What's under that kilt, Duncan?' So I was lifting my kilt up, I was that drunk – I was flashing to everybody. Graham Stuart came across and led his sisters away! All the players were coming over and pulling their women folk away. At one point, I lost my balance, the table crashed to the floor, everybody fell, but I was still standing. 'That's my centre-forward there,' Big Joe Royle said to Tommy, looking up at me.

Next morning we went back north at 10.30, crates of Labatt on the bus, and stopped off at the services on the M6. We took the FA Cup into the Wimpy! Well, might have been Burger King . . . my mind was still a fog. Waggy placed the cup on the counter and gave the order: 'Twenty burgers and chips, please.' I took the cup and was running around the service station with it. Everton fans were there, loving it.

It was a mad day, and things got madder once we arrived back in Liverpool to a hero's welcome. The parade was crazy – 500,000 Evertonians lining the roads, standing on balconies, roofs, even hundreds clinging to the steel frame of the megastore being built near Goodison. The fans were unbelievable. The importance of winning the FA Cup . . . it's a massive thing, isn't it? It's the oldest football competition in the world. On top of that bus swigging a beer and looking at all these happy fans, I didn't think about the history, I was too in the moment, too busy celebrating. As I've got older, I've thought, 'Jesus Christ, I was part of one of them. I won it.' Only 144 FA Cup finals between 1872 and 2025, and I'd won one of them. It's a historic achievement. It continues to mean a lot.

After the parade we had the big bus drive around, and then of course I ended up back in the Retro on Mathew Street, with all my crowd there. What wonderful times.

I had been in two Scottish Cup finals and an FA Cup final in the space of a few years. I thought this would last for ever. You think you're invincible when you're young. Looking back, there was a pressure being Duncan Ferguson that was weighing on me, even then. Fans and the media were interested in me, and I liked building an aura as a player. I had to live up to that mystique on the field, but I wished I didn't at times.

Take, for example, the end of that FA Cup final. Pallister and Bruce shook my hand. I very rarely shook people's hands in that era. Even after big games. It's crazy really, I'd just walk away from the players. A couple of years later, after a game at Goodison in 1997, David Beckham wanted to shake my hand. United were close to winning the Premiership after beating us 2–0. Beckham turned round, said, 'Duncan,' and put his hand out. I turned my back on him and walked away. People saw it, and asked me why I blanked him. The real reason was because I was a twat. He was David Beckham, a top player, world class, who won the league, and there's me, snubbing him. I had no reason for blanking him. I should have given him a kiss and taken his shirt off him! But I didn't. Of course, I didn't swap shirts then either. It wasn't really quite the thing you did then anyway. I wish I had. You know what? David Beckham's shirt? Eric Cantona's shirt? They'd have been nice mementos.

Back in 1995, after the FA Cup final, I continued to enjoy myself. We were up for anything as players. Daniel Amokachi, who had also come on for us at Wembley, was getting married in Tunisia to a supermodel, Miss Tunisia. He invited some of the Everton players but everyone was heading off on international duty or on holiday. I liked Amo, he was a good fella, so I said to Ray Parr, 'Let's go and surprise Amo!' Another daft idea over a glass of wine!

We flew with another mate to Gammarth on the southern Med. My party were soon stood round a pool, I was having a Scotch, and we were all having a good time. Everyone in the hotel started bowing at one point, and I laughed with my friends, 'They must know who I am.' Duncan Ferguson, FA Cup winner! Of course they never knew me at all! They were bowing to this guy who'd just arrived at the hotel. We got chatting, and it turned out this lad was a Tunisian prince who'd been dethroned, and all these people were still supporting him. Top bloke – I'd support him. Anyway, my mate got an ulcer and nearly died that evening, and the prince took him away to see his personal doctor. Our mate came back recovered, and said, 'He is the prince! You want to see his palace, man!'

We all got smartened up and went off to Amo's wedding. What an event! Amo and his bride, Nadia, who's Tunisian, came in on thrones. I was having a fantastic time and was made up for Amo. They threw petals in front of the happy couple, everyone was singing, it was beautiful – all colours and lovely outfits. Amo just looked at me in shock that we'd gate-crashed his wedding. Well, he had invited us, we'd just not replied!

'Dunc!'

'Amo!'

He couldn't believe I had come.

It was great being out there with Amo, relaxing, having a drink, enjoying the sun and the freedom. Because I knew what was coming my way.

15

BANGED UP AND BANGING THEM IN

A few days later I was up in Scotland in court, getting sentenced to a term in prison. You know the rest. I hadn't thought much about what might happen in prison while I was at Everton. Daftly, I didn't care. I was still a kid. I care now. When I think about it, I think, 'My God!' But part of me then wanted to go to prison. Stupidly, I thought, 'This might be exciting. Put me in there. It might be good. It might be interesting.' That changed the moment I went through the doors into Barlinnie. 'Jesus Christ, it's happening.' Still, as I've said, the way I got through it was by being mentally tough. I said to myself: 'It's an injustice, I've still got a job when I get out. I'm not in for really doing anything. I'm not a paedophile or something.' I lived to tell the tale.

When I got out and returned to the club, I paid Everton back. I was top scorer with ten in the Premiership during the 1996–97 season. Without me, Everton would have been screwed. And that's not being big-headed. I got us a point with two goals at Old Trafford on 21 August. For one, Andrei Kanchelskis whipped the ball into my feet, I turned Gary Pallister and shot past Peter Schmeichel. Once again, United couldn't handle me. I came down on Eric Cantona and smashed him on the top of his head. 'You and me in the tunnel,' Cantona growled. He was trying to be all brave but when I turned away from him, I glanced back and he was rubbing his head furiously.

BANGED UP AND BANGING THEM IN

I got the equaliser in the derby on 16 April 1997, not long after Joe Royle had left and Dave Watson was caretaker manager. Joe left after a disagreement with the chairman over the potential signing of Tore André Flo. 'I wanted to sign Flo,' Joe later said. 'Peter Johnson didn't want to spend the money. We ended up parting by mutual consent. Or resignation. Take your pick. I felt completely empty. It was like a divorce and took a long time to get over.' Maybe Joe was signing Flo to replace me. Another 6ft 4in centre-forward. But three days later I got the ninetieth-minute equaliser at West Ham. We finished fifteenth, two points above oblivion and relegation. I helped keep us up.

I'm throwing numbers, dates and results at you just to show that I was a player as well as being popular with the fans at Everton. I was top scorer at Everton during the 1997–98 season too, with eleven in the Premiership, and my tally wasn't fattened by penalties. It would have been easier if I'd had a settled strike partner. Howard Kendall had returned in the summer of 1997 and the club made a lot of sales to sort themselves out financially. The team changed a lot and it was a collective struggle all season. Not for me personally: oddly, I played my best football under Howard. The great man made me captain against Bolton Wanderers on 28 December. I owed Howard. This was the first time I'd been made captain of any team. Howard put big commitment in me. It was a masterstroke. I got a hat-trick of headers against Bolton that day. That Everton side was not a great one; it was partly made up of players from the lower divisions. Nicky Barmby was elite level. For one of my goals, Nicky crossed from the left, on his left foot, his weaker one, so I knew he wouldn't get a big contact on the ball. I knew it wouldn't be a deep cross, so I ran to the front post to score.

And I scored at Anfield in the 1–1 draw on 23 February – a good goal too, smashed past keeper David James with my right foot. Steve McManaman apparently two-footed me during that game but I didn't notice. I threw Paul Ince in the air at one point. I don't think 'The Guv'nor' was very pleased with me. That draw was a big point, and after the whistle I screamed 'Come on!' to our brilliant fans in the Anfield Road End. We eventually stayed up on goal difference from Bolton. Once again, Everton would have been nowhere without my goals.

I feel I led the team through that relegation battle of 1997–98. Nobody really talks about it. It's like the Forgotten Season, airbrushed from Everton's history and fans' memories. I think it's because Howard Kendall was such a great man, people don't want to rake over the year when Everton had a bang average team. Howard had been so successful as a player at Everton and during his first stint as manager from 1981 to 1987 that people almost didn't want to associate him with such a bad season when he came back to manage the club for a third time.* He got dealt a bad hand with no finance. We were really terrible. The club bought a lot of players from lower divisions because we didn't have a budget. We sold good players like Gary Speed, Andy Hinchcliffe and Graham Stuart in the January window. We were so close to getting relegated once again. Yes, that season I carried that team. The coaches used to say to me, 'That's twenty-seven man of the matches in a row you've had.' I scored nine times in my last fourteen Premiership games of the campaign to keep us up. I was Howard's captain and felt all the pressure on me; taking my club down would be horrendous. We had Coventry in the last game of the season, 10 May 1998, and were under the very real threat of going down. I was physically sick in the car park beforehand. We drew, Bolton lost at Chelsea, and we stayed up on goal difference. I have never been so relieved.

---

* Howard, of course, had also come back to manage the club from 1990 to 1993, a spell that wasn't as successful as his first reign.

BANGED UP AND BANGING THEM IN

Still nobody talks about that year. Everybody talks about the following year, 1998–99, when Super Kevin Campbell came in, and rightly so. Kevin arrived in March 1999 and scored nine in eight to keep Everton up. Everybody mentions that, but never 1998, when I went through the full season fit – and lucky for us I did. The club would probably have been gone if I'd picked up an injury. Finished. Down.

Howard resigned after the end of the season. I knew what a toll the year had taken on him. I met with Howard a lot of times during the season. We got very pally and we used to go for long lunches together. Even after the season we socialised. We'd sit at a table, go through the team, and we couldn't name many of them. The campaign had only finished a fortnight or so before. Maybe it was the Rioja or we just wanted to forget how poor we were.

'Who played up front that day with you, Dunc?'

'Who was the right-back?'

'Who was the centre-back?'

Couldn't recall. That sounds disrespectful but we honestly couldn't remember. Maybe Howard and I were trying to erase the season from our minds too!

I loved Howard. A gentleman, intelligent, knew a player, could motivate a player, great with the team, great on the training ground. All the players loved him, despite some of the results. He kept us up during the 1997–98 season and that was an achievement in itself. Howard was good with me, had me as his captain – and he always backed me when I got into trouble.

16

SEEING RED

During my playing days, I know for a fact that a lot of opposition players were scared of me. They'd phone up our centre-backs at Everton and ask, 'Is Dunc up for it tomorrow? He's not going to beat me up, is he?' And my mates would be going, 'He's not like that.' They'd come into the dressing room the next day laughing at the effect I had on the opposition. I played on it. Blanked players in the tunnel, intimidated them, and I took that on to the pitch. Don't look at anybody, don't say anything, don't shake their hand afterwards. I've mentioned this aura. I used it as an intimidation tool, so that people were going, 'Big Dunc's hard as fuck. He's nuts.' I wasn't. It was front.

Of course, Barlinnie gained me a reputation overnight, and it snowballed. In some ways I spent an entire career trying to shake it off. But I realised I could use it to my advantage, gaining a psychological hold over my opponents.

As I've said, it's not real. Everton fans know what I'm like deep down. I'm not a tough guy, I'm not a bully, I try to be nice to everybody. But, unfortunately, I've reacted a number of times to being provoked on the pitch. These incidents added to this fearsome reputation, and I'll admit I needed more self-control.

BT Sport did a football programme on hard men before the WWE Royal Rumble 2022. They looked at all the usual suspects – Stuart Pearce, Roy Keane, Patrick Vieira, Joey Barton, Joe Jordan and Julian Dicks. They spoke to Jimmy Case, Mick Harford, Norman Hunter, Billy Whitehurst, Steve McMahon, Terry Hurlock and me. 'What happens at the end of this WWE bout?' they asked. 'At the end, Duncan Ferguson emerges, covered in blood, surrounded by dead bodies with a big grin on his face' was one of the replies. I don't see myself like that. I'd be the first one out. I wouldn't see or hear the end bell. It's amazing how a reputation follows you around. I'm embarrassed about that reputation. Most of the guys on that BT Sport list were a lot tougher than me. I regard myself as a guy who was brave on a football pitch.

Still, I'll try to explain the lengthy charge-sheet against me on the pitch. When I worked later with Phil Neville, he told me that Sir Alex Ferguson always used to tell them, 'Don't upset Duncan Ferguson. Switch him off.' It was only when I was angry that I reacted. On 14 January 1995 I got sent off for elbowing the Arsenal midfielder John Jensen at Highbury. I never touched the Dane, I just pushed him and he fell theatrically, screaming 'aaargh!' He stitched me up. It was embarrassing. But that was around the time when it all kicked off with foreign players diving.

We used to call it 'cheating'. It's 'simulation' now, as if that word makes cheating more sophisticated and acceptable. Everybody dives now. It's part of the game. In my day, we'd never dive. It definitely wasn't for me, anyway. But Jensen dived, let out a stupid wee scream and got me sent off for no reason. The referee Robbie Hart never even saw the incident but must have heard Jensen's cry, turned round and sent me off. Never a red card. 'It was a shove,' my manager at the time, Joe Royle, said.

Three seasons later, on 14 February 1998, when Howard Kendall was in charge at Everton and had just been presented with his Manager of the Month award, I got sent off against Derby County at Goodison. Howard defended me. I'd been on my best behaviour for Howard all season: only five yellows in twenty-four games, which was good for me. We were in a relegation battle and the manager, who I greatly admired, needed me. In the Derby County match, players were pulling my shirt and blocking me all game, doing everything to stop me reaching crosses and corners. My team-mate Carl Tiler flicked the ball on, and I was just about to turn to score when Paulo Wanchope grabbed me. I know it was Valentine's Day, but come on. I flattened him. Howard tried to stick up for me as his captain. But I'd flattened Wanchope. I wasn't proud of it. I was bang out of order. I put Everton at risk of relegation. I let the great man down. I know Wanchope rolled around, and that was all the ref Steve Dunn saw. I was off, when the original foul was Wanchope's, but what I did was indefensible. Everton had to survive seventy-four minutes with ten men and eventually lost without me.

Everton fans were so angered by Dunn's performance that some wrote to the FA at Lancaster Gate demanding he apologise to me for his mistake. There was no mistake. But I appreciated the fans' support. They always had my back. I listened to Howard afterwards saying a penalty should have been given for Wanchope pulling me back. I did agree with Howard's post-match view of Wanchope's reaction. 'That part of our pitch is very even,' Howard told the press. 'I don't think it needed rolling!' Howard would never fine a player. He would ask them to pay for a team night out instead, which would probably be a Chinese meal. As it happens, the club had organised a trip away to Cyprus a week later. There must have been an international break. I had to foot the bill because of the Wanchope red card so I paid for a big night out while we were in Cyprus: meals paid for, drinks paid for, nightclubs boxed off, the lot. The bill came to £25,000. Madness. My team-mates over the years must have thought it was always a free bar. Marbella trips, end of the season, again all on me. But, to be honest, it was my fault, not theirs. I always wanted to be the big man and pay all the bills.

Opponents throughout my career often tried to control me by grabbing me, and refs did nothing about the grappling. A few years later, on 1 April 2002, I got sent off by Steve Bennett at Goodison for punching Bolton's Fredi Bobic. He'd grabbed me, and I reacted to shake him off. My manager at the time, David Moyes (Moyesy, who we'll meet properly later in the book), read me the riot act in the dressing room, especially as he'd just given me the captaincy. Moyesy didn't appreciate my reaction of a right hook to Bobic's solar plexus.

'Big man, what were you thinking? You've let us down massively.'

'I know, gaffer. I thought it was Kevin Nolan.' It was a case of mistaken identity. It was me, it was my punch, but I thought it was the Scouse kid Nolan. He was trying to be a bit smart with me. I knew he was a Red, and I thought it was him. I hit the wrong guy. Fortunately, we'd won 3–1.

'You could have let the rest of the players down,' Moyesy said.

'I was out of order, gaffer.' I apologised to Moyesy and the team.

I was an angel for the next two years. Unfortunately, I lost my halo. I went back to my old ways. I'll never forget Everton's visit to Leicester on 20 March 2004. I was booked for putting a hand on Leicester defender Nikos Dabizas and then just before the break I grabbed his team-mate, midfielder Steffen Freund, and wrestled him to the ground. Freund kept on fouling me, he was just doing his job, and I was getting nastier. Ref Barry Knight gave me a red, so I argued with him, and then got Freund in a head-lock. Another red. On my way off I made sure I gave the Leicester fans some stick. They deserved it. They were giving me wanker signs so I gave them a fuck you, up yours gesture back. I had no problem giving it back to fans who baited me. Earlier in my career, in

August 1995, I had absolutely wound up 8,000 Celtic supporters when I scored in Neville Southall's testimonial at Goodison. I celebrated that goal in style, as an ex-Rangers player should.

But back to that Leicester game. Moyesy stood up for me: 'I believe Duncan Ferguson is a victim of his reputation.' I still got charged by the FA and had to go down to St Andrew's, Birmingham City's ground, for another disciplinary hearing. I really couldn't care about them. Just old boys from the FA having a go at young players. But Everton didn't want me to get a big ban. They needed me.

On the way down, the club secretary, David Harrison, who's now at Manchester United, said to me, 'What's your defence going to be, Dunc?'

'Well, there isn't really one. I'm bang to rights. Freund's a knob, he deserved a throttling, and the Leicester fans were twats, so I told them so.'

'OK, Dunc, I was hoping for a slightly stronger defence.'

'OK, David, I've got a defence for you. Remember the last time I got sent off, it was that lad Bobic from Bolton. He's German too. Like Freund. I just have this thing about Germans.' They always beat Scotland after all!

David laughed. He didn't seem sure it was the most convincing defence.

So we went in, and this FA judge fella began, 'Mr Ferguson, this terrible incident . . .' and then asked me why I'd tangled with Freund.

I explained I had a thing about Germans – first Bobic, and now Freund. 'I was only getting them back for the war,' I joked.

David could hardly control himself. 'Oh, for God's sake!' I heard him whisper to himself.

The FA didn't buy my German defence. They banned me for four games and fined me £10,000. Of course, I've really got nothing but respect for German players. I was just a bit immature then.

I had some tight battles throughout my career with some of the toughened old centre-backs. Arsenal's Tony Adams was always hard to play against. He smacked me right in the nose once.

'I didn't mean it,' Tony insisted.

'I bet you, you did.' And he did.

Fast forward a couple of decades, to when I was Forest Green manager in 2023. I was in a wee coffee shop on my own in Cirencester, thinking, 'I don't know anyone here.' Next minute, knocking on the window, it's Tony Adams! He's got a house down there. God, he was looking fantastic, at his playing weight. 'Tony, God almighty, you look fit enough to play.' He came in and sat with me for fifteen minutes, passed me his number. Nice guy. He never mentioned the elbow. I remember. But I forgive him.

The Liverpool defender Sami Hyypiä said in his book that 'it's really unpleasant to play against Ferguson, because he always plays a bit wrong and uses his elbows'. OK, fair comment. I once flattened Sami at Anfield. He was getting the better of me so I just came across and banjoed him with the elbow. I watched the ball, bang, put him clean out. Hyypiä got stretchered off, came back on, and right away I had respect for Sami. I thought, 'Not only are you good, you're a brave bastard as well.' 'It was wrong what I did, it was out of order,' I told him as he came back on. I bumped into Sami a few times later in Liverpool and always got on with him.

Gary Pallister from Manchester United was one of the toughest I played against, more difficult than Steve Bruce because he was so tall. If I had height advantage over a player, I'd destroy them. I was a leaper. The bigger the player, the more even the battle. Brucey was a bit smaller, and he was coming to the end of his career when I played against him; Pallister was a harder opponent.

The Hermann Hreidarsson incident at Charlton Athletic on 28 December 2004 was not one of my finest moments. He was a big tough Icelandic defender who believed he was a bit of a boy, he really fancied himself. Franny Jeffers told me about him. Franny was a friend of mine from his days at Everton and was now at Charlton. Franny wasn't playing that day but I saw him at The Valley before the game. Good lad. When I came on for Marcus Bent in the seventy-fourth minute, Hreidarsson was pushing me and winding me up. That got my blood boiling. I waited nine minutes and then flattened Hreidarsson. I elbowed him in the face and he was poleaxed. I shouldn't have, I was totally out of order. I'm so remorseful now. The guy didn't deserve it. No matter what I'd heard about him being a handful, it was a cheap shot by me. Mike Riley sent me off. He'd only just noted me coming on. I was in the dressing room after, and the door went and I thought it was somebody coming in for seconds. It was Franny Jeffers running in, going, 'Dunc, I'm absolutely made up you did that. He had it coming. He's been pushing people around at training. I cannot wait to go into training tomorrow, wind him up and say, "Big Dunc showed you, son!"' Expensive, though. I got a fine of almost £60,000 off Everton and a three-game ban off the FA. I bumped into Hreidarsson in Marbella a few years later and we got on great and I did apologise.

I'm trying to keep track of all the red cards. I'm not proud of it. A year or so later, on 31 January 2006, I had a run-in with the defender Paul Scharner at Wigan. People often ask me whether it was a physical thing with Scharner. Yes, I punched him in the solar plexus. I was getting older, my powers waning, getting a bit more narky, and he gave me a push in the box so I hit him. I got sent off for violent conduct – my eighth red. I equalled Patrick Vieira's record so I was in good company.

I wasn't expecting Scharner's team-mate, wee Jimmy Bullard, to ask me, 'Are you all right?'

'No problem, wee man,' I said to Bullard as I walked off.

I don't know why but this little man said, 'See you in the tunnel, Dunc.' What?!

'I wouldn't have done that,' I heard Bullard's team-mate Lee McCullough telling him.

I'd still waited in the tunnel for Bullard. He didn't want to come in at first. He realised he was not in the same weight division. When he did, I had a few words. Funnily enough, two weeks later I was at Goodwood races and Jimmy was there. His teammates pushed him in front of me! I laughed, 'Don't worry about it!' I was getting stuck into a beautiful cigar and a nice bottle of champagne.

But back to Wigan. As I came off the pitch there was a melee, and I just put my fingers in right-back Pascal Chimbonda's eyes. I got a seven-game ban. I was only on the pitch for eight minutes. Moyesy told the press that I deserved to be sent off. 'I can't defend him.' I had no defence.

'You've let everyone down,' Moyesy told me. That time I was frustrated with myself. I was starting to come to the end of my career by that point; I wasn't the same player.

Football's a physical game. I even attacked some of my teammates during my career, one or two in the dressing room. One was the Everton midfielder Don Hutchison. He was a bit of a mouthpiece, especially with the younger players. We were building up to a game with Liverpool, and Don was on the training ground mouthing off to people. I didn't like it. He was picking on young kids like Danny Cadamarteri, a talented forward at the time. I stopped the training. I didn't like what he was doing but Don didn't deserve what was coming. It was the way Don was, very competitive, but I didn't like it.

'Shut it, Don. Don't speak to them like that or I'll flatten you.'

Don bit his lip, which I'm glad he did. I didn't want it to escalate. I fronted Don up and he swallowed it. When we played Liverpool three days later, Don came in, sat down next to me and was mouthing off.

'You red-nosed twat [he had played for Liverpool], shut your mouth,' I told him.

Hutchison said something under his breath, and I flew at him, grabbed him and threw him all around the room, over the physios' table, everywhere. Everybody jumped in, and Archie Knox and my old pal and manager Walter Smith, who had joined Everton at the end of the 1997–98 season from Rangers and would be at the club until 2002, came between us and tried to stop it. I'd never have punched Don. I only grabbed him and roughed him up by his neck and then I threw him.

Tommy Gravesen was another team-mate of mine and I didn't like some of his actions. The Dane was aggressive to young players. I felt as if he'd pick on them, and mouth off. So one time I waited until he came in the dressing room and then just threw him around. I didn't punch him. He used to have a terrible habit of . . . well, I really don't know how to describe it. He'd try to pin a young player like Leon Osman down on the ground and wrestle them. I didn't like what he was doing. I had to have a few words with him. He tried it on me a wee bit and soon got the message: don't. He thought he was a bit of a boy. He pushed me. I gave him a wee tickle on the arm. Tommy got the message.

'Dunc, can I come and move my gear and sit next to you?' he said.

Maybe he was all right after all! In the end, I liked Tommy Gravesen, a good guy but a bit different.

Throughout my playing career, because my style was aggressive I often got punished by refs. But there were times when I got sent off for daft things, like against Blackburn at Ewood Park on 21 September 1996. David Elleray sent me off for what he called 'industrial language'. Rubbish. I sang, 'Who's a baldy bastard? Who's a baldy bastard? Na na, na na.' There were lots of receding hairlines on that pitch, one of them being Elleray's. He took offence. Another red. I wasn't singing loudly or shouting in his face, I just made sure he heard me. Tim Sherwood, Blackburn's captain, even tried to rescue me. He ran up to Elleray and said, 'He was singing at me, ref!' Tim's got big, long hair, so I sang, 'He's got hair down to his knee' – the Beatles, 'Come Together'! Elleray still sent me off. Help!

While we're on refs, there's a photo of me in the Liverpool derby at Goodison on 11 December 2004 shouting at the referee Steve Bennett. He's leaning backwards as if by the force of my words. It's now a famous picture, and I get asked to sign copies of it by Evertonians. I guess it sums up my approach to authority. I didn't have a problem with refs. It wasn't them, it was me.

17

LEAVING HOME

'Don't go, Duncan! Stay!'

I was in a car leaving Goodison Park late on 23 November 1998. Destination: Newcastle. Everton fans were clinging to the car and pleading with me not to go. I was torn. Ruud Gullit had made it clear how much he wanted me at Newcastle. I was his first signing. I'd be playing alongside Alan Shearer. 'You'll cause havoc on opposing defences,' Gullit had told me. When he became player-manager at Chelsea in 1996 he'd tried to get me to go there as well. Now he wanted to sign me for Newcastle.

In fact the move was forced on me – Everton wanted me out.

By chance, Everton were playing Newcastle that November night. Walter Smith pulled me into his office that morning. His words chilled me to the bone: 'Everton are inviting offers for you.'

'What?!'

'The club are looking to sell you if the money's right. I don't want to sell you. The chairman does.' Peter Johnson was coming under pressure from the bank, apparently, and I was Everton's most saleable asset.

I sat there listening to Walter, stunned, heartbroken. I'd just been talking to Dennis Roach about extending my deal at Everton. This was the chairman's doing – Peter Johnson was selling me. Everton didn't want me. They just wanted the money.

LEAVING HOME

By the afternoon, I knew Newcastle were interested. I met with Walter again.

'I don't want to sell you,' Walter said, and I believed him.

'Good. I don't want to go.'

'But the club are chasing money, Dunc. Newcastle have got a few quid. And we're struggling here.'

'I still don't want to go.' I'd only recently scored against Manchester United. Again. I was Walter's captain. 'I'm happy here,' I told him.

I then got a phone call from Dennis. 'This is happening, Dunc. Everton want it done. The board don't want you any more. You need to go.'

I didn't want to leave. I was suspended for the Newcastle game but I went, watching on, supporting the lads – such a weird feeling. My old team, the team I loved, against what could be my new team within twenty-four hours. Sue Palmer, Everton secretary, came looking for me.

'Newcastle want to talk to you upstairs after the game in the chairman's office,' Sue told me.

As I walked up the stairs with slightly weary steps to speak to them, Walter and his assistant Archie Knox came down.

'For God's sake, Walter, I thought you'd have fought my corner a bit harder to keep me.'

'What are you talking about, Dunc?'

'You know what I'm talking about. You've agreed £8 million with Newcastle for me. I'm about to talk to them right now.'

That was the first Walter said he'd heard about it, passing me in the corridor. I believed him. Walter looked stunned. He was in shock.

I went up to Peter Johnson's office. Gullit and Dennis were in there, getting the deal sorted. Word spread and Everton fans made it very clear they wanted me to stay. My dad was so grateful to the

173

fans for their support that he went into the Winslow, a pub opposite Goodison, to thank the fans that night.

But the club wanted me sold. Everton did well out of me. Bought me for £4.3 million, sold me for £8 million and got four years' work out of me.

I travelled to Newcastle to sign the contract. I still didn't want to go. Walter phoned.

'Duncan, the fans are kicking off.'

'I know, I know. I'm happy to come back, it's not a problem. I won't sign the contract. I'll come back.' I didn't sign the contract for two or three days, hoping that Everton were going to say, 'Do you know what? Let's pull the plug.' But they never did. They needed the money. They wanted me off the books. So I signed.

The fee was £8 million. My financial package was £9.2 million over five and a half years.

'What are you getting, Dennis?'

'I'll take the £200,000.' Conveniently, he took the £0.2 million. That was Dennis for you.

'Oh, right.' Fair enough. What I didn't know was Dennis was getting paid by Newcastle as well. I know I got a salary of £38,000 a week.

I scored twice on my debut against Wimbledon on 28 November. Two flukey goals! I always play quite well on my debut. I hit the first one into the ground, then a fortunate header. I ran off to celebrate with the fans, my baggy shirt flapping around them. Everyone wore their shirts big then. And I got to play with Alan Shearer. I've seen some great strikers. Thierry Henry was an unbelievable player, Wayne Rooney and definitely Alan.

I liked Alan. For some reason, people ask me what Shearer was like. Some people didn't get on with him. I always got on with Alan. But we never spoke to each other when I first went to

Newcastle. He was at one end of the training field at Chester-le-Street, I was at the other. He was coming back from rehab at the time. I was coming into the club as a centre-forward on big money and I'm not sure what money Al was getting.

Alan was a fantastic player, the best. We soon began to play two-touch all the time at training. Quite a crowd would gather to watch us, including all the players. We'd play in the gym, in the kit room, in the boot room, in the dressing room, always two-touch, me and him. We were the best at it. When me and Alan were fit, we were unstoppable. Right foot, left foot – unstoppable.

We became very close. 'When we're in the tunnel I look across at the other team, Dunc, and they're looking at you and I can see their fear!' For three to four months nobody could handle us.

Even to this day we keep in touch. My wife Janine and his missus Lainya get on very well. At the millennium, Lainya phoned Janine and invited us over for a party.

'I'm not fussed.'

'Come on, let's go,' Janine said. 'It's a nice gesture.'

So we went to this party in Alan's house. I was thinking there'd be 500 people there. Al's popular, knows everybody. I took my last two bottles of Cristal champagne. I marched up to Alan's house, banged on the door, he opened, and I went, 'Here you go, two bottles of champagne – Happy New Year!'

'I've heard about this stuff!' Alan said. He never opened it, just stuck it in his fridge! Rightly so.

I looked around. There was nobody there. Just five couples – me, Rob Lee, the late, great Gary Speed (God bless his soul), the physio Paul Ferris, and a cricket player called John Morris, who'd played at Durham. I soon learned that Morris's claim to fame was that he was with David Gower in the Tiger Moth plane that flew across a cricket ground in Queensland where England were playing in 1991. Good guy, anyway. That's all who were there. So for Alan to invite us was special. You'd think there'd be hundreds there, but we had ten people and his kids on a karaoke.

I always wanted Alan to be Newcastle manager. I always thought that was his destiny. He was caretaker for a few months in 2009 but was never given a proper chance, really. He had a hard break on it.

Initially, I got on well with Ruud Gullit. He obviously rated me. He'd tried to sign me for Chelsea. I got on another FA Cup run in 1999. I came on in the semi-final against Tottenham at Old Trafford that went to extra-time, played really well and changed the game. I got the better of Sol Campbell, and in the end he gave away a pen with a hand-ball from my pass towards Gary Speed. But I was fighting another injury by the time we got to Wembley to play Manchester United in the final on 22 May. I came off the bench for Didi Hamann and put myself about, caused some problems. I set up a chance for Silvio Marić but I was struggling. We lost anyway.

I fell out with Gullit big-time later that summer. Newcastle fans always mention that infamous Sunderland game on 25 August when Gullit started me on the bench at St James' Park. The thing nobody talks about is that I was coming back from injury. I was always going to be on the bench. But Alan was also on the bench, and he was 100 per cent fit. Alan was raging. Gullit just didn't like Shearer. Alan was a fantastic player, and maybe Gullit was jealous of him. Two world-class players clashing, who knows? It happens. Anyway, before the Sunderland match we played a game in training, eleven v. eleven, and me and Alan were in the reserves, against Gullit's first XI. Gullit kept shouting at his players, 'Keep Alan on his left foot. Keep him on his left foot.' So Alan smashed one in the corner with his left. Because Alan was fantastic. I scored a header, we won 2–0, and normally

LEAVING HOME

Gullit would have changed it around, pulled you out and put you in the other team. But he never changed it.

Obviously, this was all Gullit trying to get Alan out of the club, which seemed incredible as Alan had so much to give. He was one of the best strikers England ever had. And when Newcastle got beat 2–1 by Sunderland in a deluge at St James' Park, Gullit came out with a few bad statements, saying it was because of Alan and me. Some rubbish that 'the game slipped away from us' when Alan and I came on. I was upset because I'd been dragged into Alan and Gullit's broken relationship. I was steaming, so I got up early in the morning, the Thursday, and shot in to see Gullit. Beat Alan to it – he was still on the school run!

I just gave it to Gullit, absolutely hammered him. The Scottish boy, Steve Clarke, now Scotland manager, was in there. I didn't even know who the assistant manager was then. I didn't care. I was too busy giving it to Gullit. 'You're out of order,' I told him. I called Gullit every name then stormed out. Just as Alan was storming in!

'All right, Alan,' I said as I marched past.

'God Almighty, big man, you beat me to it,' Alan laughed. Like a double tag team! Gullit didn't know what hit him. He was gone within forty-eight hours.

I never really settled at Newcastle. It started to build up within me. Our Italian defender Alessandro Pistone got it one day. I had a right go at him and he didn't deserve it. He was swearing at me in a five-a-side game. 'Look, mate, shut up,' I said. He wouldn't. 'I'll see you inside,' I told him. I chased him into the physios' room and threatened him. I shouldn't have. I was angry with myself and Pistone just happened to be in the firing line. He got the brunt of my frustration. I liked Alessandro, great guy, who invited me to his wedding. We were pals when he later moved to Everton and I was back there.

At the Newcastle Christmas party in 1998 we all got a gift off the other players, and mine was a prison shirt. I got off lightly. Didi Hamann got a copy of *Mein Kampf*. I remember Alessandro received a sheep's heart.

When Gullit lost his job, Bobby Robson came in and got the best out of Alan, who was low on confidence because of Gullit. Everyone needs a pat on the back, and Bobby gave him good advice. Alan was playing with his back to goal a lot, and Bobby said, 'Run in behind more.' It worked. Alan was phenomenal throughout his career. I was good in patches. Bobby was a really great guy who'd seen and done it all, like I would later experience with Carlo Ancelotti.

I loved playing for Bobby. I was strong and I destroyed Tottenham, and Sol Campbell, in the FA Cup on 22 December 1999. Warren Barton crossed, I headed on to Gary Speed in front of the Leazes End, and that started the rout. 6–1. Four days later, I scored a glancing header past Sander Westerveld, the Liverpool keeper. I was the targetman, I played for the first ball and Alan would feed off me. Three weeks later, I scored two in the first four minutes as we blew away Southampton at St James' Park. Bobby just brought the best out of me.

Bobby was hilarious. In an effort to keep himself fit he'd try to do sit-ups on the grass with us all in pre-season and sometimes needed helping up.

I got to the gym too. I bulked up at Newcastle.

'How much weight do you lift in the gym?' my doorman mate, my minder, asked me.

'I lift light weights, keeps you fast and slim. I look to be in the gym all the time.'

'Why don't you lift a bit heavier?'

'Because I like to be sharp and fast.'

LEAVING HOME

'Start pumping the weights. Eat five times a day, start taking protein and build yourself up and be a man mountain.'

I'd go in the gym at Newcastle in the morning, and all the lads were in there. I'd do some heavy weights. I think the lads were impressed.

'All right, lads?' I'd say, and walk out.

Normally my fighting weight was 13st 8lb, 13st 10lb, 13st 12lb, 14st max. I pushed myself to 15 stone. I got on the punch-bag, absolutely battered it. Look at the pictures of me at Newcastle. My neck was huge, my shoulders broad. I was pushing everybody around.

I enjoyed my football more under Bobby than Gullit. 'You're not missing training like I heard you were doing when you first came here,' Bobby said. 'You and Alan are the most in-form partnership in the Premiership.' And we were, for three or four months. We scored thirteen goals between us in sixteen consecutive games under Bobby.

Yet I had a terrible injury record at Newcastle. The physio Paul Ferris used to bring a ball into the treatment room to keep me busy because I was always in there. My injuries stopped me from getting to where I should have. I put it down to that broken toe and my lifestyle. Maybe all these muscle injuries wouldn't have happened if I wasn't drinking and was in my bed at ten o'clock, which is what everyone does now. Hydration and rest are key. I never knew what water was. They were stretching, I was dancing around. So I got the injuries and I believe that killed half my career, really.

I played only forty-one times for Newcastle because of problems with a hernia, calf and hamstring. I had ten operations. Double hernias, pubic bones, sciatic nerves. I've got a scar a yard long right down my bum. Footballers don't get hernias these days, due to all the core exercises they do. But back then, no one did the exercises, and because I had big, long legs, I was weak and susceptible in that area. I was getting double hernias a lot.

When I was fit and in form, I felt untouchable. I gave the fans some moments. We played Fabio Capello's Roma at St James' Park in the UEFA Cup on 9 December 1999 and I worked over their Brazilian defender Zago. We clashed at one point, he went down, trying to get me sent off, but the ref wouldn't fall for it. Newcastle fans didn't forget and hammered Zago.

They never forgot the way we battered Manchester United on 12 February 2000 at St James' Park either. I scored one of my best ever goals. Alan turned Rob Lee's long ball my way. I was on the edge of the area, with my back to goal, Jaap Stam close by, but I swivelled and struck the ball on the volley past Mark Bosnich. Sir Alex must have thought 'here we go again' and described my goal as 'a marvellous hit', which was praise indeed. I gave Stam one hell of a time. Bobby was also very complimentary about me, and actually turned all Churchillian: 'Duncan fought Jaap Stam in the air, he fought him on the touchline, he gave him a torrid time. I don't think Stam enjoyed it one bit.' Bobby was right and Stam was some player. 'He probably found Ferguson the toughest, most awkward striker he's played against this season, and that includes the Champions League,' Bobby continued. 'Big Duncan is beginning to enjoy his football again.'

Yes and no. Newcastle was a difficult time for me because of my injuries, and my wife couldn't settle in the city. The facilities at the club weren't the best. We trained at the Riverside, Chester-le-Street, home of Durham cricket. Not ideal. I definitely got on with the Newcastle fans. Kids came up to me after training as I got in my car. I'd get out, open the boot and dish out training kit. They loved it. But my relationship with the club lacked the intensity of my bond with Everton. A month later, when we played at Goodison on 19 March, I was reminded of

LEAVING HOME

what I'd been forced to give up. Those passionate Everton fans, that special feel of Goodison, that connection with a club and a city. Goodison was home to me. Everton mean so much to me. Before the game there were Everton fans in the hotel coming up and showing me their Everton tattoos and saying, 'Duncan, we love you. Come back.' Everton fans were even in the dressing room before the game. Newcastle won 2–0, but my head wasn't in it, my heart wasn't in it. After our second goal, from Kieron Dyer, I just jogged back to the halfway line. I couldn't celebrate Everton losing. It was an incredibly difficult day for me.

Every time I got changed for a Newcastle game I'd look at my Everton no. 9 tattoo on my left bicep. Only cost me £40 from Sailor Jack's! I got the ink done after Barlinnie. After the fans wrote all those wonderful letters that got me through those long, lonely days and dark nights, I got a competition going in the local Everton paper and I promised I'd put the best design on my arm. Which I did. Artwork selected by a fan. God, I missed Everton. I needed to go home, and so did my missus. We had a three-month-old baby. It was time to return.

18

GOING HOME

Newcastle are a great club and I did like being up there, but my wife didn't. Janine couldn't settle. We had just had our first child and Janine wanted her family around her, In the pre-season of 2000–01, Bobby Robson pulled me in and said it was time I moved on.

'Bobby, I'm not going to move anywhere unless it's Everton,' I said.

'Well, Everton want you back. But they're only paying £4 million, Dunc. It's not enough. I've told the board that. You're worth more than that.'

I wouldn't have left Newcastle for anybody else. But because it was Everton, because Janine wanted to go back, I agreed to go. There was a major problem, though. I was entitled to compensation as I hadn't asked to leave. I was on big money at Newcastle, £38,000 a week, with three years left on my contract. It got messier and messier. Bobby accused Dennis Roach of 'hijacking' and 'delaying' the deal. Bobby claimed Dennis had demanded £700,000 on my behalf to leave. Dennis would have got a cut of that, Dennis usually did, no surprise there, and he had a point. My deal at Newcastle lasted until 2003, so they would have owed me nearly £6 million in wages. Dennis said he asked for £250,000. Newcastle wouldn't agree, so I just sat tight – well, got on a flight.

I joined the Newcastle squad in Barcelona for their friendly on 13 August with Espanyol. I didn't play.

My planned Everton medical for 16 August was cancelled. I felt for Walter Smith. I caught him on TV and could hear his frustration. 'Having agreed a deal with both parties on Friday we were very hopeful of signing Duncan. We are extremely disappointed that the deal will not now proceed.'

Dennis went public on the day I was supposed to be having that medical on Merseyside. Instead I was kicking my heels on Tyneside. 'People of Duncan Ferguson's quality should not be treated in this way,' Dennis said. 'Duncan has told me he will fight for his place.'

Newcastle didn't want that. They wanted the deal to go through while paying me as little compensation as possible. So did I. It was a stand-off. I wasn't bothered about the compensation. I walked away from the contract. I never got a penny. It was never about the money for me. Newcastle were furious with the delay as they wanted to use the money to buy Craig Bellamy from Norwich City. During the delay, Coventry City nipped in and got Bellamy.

That's when it all kicked off with what Dennis was doing. Bobby tore into him. 'When the Ferguson deal was cut and dried, it was two plus two equals four,' Bobby said. 'But some people tried to make it six and we wouldn't be party to that. I'm very angry about it.' Typical Dennis.

Eventually, the deal went through. But the FA accused Dennis of breaching rules on 'double' payments on my deal and also five others. Newcastle believed Dennis was being paid by both Everton and Newcastle. Agents doing two-way deals? He was just greedy, Dennis, he just couldn't help himself. He got charged by the FA with seeking or receiving irregular payments for my £3.75 million move and another deal, Paulo Wanchope's £3.65 million transfer to Manchester City from West Ham. Bobby and Joe Royle both complained to the FA about his conduct. Dennis was accused of demanding £350,000 from Newcastle. I got dragged in as well about paying him. I denied it. I got him off the charge. I had paid him. I just could not grass him up.

Anyway, I was going home. My wages were much reduced, down to £21,000 a week. Look, it was still great money. I know how lucky I was to be well paid to do something I loved, but players look at the TV cash pouring into clubs and want a slice of it.

Everton had come back in for me because Bill Kenwright's consortium had bought out Peter Johnson and Bill loved me as a player. He wanted me back, almost as a statement signing – 'Look what I can do.' Walter also wanted me back. 'The prodigal son returns!' was his message to me. I was desperate to get back. Everton's my spiritual home.

When the move finally went through on 17 August, I spoke at a news conference at Goodison that afternoon. 'Everton's in my blood,' I said. I also claimed I was '100 per cent fit', which wasn't completely true. I came back from Newcastle with terrible injuries. I've still got a big scar on my calf, which at the time I kept pulling over and over again. So I came back, but I was struggling. I was down at Rodney Street clinic in Liverpool under the Doc – great fella, old school.

'How's your injuries, Dunc?'

'I've got no injuries, Doc. Look at me, man. I'm fit.'

'Come on! Have you got a calf injury?'

'No, I'm fine, everything's cool.'

'You're not right and you've not been training properly in pre-season.'

'No.'

Walter phoned down and said, 'Look, how is he? Has he passed his medical?' Walter just wanted the Doc to pass me. 'If he's all right, he's all right. Let's just get him signed.' I had my scans and somehow was now an Everton player for the second time. I had a calf injury. I hid it.

Walter put me on the bench for Everton's first game of the season, away at Leeds on 19 August 2000. He gave me half an hour – I came on for Stephen Hughes. My calf wasn't right but I eased myself in. In the next game, against Charlton at Goodison, I was warming up and more than 30,000 fans were screaming, 'Duncan, Duncan Ferguson!' I pulled my calf, again. I knew I was going to because it had been tearing like anything at Newcastle. The pain was excruciating. I had to go downstairs in the tunnel because I was white as a ghost. 'What am I gonna do?' I asked myself. The calf was that sore. I went back out and walked up and down. The game started, I was on the bench, and I went back into the tunnel, trying to stretch my calf, trying to hide, because I couldn't run up and down. This was my second home debut, all the fans were there, expecting me to perform.

In the second half, Walter came down, because he sometimes sat upstairs, and saw me.

'You're going on, Dunky.'

'Sound.'

Mark Hughes came off after sixty-seven minutes, and I went on with a torn calf. I could hardly move, and scored two goals. How on earth I managed it, I don't know. Incredible. I just had to get through it. Tommy Gravesen slid me in, on to my right foot. I'm not strong on my right side, I hesitated, remembering I've got a torn calf, but I got the shot away and it went through the goalie's legs. It was emotional. To get off the mark and score on my second home debut was special in front of those special fans. I knew I wouldn't be back in front of them for a long time. Then Franny Jeffers played me through and I scored with my left, off a deflection from Richard Rufus. Another two lucky goals! I always get lucky on my debut.

I watched *Match of the Day* that night. Alan Hansen was on and he said, 'I'd love to be in that dressing room, Gascoigne and Ferguson. Oh, cancel that! I wouldn't want to be in that dressing room! Too much fun and games!' If only Hansen had known.

Paul Gascoigne was a genius but a lost soul by the time he came to Everton. I liked Gazza but I saw him as someone I didn't want to be about. I was hearing that he was causing trouble in the city, and was lucky he never got hurt on a number of occasions as some other players in Liverpool have done when mouthing off too much. Gazza at times wanted to socialise with me but I could never be with him. It would cause me problems. I got on really well with Gazza but he was going through a difficult time with his own demons.

One day, Gazza tried to sell me a car from a boy in Middlesbrough. Gazza said it was a 55 AMG Mercedes – just what I wanted. Gazza's mate brought this Mercedes down and I paid the boy £65,000 with a cheque. He went back with the cheque and left the car. Richard Gough, down playing with Everton at this time, clocked it.

'You know, Dunc, that's not a 55 AMG. I've got one.'

The reason I wanted the car was because I'd seen Richard with one.

'What do you mean?' I knew next to nothing about cars.

'That's a 430. There's no badges on it.'

I went off and found Gazza.

'That's not the car I wanted, lad.'

'Well, that's the car they've gave you.'

'Get the boy on the dog and bone.'

Gazza didn't want to call him.

'Give me his number, then.'

So I phoned the boy up, this Joe.

'Look, lad, that car is not a 55 AMG. I want my money.'

'It is what it is,' he said.

'See that cheque, it'll bounce. If you want your car, you'd better come down and get it.' I rang off.

Gazza was standing there, twitching. 'Dunc, these are heavy people, these guys will come down and these are serious people you're dealing with.'

'Gazza, you tell your mate to come down or there will be no car. The car will be gone and he'll have to get it off my mates, and believe me, Gazza, your mates from Middlesbrough won't get that car back.'

Gazza was shaking now. He thought his mates from Middlesbrough were heavy. Well, they probably were. My mates from Liverpool were a whole lot heavier. It's Liverpool, isn't it?

Gazza had to sort his Middlesbrough mates. They must have driven at 200mph from Middlesbrough to get there. Lucky for them because it would, I'm sure, have cost them a few quid to get it back.

I like Gazza, but I wasn't surprised when he moved on from Everton after two years. He wouldn't have survived in Liverpool the way he was acting. Players have their peak. Gazza was once a world-class player, idolised by England, but his powers were leaving him. He was past his peak at Everton. He was thirty-three when he joined, in the twilight of his career, and injuries and lifestyle had taken their toll. There were still some moments of genius. David Ginola was one of the best, but was thirty-five when he came to Everton in 2002 and he wasn't very good in his seven games. Like Gazza, Ginola was once a great player but it never worked out for him at Everton. Time is one opponent you can't beat, however skilful you are. Unless you're Cristiano Ronaldo.

Anyway, the day after the Charlton game, I was on the treatment table, and Walter came by.

'Big man, don't be worrying about it, you'll be back as soon as anything. You'll be back no problem, it's only a calf strain.'

I knew different. I'd been hiding an injury. I was worried I was about to let Walter Smith down again. 'All right, boss, no problem.' I was out for four months and needed an operation on the calf.

After they operated on me I eventually got back playing, but the calf was a wee bit swollen. I carried on playing. One day I said to the physios, 'My calf's not right here.'

'Nah, there's nothing wrong with you.'

'Look at this calf!'

I'm lying on the physio's table, in front of the players coming in and out, and the physio starts pushing my calf, and it bursts. Two pints of blood come spurting out all over the physio's table, all over the place, all the players going sick at the sight. It was disgusting, this congealed purple mass of blood and pus rolling down my calf, big lumps of it. It was hitting the sinks, flying up to the ceiling. The physio kept squeezing and it just kept pouring out like an unstoppable plum-coloured river. The bleeding only slowed after about an hour and a half.

'You'll have to go to the hospital.'

'Yes, no problem.'

I jumped in a taxi, went to the hospital on my own and the medics were waiting for me.

'You've lost two pints of blood?'

'Yes.'

'What's going on?'

'You tell me.'

It turned out that when they operated on me, they'd cut something, and the blood had built and built in my calf, festering and congealing.

I had loads of injections. I had one when we were playing

GOING HOME

Liverpool at Goodison. It was pissing it down, the rain was freezing cold, and Everton needed to win. I had a double hernia and they brought the surgeon down to Goodison with the white mask on to give me an epidural. They plunged a big needle right in my stomach, and one right up my pubic bone at the same time. Boom. Big long needles.

'You might be numb from your waist down for a wee while,' the doctor said.

'Well, that might be a bit of a problem, considering I'm playing Liverpool in a minute,' I replied.

It was horrendous. And I went out to play against Liverpool.

'That's never going to happen again,' Everton's physio said to me. 'Where are you sore?'

'Just about here,' I replied, and pointed all over.

Mick Rathbone reckoned he'd 'never met a player with such a high pain threshold'. I remember when Mick, nicknamed 'Baz' after the actor Basil Rathbone, came to Everton in 2002, and I introduced myself: 'I'm Big Dunc, I've finished a few physios' careers.'

'I'm Baz,' he said, 'I've finished a few players' careers!'

We immediately got on, which was just as well as I would spend a lot of time with Baz. Unfortunately.

We had some right characters at the club in those years. I loved Wayne Rooney, good fella, known him since he was a boy. He had written to me when I was in Barlinnie. He's got a picture of when he was eleven with me and his brothers John and Graham; he used to hang around Bellefield, wanting an autograph off me. When he joined Everton, Wayne had followed me around. I was always wary of his age but he loved being around me. We were in the gym one day, doing some weights, and Wayne saw these boxing gloves. He pulled on the right one and I put on the left and we sparred. He was useful. I was trying to duck out of the way and he caught me on the forehead. I never took up his offer of sparring again! A couple of weeks later, on 1 October 2002, we shared a pitch against Wrexham in the League Cup and Wayne, still only sixteen, scored twice. I knew he was destined for the top. Wayne was special. He was one of the two best players in the Premier League – Wayne and Alan Shearer. I had so much respect for Wayne as he handled everything well. I crashed and burned as a British transfer record. He handled everything impeccably.

I loved watching his career take flight. We've stayed close. I went to his wedding to Coleen in 2008 on the Amalfi coast – sixty-four guests invited and I was one of them. Westlife played. What I love most about Wayne is that he's never changed. He's stayed very down to earth. I knew about his ability from when he was fourteen. Everybody knew about Wayne. I laughed when people said 'he's a kid'. Already he was a man, strong physically and mentally. Wayne was a school champion runner, ran like the wind, and he could play. When he came up to the first team, I could see it right away. He was already developing into a world-class player. He had the technique. When he connected with the ball, I could see and hear how good he was. It was the precision, the sound, the way the ball moved, and how quickly it moved through the air. So much of his game was instinct. But it was also about his intelligence. Wayne analysed the game. It wasn't yet a time of looking at video clips. Laptops were only just coming in then. Wayne learned on the street like I did. He was aggressive in the challenge, tactically good, and knew where to run. He learned by watching older players like me.

Watching Wayne learn reminded me of how I became good at pool. I'd watch the best boys playing, because they thought six steps ahead. So I learned and I became really good. I took on my brother-in-law, John Parrott, at pool and beat him 5–4. It was a christening. John's a world champion snooker player but I was good at pool, really good. I'm not sure to this day whether John let me win. Before you hit the ball, you read the table. Wayne was like that with a football. He worked ahead.

Wayne looked up to me. I used to sometimes drive him and drop him off at his house in Croxteth. But I was a bit wary because I had a bit of a reputation. I was doing things I shouldn't have been doing and Wayne was young. There were fourteen years between us. So I kept away from him a wee bit. I didn't want to be seen as if I was leading a young lad astray, which I wasn't, but I probably wasn't the best role model, was I? Wayne came from a good family – I get on with all of them and they all love me. Wayne is a good fellow, a Scouser, hard as nails, boxing family. He came to my kids' christenings, came to the house. We were close back then and he'd ask me for advice. 'I'm going to Newcastle,' he told me in August 2004. He'd just come back from the Euros and was hot property because of his explosive performances for England. Everton were keen to sell him to Newcastle. Kenny Shepherd, who worked with Wayne's agent Paul Stretford, had good connections at Newcastle. His dad Freddy was chairman after all.

Newcastle had bid £20 million.

I advised Wayne. 'You're not going to Newcastle,' I told him. 'Great club, but not for you. Don't go there, son.

'I need to get out, Dunc.'

'I'm sorry to hear that. But don't go to Newcastle.'

We were at Bellefield one day that August, and Wayne came into the canteen. He'd gone in to see David Moyes, Everton's manager since March 2002, and they'd argued over Wayne leaving. There was talk in the *Echo* of Newcastle being interested.

Everton wanted him to go there because they'd get more money. Wayne came back down followed by Moyesy. They were still at it.

Suddenly, Moyesy came into the dressing room. I jumped up and got out of there as quick as I could. I didn't want Moyesy thinking it was me who somehow put Wayne up to it. I hadn't. It was none of my business. So I dropped my shoulder and got out of the firing line.

Eventually, Wayne went and talked salary with Manchester United. Everton wanted to hold on to Wayne and offered him £50,000 a week. Everton couldn't afford that. No chance! Everton didn't have £50,000 a week to give him. It was just a gesture to appease the fans. Anyway, he accepted United.

Wayne lived on the same road as me in Formby. The day he signed for Manchester United, he came over and asked, 'You got any of that champagne, that good champagne you keep, that Cristal?'

'I've got cases of it! The ones the burglars didn't manage to get their hands on.'

'Can I get some? I'm signing for Man United!'

I gave Wayne a couple of cases of Cristal and he went off down my path. I would miss Wayne for Everton, but I wished him all the best on his new journey.

Me and David Moyes fell out along the way. He sent me home from Bellefield on 17 November 2003 after a loud disagreement. Moyesy had become frustrated by my injury record. I'd managed the full ninety in the League Cup against Charlton on 29 October but then got the flu. What with being ill and sent home, I didn't play for two months. Moyesy went ballistic. I thought I might have to move on.

When Moyesy first joined Everton our relationship started

GOING HOME

well. He said all the right things to me. He'd heard I was the top boy in the dressing room. He told me that I was his captain. Everton were fifteenth in the league at the time, and there were only nine games to go until the end of the season. Moyesy said to me that no matter how we did it, we had nine games to keep us in the division. I told him that I would do anything to keep the club up. And I was true to my word. I scored the winning goal in Moyesy's first ever game for the club against Fulham in a 2–1 victory. I scored again in successive games against Derby County and Newcastle United. Three goals in three games. But then our relationship took a turn.

During the next match I got sent off against Bolton for throwing a punch at Fredi Bobic (as I mentioned earlier in the book, I thought it was Kevin Nolan). Moyesy was rightly angry, but I felt his reaction went too far. He wanted to fine me two weeks' wages. As captain under Howard Kendall and Walter Smith, they had never fined me as their leader on the field. The worst they made me do was pay for the team's Chinese meal on a night out (although that could be expensive!). I felt that fining me as captain showed a lack of respect, and perhaps was a mark of Moyesy's inexperience as a manager. I was particularly aggrieved because I had only just come back into the team after injury. I had paid £20k of my own money for rehab in Portugal, in order to get fit to help the team with the relegation battle. I pleaded my case to Moyesy and the board, and eventually they reduced the fine to a single week's wages. I would score again that season when I returned from suspension. And of course the club stayed up. But our relationship after that point was never quite the same again.

Moyesy was only thirty-eight. He was just learning, wasn't he, how to deal with guys like me. It couldn't have been easy going into that dressing room. Moyesy was a young guy, in his first big job, and I wasn't easy to control. He was enthusiastic, really on top of you, really hands-on. Good manager. Me and Moyes definitely clashed, but we'd clash in his office, never in front of people. I had too much respect for my manager for that.

We had survived relegation at the end of the 2001–02 season. But after another season, Moyes wanted me out of Everton. I knew my injury record wasn't good, that I was a senior player and he wanted to make changes. Fine. But do it properly. I came back for pre-season fit and ready to train hard. I carried over a suspension into the new season.

'I want you to leave,' Moyes said.

The summer 2003 Premiership transfer window closed but the Championship one was still open as, back then, the rules were different.

'Could you not have told me a month ago?' I asked.

I felt like Moyesy was sending me to the Championship. I didn't want to go to the Championship. His old club Preston were getting touted as being in for me.

Moyesy had said a lot of stupid things, as I've done, and he did again now. It was an aggressive conversation, very heated. He didn't want me to go to a Premiership team. That's why we fell out.

'You'll never play for Everton again,' he told me.

'You can't determine that, it's got nothing to do with you,' I replied.

'What do you mean? I'm the manager.'

'I don't give a fuck if you're the manager, I'll play in this team again.'

'I won't pick you.'

'You will.'

'What do you mean? I pick the team!'

Moyes had committed the cardinal sin: you should never tell

a player he'll never play again. Never! You can think it but don't say it. It'll just come back to bite you. Your squad will get injuries, suspensions, players will lose form, it's a long old season.

'You're sixth-choice striker here,' Moyes told me.

He might as well have said fiftieth! Everybody was in front of me. But I knew I'd be back. I guarantee he's never said that to a player again, because I was back playing within three months. I came on against Liverpool and took a free-kick. I never take free-kicks usually but I took this one and hammered it against the bar. We lost.

Moyesy thought I was finished. He put me in the reserves. He didn't quite put me in the Bomb Squad, the wee group that trained in the rain with the Under-21s, but our relationship was broken. We never spoke to each other. But I was fit, I trained hard. I knew I was starting to do well because after three months of walking past me in the corridor at Bellefield in silence, Moyesy one day said, 'Morning.'

I didn't reply. I just walked on.

The next day, same thing: 'Morning.'

I blanked him. Moyesy must have hated me. A player shouldn't blank a manager. I was childish, immature. I should have accepted his 'good morning'.

This went on for weeks.

'Morning,' he said again one day.

'Stop saying "morning" to me, will you?' I told him.

'Get up the stairs,' he said.

I went up the stairs to his office and we had it out. We properly had it out. Verbally. It got heated and it could have come to blows, who knows? I was standing. Moyesy was behind his desk. We said a lot of terrible things. I said a lot of hurtful things about Moyesy. I called him for everything. I gave him the Bells of Shannon. I exploded and he gave it back. Moyesy actually showed a lot of restraint. Everybody was in next door, all the coaches, listening in. The players downstairs on the bikes could hear us.

'Look, you're out of your depth and I've got absolutely no respect for you at all and I never will do.' That's what hurt him. But I did have total respect for David Moyes. We all say stupid things. I think that's what killed me in the end. He had to show me the door.

'Right, get out, get out and don't come back. Fuck off. Get out the building!'

'Fucking whatever.'

I went downstairs, took a shower and calmed down a wee bit. I thought, 'Let's go back up, let's try and shake hands this time and try and calm it down because we all say daft things.' So I went back up, and this time all his coaches were with him.

'Look, do you seriously want me to go home?' I asked.

'Get home and don't come back,' Moyes said. I didn't blame him.

OK. I left and sat in my house for two weeks. Every day I phoned up Sue, the manager's PA.

'Sue, tell the gaffer I'm sorry. I want to come back in.'

'I'll tell him, Dunc.'

'Tell him I'm really, really sorry, Sue.'

'OK, Dunc.'

In the end I told Sue, 'Tell him I love him and tell him I shouldn't have said the terrible things I said.'

Eventually the Professional Footballers' Association got involved – not from my side, but maybe Everton took a bit of advice from the union that they'd have to get me in for training at some stage. I got myself back in and it was fine. We shook hands and both agreed to 'move on', which I was grateful for.

'I should never have said what I did,' I told Moyes. I did respect him. I just said what I said to hurt him at the time. When you're in an argument you just say the worst things you can, don't you? I didn't mean it. Maybe he meant the things he said about me never playing again but he probably learned he shouldn't have said that. In the end Moyesy gave me another year because I wasn't finished.

A few months later, on 22 February 2004, Dennis phoned me up and said, 'Do you fancy going to Qatar?'

'Where?'

'Qatar. Look, Moyesy's at Everton, the club want you off the books. You're getting older now, Dunc. Go to Qatar, get a few quid. It'll be great for you.'

'I'm not going to Qatar. I'm playing for Everton. And I can't take time off to go to Qatar. I've got training.'

'No, don't worry, they'll give you a few days off. I've sorted it.'

So I flew out to Qatar with Janine. It was a time when the country's development was just starting off, they were just beginning to build things. Dennis had everything prepared, as Dennis always did.

'A lovely guy called John's picking you up. He'll drive you in, he'll show you a villa, he'll show you around,' Dennis said. 'Don't talk about money.'

'No problem, Dennis. I'll leave the money side to you, don't worry.' Of course, I put the phone down knowing full well that Dennis was saying 'don't talk about money' because he'd done some deal, hadn't he?

This John guy said he'd show us the stadium, and to meet him in the hotel reception in an hour. We came down in the lift and Janine had a miniskirt on and a low crop-top, and all the local men were staring, and she had to go back upstairs and get changed. We didn't know the local dress-code.

John drove us around, and took us on a tour of the stadium. 'One of the royals will put you in his team,' he told me.

'What?'

I'd just scored against Southampton, I'd scored in the Premiership. I was playing well, I was fit.

'John,' I said, 'it's great, a lovely place, but I get good money in England.'

'It's really good money here, Dunc.'

'It's all right – £4 million, tax-free.'

'Four million? Who's told you it's £4 million?'

'It is £4 million, isn't it?'

'No! It's £6 million!'

'Well, I heard it was only £4 million!'

The deal never happened, because Dennis was greedy. He couldn't help himself, Dennis. I loved Dennis. When he died in 2019, of course I was sad. I still liked him. If he'd just been up front with me I could have been in Qatar. As it happened, Moyesy gave me another year, because I wasn't finished. I dropped to £12,000 a week, though. But I was still at Everton.

In January 2005 Moyesy brought in James Beattie from Southampton for £6 million to replace me. I was fine with Beattie. I like James, but he wasn't at my level. I knew from the first training session that he wasn't Shearer or Rooney. Beattie was a good player and played for England but he wasn't ready to lead the line for Everton. A bit like when I wasn't ready to lead the line at Rangers – a big-money signing, but not ready.

The coaches could soon see, after training, that Beattie wasn't top level. He wasn't ready to take over from me. They probably knew they'd made a boob, and of course I let them know that. I'd walk by Moyesy and go, 'How much?' That happened to me at Rangers. Didn't mean James Beattie wasn't a good player.

Moyesy took the armband off me and gave it to Alan Stubbs for 2004–05, and then David Weir in 2005–06. I sensed my influence declining.

GOING HOME

'You're back to being my captain,' he then told me.

'I don't want to be your captain,' I said.

'You won't be my captain, you'll be Everton captain.' That's how he got round it.

'OK, give me it.'

New players had come in, like Mikel Arteta in February 2005. Mikel was a great footballer and he's doing fantastically in management at Arsenal now. You wouldn't think it but he was a quiet assassin. Good footballer, nice fella, but he could be a right little nasty bastard. He'd leave his foot in. He caught me in training, went right over the top of the ball and did me! Mikel was quiet but hard and a wonderful player. A couple of months after Mikel joined, we got a free-kick on the right against Manchester United at Goodison and Mikel went to take it. I'll never forget the incredible atmosphere or the goal! I stood offside, knowing United's players would drop back and knowing that Mikel would deliver. I got away from Rio Ferdinand and headed past Tim Howard and the roof came off Goodison. Mikel's like all good players: he's got that fire inside. He's a winner. He was always a nice, passing, technical player, and it's no surprise to see Arsenal play good football.

19

TAKEN TO THE COLLINA'S

Mikel played in a game that still angers me to this day. This was the controversial Champions League play-off second leg against Villarreal on 24 August 2005.

Yes, the Pierluigi Collina game. We'd lost 2–1 at Goodison before travelling to El Madrigal, so the qualifier was difficult enough without thinking the ref was against us. Collina was a famous Italian referee, well respected in the game, the best referee in the world. Until this game.

Collina blew for a free-kick after a minute, and I knew then we were in trouble. But we fought. Even when Juan Pablo Sorín made it 3–1 on aggregate, we never gave up. Mikel scored a cracker at the seventy-minute mark with a free-kick and everyone sensed the momentum turn our way. Villarreal's fans became agitated. So did their players. Our magnificent fans were behind the goal we were attacking and they believed. We believed. We went for the jugular. Mikel whipped in the perfect corner for me. I rose and absolutely bulleted the header into the net. 3–3.

Collina immediately ruled it out for a foul. Absolutely ridiculous. I was seething. I stormed up to the Italian. He gave me his famous bulging-eyes treatment. I couldn't get any sense from him. He mocked me, pointing to his ear. 'I can't hear you. I can't understand you.' That's all he said to me. He was just blanking me. Did Collina chop a goal off because he didn't like me? It's human nature; people do it, don't they? Don't like you, bang, no goal. VAR would have sorted that in seconds. It was a perfectly good goal, no dispute. In my mind, it felt like they didn't want another English team in the Champions League. Everton had finished fourth but Liverpool winning the trophy in Istanbul meant they were in and we were in this play-off.

I listened to Everton fans and they felt Collina basically cheated us. I agree – he was shocking. I just didn't understand Collina. Even now it makes no sense. It was a perfectly good goal, but for some reason he found fault in it. He saw an infringement somewhere, but, you know, if you want to find an infringement you'll find one, won't you? He said that Marcus Bent pulled a shirt. Nonsense. Marcus was the one having his shirt pulled.

I listened to what Collina said later: 'At that time I was looking at those players, Bent and his Spanish opponent, and I've seen something that probably television didn't show. Clearly Duncan Ferguson didn't make any foul but I didn't punish him for a foul. I punished Bent's foul.' That wasn't correct, was it? It was a clear header. I don't give a damn who's holding who 10 yards away. It doesn't matter, does it? It was just a clear header, and basically Collina stitched us up that year because Villarreal went to the semi-finals, and lost to Arsenal. Collina denied us that chance. We could have put that game into extra-time.

In the dressing room afterwards everyone was devastated and angry. That incident got highlighted more and more as the hours went on. Everyone could see it was wrong. And what did Collina do? Immediately retire. Why on earth was he allowed to referee such an important game in the first place? Everton have never had answers from UEFA.

20

ENDGAME

As that 2005–06 season wore on, I knew my days were numbered. My contract was up. My time was up. My body told me that. I spoke to Moyesy at Christmas time. 'I'm not the same player, gaffer. I'm not having the same impact off the bench.' I was dead honest with him.

'Duncan, you are so honest. I respect your decision.'

I instigated the end. I didn't want to play anywhere else. I wanted to finish at Everton in the Premiership. I wanted to be remembered as a good player, not a journeyman who fell down the divisions, nicking a few quid here and there. I turned down plenty of opportunities to do that.

What really stuck in my throat – and this is the real reason I fell out with Moyes – was that my time at Everton didn't end the way I felt it should have. Show me the respect I deserve for all the work and goals, and for everything I've given Everton Football Club. I put my body on the line for Everton and look at the state of it. Battered and bruised.

My leaving of Everton Football Club wasn't done properly. I know they never are. I consoled Leon Osman when he finished at Everton in 2016. He never got a lap of honour, never even got on the pitch for the last game of the season against Norwich City at Goodison on 15 May. Leon stayed on the bench, even though we were 3–0 up. Afterwards, Leon was in the car park crying his eyes out in the back of his car because his career was over, and he never got a proper chance to say goodbye to Goodison. Somebody who played 433 times for Everton deserved better.

The date I'll never forget is 7 May 2006 – West Brom at Goodison. I knew when Moyesy gave me the captaincy that was it. The end. I never got told I was getting released before the game. It dawned on me on match-day.

'You're the captain, and there's your captain's armband,' Moyes said to me when I walked in the changing room.

'I don't want the captain's armband.'

'No, Dunc, I think you should take it.'

I knew then. That was Moyes's way of telling me 'this is your last game'.

Look, I'm not really blaming David Moyes. I expected that to happen. As a footballer, it rarely ends in the way you want it to. Moyes should still have told me the week before so that I could prepare myself properly to say goodbye to the fans.

'Look, it's your last game, get your kids in.'

Fortunately I'd got wind just in time that this was the end so I'd managed to get my kids to Goodison and got them on the pitch. I wanted them to see me go out in style. In front of my second family, the Everton fans. The Everton and West Brom players gave me a guard of honour. I couldn't have scripted the game better, really. We got a pen in the last minute. I wasn't on penalties, Mikel was. James McFadden took the ball off Arteta and gave it to me. I stood in front of Gwladys Street, and looked at all those amazing people who'd supported me through thick and thin. They weren't just fans to me any more, they were friends for life. The whole of Gwladys Street started singing my name.

I didn't want the penalty. Going up, I knew I was going to miss it. I had no power left in my legs, my hamstrings were gone, my calves were long gone. I was absolutely petrified. All I thought about was, 'Dunc, you're missing this, it's going to be a disaster.' I was cramping up as I put the ball on the spot. 'If I miss this, it's going to haunt me for the rest of my life,' I thought to myself. My kids were watching my last touch as a footballer. I was shaking, my heart racing. Somehow, from deep within my body and soul, I summoned up the strength for Gwladys Street, for one last kick in front of them, one last chance to give joy as a player to these people I love and respect so much.

It turned out to be two last touches. The worst penalty you've ever seen. I duffed it that slowly that it hit Albion's keeper Tomasz Kuszczak, who fumbled it back to me. Can you imagine, your last kick of the ball and you miss? Disaster – I'd think about it every day.

As the ball came out, I just put my right foot through it. When it went in, I was made up. It was a great moment. Somebody was smiling down at me, one of the few bits of luck I had in my career. I should have taken more penalties for Everton. I took only ten, scoring eight, but I'd never forgotten missing one against Motherwell when I was eighteen. I shied away from them.

During the lap of honour I struggled with all the emotions – pride, heartache, grieving in a way that my Everton career, my whole football career, was over. I celebrated afterwards with fans in a local pub. What else could I do?

I got called into the manager's office the following day. I was at Bellefield in a big queue with youth players waiting to be released. I couldn't believe it. Emotions were running high. That's when I was told. That's why I had the fall-out. I knew the day before that my time was up, but this was the club making it official, and me hanging around with kids crying their eyes out. I'd given Everton everything, and here I was standing in a queue in a corridor with kids they were discarding. Surely the manager could have put me to the front of the queue. In fairness to David Moyes, he didn't know I was in the queue.

So that was my big falling-out with Moyesy. I went into his office. I wouldn't shake his hand. I pushed his hand away.

'Well, Dunc, this is the end,' Moyes said.

'You go and fuck yourself,' I replied. The release meeting was only ten seconds. The door was still swinging on my way out.

Maybe Everton could have shown me a wee bit more respect. After all, I was a senior player who had given them ten years, I'd been captain under three different Everton managers, and was at that time their all-time leading Premier League goalscorer.

And even after all that, when I retired from Everton, Harry Redknapp phoned the house. He wanted to take me down to Portsmouth. He offered to double my money to £24,000 a week. 'Come down when you want,' Harry said. Paul Jewell at Wigan wanted me too. We had lunch. I couldn't do it. I wanted to finish at Everton and remember myself as an Everton player.

The next day I phoned Howard Kendall. I needed to be with somebody I trusted, and Howard was a mentor to me. I'd only been one year with Howard as a player but I knew him as a friend so I went to him the next day and sat with him. I told him about what happened to me at Everton. We spoke about my path ahead. I took so much comfort and advice from the great man.

'Go into coaching,' Howard told me. 'Go into management. You're a great speaker, you were my captain, you've had great times, you've pulled the club round.'

In the end, my head wasn't right for that. I decided to go to my place in Mallorca for a few years. I put myself in exile. I cut myself off in Mallorca. I didn't even have a mobile phone.

I wanted to get away from Everton because the club was on my doorstep and still in my heart.

My kids were young and I had a few quid. I did a deal to sell my Formby house for £7.5 million. Yes, that's not a misprint. I'd bought it for £2 million. The boy who bought the house gave me £5 million up front and we shook hands on him paying me the £2.5 million when he had it. Another stupid move, shaking hands on £2.5 million. I went to Mallorca and did stupid things. I bought a €4 million villa.

After a year, I got bored. Even the beautiful surroundings lost their beauty through familiarity. A year later, I wasn't looking at the beach any more because it didn't change. Still golden. I wasn't looking at the sea because that stayed the same. Still azure. The heat got to me. I began to realise I was still young, only thirty-four. That's old for a footballer but not out in the real world. I was a baby, really, but hadn't realised it. So I went to the gym and did a bit of running, feeling the need to start earning again.

I look back now and wonder where my career would be without those five years in exile. I look at Mikel Arteta and see how he cracked on. He played his last game for Arsenal on 15 May 2016. On 3 July, he was appointed as Pep Guardiola's assistant coach at Manchester City. He took forty-nine days off! I took five years. The game's changed because, normally, fifty would have been about right as a manager's age but now it's like thirty-five or forty. I missed the game.

I was thinking I was young enough – I'll come back at thirty-nine and manage. But nobody reached out to me. I was on my own anyway. I've always been a loner. I've always had only one or two close mates. In football, really only Howard. He'd always come and visit on his regular Magaluf trip. I'd take him up to the posher end of Mallorca. We'd go out for lunch and end up going out singing. We'd end up in a bar with a piano, often with Paul McCoy, one of Howard's best pals. Paul was a great singer, in a Beatles tribute band called Penny Lane, and he did a brilliant

ENDGAME

Frank Sinatra impression, so it was always a good night out when he was over. Lovely times.

But I missed Everton, I missed Goodison, I missed home. I left as a player but Everton never left me. One of the special nights of my life was being voted into the Gwladys Street Hall of Fame on 11 March 2009. I flew back and it was unbelievable: 700 paying guests for 'Duncan Ferguson – Braveheart'. It meant so much, and I told them so. 'I'm very, very proud,' I said. 'I've played for other quite big football clubs, but when I think about my career I only ever really think about having played here. I never had a relationship at those other clubs like I had with you. I was proud to be captain of Everton under three different managers. When you've played for Everton, other clubs are nothing – nothing!' That got a cheer.

I'm loved by Everton fans. The football's a part of it but it's also because I care. The guys who were in the great Everton teams who are not loved, that's because they never put that time in. I went to an Everton party in Goodison once, a big marquee, packed with players and managers. I looked around and there was Colin Harvey and Alan Ball. Bally was loved too. Graeme Sharp, Peter Reid – every single great Evertonian you could think of. I'd never put myself in a category of being better than any of them because I wasn't. They were all better than me. They just weren't loved like me and Bally. I was put on a table in the corner, miles from the stage. But from the stage to my table there were hundreds of people queuing up to meet me. I'm talking about the biggest legends in our club, guys I loved and idolised. I had an attraction to people. They loved me. Probably something to do with the jail sentence, running about in the city, spending time with them.

'He's one of us,' Everton fans said. 'He's in the Buzz, he's in St Anne's police station, he's running about with that firm up in Huyton, he's a great guy, picks up the tab for local kids at the ice cream van.' Players who've got a far better record than me were never like that. Some of them don't get it. They just think it's about goals. But it's not about any goal, it's about patting somebody's head and saying, 'Are you all right, wee man?' It's about shaking a hand, about a smile, spending time with fans. It's about human contact. I cared about the fans. That's worth more than brushing by some of them – which I've seen, which I see all the time, pushing people out the road and not spending a bit of time with them. I never did that, and that's why I'm loved by Everton fans.

I don't think I've done many bad things in my life. I don't think there's many people in Liverpool who'd ever say I've done them a bad turn. When I was coaching at Everton's new training complex, Finch Farm, I always tried to be my best – be a good coach, be a good person. In the city I've done a lot of good deeds, visiting poorly people in hospital, helping charities, giving people money, giving £30,000 to £40,000 worth of minibuses to kids' charities. Other little things, like when the players were at Alder Hey Children's Hospital and there was one kid, obviously struggling, so I let the others go on and just sat with him, gave him a big bear hug. When I got back to Bellefield I sorted a scrapbook, got all the players to sign it and sent it to the kid.

Every day something happens. I was coming out my car one day and a car stopped, window rolled down and this mum said, 'Duncan, look, I just can't thank you enough for what you've done for me.'

'What have I done for you?'

'You went to see Liam up at Norris Green. He was dying two years ago, do you remember that?'

'Oh, I do remember, yes. There was a big firm of yous, wasn't there?'

'Yes, there was about thirty of us in the house.'

I did it because I cared. It didn't matter to me whether they were Blues or Reds. I heard about it, I was in Norris Green, I went round, no cameras. I went in through the house, up the stairs, and I comforted the lad when he was dying of cancer. Liam was about thirty-five, poor lad – no age. I came back downstairs and spoke to the family – Everton fans, Liverpool fans. All the family were there and I went to see their dying son and brother and husband. So, yes, I did remember when I was stopped in the street.

'Are you an Everton fan?' I asked the woman in the car.

'No, I'm Liverpool. We'll never forget what you did for us. We don't forget.' Blues and Reds, I get on with them all.

It's about doing the right thing. If you go back to when I was playing football it was the exact same. Do you know how many people have come up to me that I've given a pound to, given a lift home or spent a bit of time with? Hundreds, probably thousands. People don't forget. These guys aren't ten any more, they're thirty or forty, and some of them are running these estates, some of them are standing on these doors. So before I knew it I had a support network around me I didn't even know about. I was just being me, giving kids pounds at Bellefield as I got on the bus – 'There's a couple of quid for you.' I've even dropped kids off, but you wouldn't do it now, would you?

'What are you doing walking round here? Where are you from?'

'Bootle.'

'Come on, I'm going by that way. Get in the car.'

And I'd drop them off in Bootle. I've done it my whole life and everybody knows. That's why I get the respect. Scousers don't forget.

'What are you short of?' I ask people. Kids in Great Ormond Street Hospital in London, Mum and Dad can't get up and down on the train, too expensive. 'Here's £1,000,' I'd say. 'There you go, get up and down on the train.' £1,000, £3,000, £5,000 – whatever they needed, whatever I had in my pocket. It's just the way I am. Even Janine says, 'You have to stop.' But why? If I've got a bit of money in my pocket having played football and somebody needs a bit of help, I'll give them it, that's it. But, of course, Janine was right. I did have to stop.

'Here's £20,000, take it.' I was young and didn't realise what I was doing. I loved the city, I loved the people in it, and if I could help, I would. I thought the money would always be there. I didn't realise I was giving away my kids' money. I'm struggling now, skint, and nobody's helped me out, nobody's given me £1 million, and rightly so – why would you? I was mad, I was crazy. My generosity is a definite weakness. But it was my nature. I don't want a pat on the back. But do you know what that's called: it's called being a mug.

'What's happened to your money?' my dad asked me.

'I've been mad, gave it away to everybody.'

'No, you're not mad,' he said, 'you've just been loyal and generous. It happens, you'll learn, you'll change a wee bit.'

I have a bit. But if I had £100 million, I'd still give most of it away. I just like helping people. I enjoyed going into Alder Hey with Everton at Christmas. I was first in and last out. The team bus left without me a couple of times. I'd be in the hospital talking to the kids. People would go past and say, 'There's Big Dunc.' I was popular. They'd stop and talk, word got round, so I'd be in all the wards. I tried to help everyone. I'd listen closely to other people's stories. I made sure I went round everybody. If I'd missed one person I'd have felt I'd become a twat, that I'd broken their hearts. I'd hate that. I'm sure I've not been right with everybody, I've maybe sometimes brushed by somebody not meaning it, but if there's been a hundred, I've seen and spoken to ninety-nine of them. For me to sign an autograph or spend a bit of time with somebody . . . come on, it's a pleasure for me. Young players won't do it like me. That's why I've been so loved in the city.

I've sent so many video messages I can't even remember how many. There was this guy called Jack Simmons, whose brother Tom was slacking in school in 2021. So I sent him a video.

'Hiya, young Tom, you all right, son? It's Duncan Ferguson here from Everton Football Club. I just wanted to wish you all the best, pal. Your teacher, old Tom, has told me you've been fucking slacking off a wee bit in your photography, is that right? We cannae be having that, mate. You better get your finger out and make sure you get the fucking results. And if you get the results right, and you stick in, I'll come and see you. And I'll take you for a bit of lunch and I'll come to your house or something, aye. We'll sit down and have a wee chat. Is that all right, mate? So you make sure you stick in. Don't fuck the job up. Anyway, look, here's Goodison for you. What do you think of that? Hopefully you'll be back soon, lad, eh? Stick in, son. God bless, from Big Dunc, take care.'

I didn't know Jack was going to post the clip on Twitter (now X). It went viral, as they say, and two million people watched it. Anyway, Tom got stuck in at school, got the results, so I took him and Jack out for a bit of food. Nice lads.

I love doing wee things like that. In May 2024 I went to see Tommy, still on the same estate at eighty-three, starting to struggle a wee bit. I went to his door, and opposite him lived a wee ginger-headed lassie who was now a wee lassie no more, at twenty-three. She was sitting outside on her step.

'Are you all right, love? Do you remember me?' I asked her.

'Of course I remember you, Big Dunc.'

'Where's your sister?' I asked.

'She's married now, Dunc.'

They were twins, three-year-olds when I first met them. I'd be over at Tommy's, the ice cream van would come round, and I'd shout to all the kids, 'What do yous want?' And they'd all come round and I'd give them all ice creams and pounds. She remembered that.

There's thousands of stories like that, so that's why I'm loved.

I used to do the same in Mallorca. On a Friday night I'd go down to the square, set up a table, put water and cans of Coke on it and play a wee football game with all the kids. I'd pay for it all.

I decided to move the family back home from Mallorca because I missed my Everton family. My head was drawn to Everton as my heart always was. So I swallowed my pride and called David Moyes. I phoned Sue and she was made up. I told her I wanted to see the gaffer. So we spoke on the phone.

'I need to come and see you, gaffer. I want to go through a few things with you.'

'Dunc, I've been waiting for this phone call for five years,' he said.

I went to Finch Farm, where the team had moved from Bellefield, and put my hand out to Moyesy. 'I never shook your hand five years ago and I felt bad about it, gaffer. I didn't feel like a man, it's been playing on my mind, and I'll respect you if you don't shake my hand now.'

'No, Dunc, I'll shake your hand.'

So we shook hands. It meant a lot.

'Sit down, Dunc, I'm glad you're here. I've been meaning to talk to you for the last five years. I've been waiting for this.'

'Look, I'm sorry what happened the last time we met. I was out of order when I stormed off and told you to fuck off. I'm sorry. I was steamed up.'

'I didn't know you were standing in the corridor for that long,' Moyesy told me. 'I didn't know you were in line with the kids.'

'Let's forget about it,' I said.

So that was the time I kissed and made up with Moyesy.

And that's also when he said, 'Dunc, I've got a job for you. I want you to become an ambassador for Everton.' Moyes wanted me to be this recruitment boy who'd go into people's houses, talk to the parents, meet the kids and try and get the twelve-year-olds and the fourteen-year-olds to Everton because Kenny Dalglish was doing it at Liverpool.

'Who's better to do it than you? Who's bigger?'

Moyesy knew I could talk and he knew I was good with kids as he'd seen me in action at Alder Hey. Moyes would tell you that I was the best person he'd ever seen in that environment with poorly kids. He wanted me now to focus on recruiting kids for the club.

'We're losing out on a lot of good kids and I want you to counteract that. You're the only person I can think of that can do that.'

'Brilliant, thanks very much, I'm made up,' I said, 'but, to be honest, I want to be a coach.'

Moyes did not know what to say. Maybe he was surprised. He didn't know I was going through my licences.

'Really,' I carried on. 'I want to do my B licence here and I want to coach here and learn my trade here.'

He didn't know what to say. It wouldn't have been a good look for Everton if I'd gone to Tranmere to become a coach. But he was kind enough to agree. He agreed this was the best place for me.

'You should come back to Everton. You need to be seen to be coming here, you're one of us.'

I was back where I belonged. It meant a lot when I heard Moyesy say, 'If you look at the Everton legends in the eyes of fans, greats like Peter Reid, Neville Southall, Kevin Ratcliffe, Graeme Sharp and that crew, Duncan is maybe the only [recent] one who could put himself close to those players.'

*

Having rebuilt my relationship with Moyesy, I then put the past further behind me on 2 June 2011 by paying £950 to enrol on the Scottish Football Association's UEFA B licence course at the National Sports Training Centre at Largs on the west coast of Scotland. I washed away the bad blood between me and the SFA in the Firth of Clyde.

Then, nearly five and a half years after leaving Everton, I started at their academy on 17 October. I shadowed the academy manager Alan Irvine, who I knew well. We'd played together at Dundee United and Alan had coached me at Newcastle and Everton. It was good to be back in the Everton fold. All my memories are here, in this city, really. Certainly Everton was the time of my happiest memories. My kids were born in this city in Liverpool Women's Hospital. I love Liverpool, and I love Scousers.

I must do. I married one.

21

THE LOVE OF MY LIFE

'If I hadn't met you, I'd still be single.' That's what I always tell Janine, and it's true. She's beautiful, special and kind. She's looked after the kids and she looks after me, keeps me calm. Janine's always been there for me, always been strong. She's been great. Probably done well to stay with me over the years, particularly when my drinking was becoming a problem.

The first time I met Janine Tasker I knew she was the one. I saw her on the dance-floor in the nightclub the Buzz, and that was it. It was the Tuesday before the 1995 FA Cup final weekend. Some local guy that we knew, a boy called Warren, organised a going away party for Everton fans. A going away party! That's a good angle to make a few quid, a party, I should have guessed he was a Red! Just get drunk before we go off to Wembley to play football! I wasn't going to go. I'd been off the drink for about six weeks because I was trying to get fit after a double hernia.

'Duncan, you'll have to come down,' Warren said.

'I'm not coming down on a Tuesday night, mate, to the Buzz.'

'Dunc, I've sold these tickets, I've told everybody you're going to be there.'

Christ. So, as it happens, my sister Iris and some of her friends were up visiting me. They accompanied me to the celebration party before the celebration party. Iris couldn't believe the relationship I had with the fans. She was proud of her brother. Women were coming up to me asking me to sign all their body parts.

Then I looked across and saw Janine on the dance-floor and my world changed. When you know, you know. It's true. I knew she was the one. She was with her friend, and then they went to the bar. I was with Gary Ablett, God bless him, and he went over to them. He was single at the time, and was talking to the two of them when I arrived and cut across him.

'Hi Gary, are you introducing me?'

Gary introduced me to Janine. I knew immediately I wanted to be with her. I'd had plenty of practice so I just knew. Janine's a cracker, a really nice person, the type you warm to the moment you meet them. Everyone liked her. All the men chased her at one time or another.

'Nobody caught me!' Janine told me.

She was a looker, still is. But she wasn't that fussed about footballers. Still, she knew who I was. She'd seen my signing at Everton on TV in 1994. 'Mum, Mum, come through here, look at this fella on the telly! Look at his red jacket!' People said it was red, but it was orange. 'Like turning up in a green suit to sign for Rangers' one of the sportswriters said. People still come up and mention the jacket. Definitely orange, not red, but we'll move on. Anyway, the standing joke in our family is that Janine knew me before I knew her.

I was really enjoying talking to Janine at the bar but noticed she was shaking. I later found out she'd come out of a relationship only a couple of months earlier and some of her ex-boyfriend's mates were in the Buzz. They were clocking me talking to Janine. Anyway, nothing happened, we went our separate ways. I headed south to Wembley.

I found out she was the sister of Karen, the girl John Parrott was

THE LOVE OF MY LIFE

seeing. I was on the pitch at Wembley, shouting to John, 'Give me Janine's number, John!'

'No, no, no!' John didn't want me anywhere near Janine! I had a terrible reputation at the time. And rightly so. What's a boy to do when he's on his own in Liverpool?

I was in Mathew Street a while after the cup final, during the Beatles Festival, drinking with my mates George, Tommy and all my other pals – Big Terry, Fat Stan, Scottish Ged, Black-headed Graham, Ginger-headed Graham, John Parry, all the crowd – and Janine and her pal came walking by.

'All right, luv,' Tommy said. That's when I asked George all about her. 'She's from a nice family,' George told me.

Eventually, Janine came in to Retro and I got to know her better. I got her number and we agreed to go for lunch for our first date.

'Come round and pick me up at the training ground,' I told her.

Janine came to Bellefield, parked the car, I came out, opened the front door and she leaned across and said, 'Do you mind lying down on the back seat?' I thought it was a bit forward for a first date!

'I do mind lying down on the back seat!' I'm 6ft 4in. I sat in the front and we drove out. Janine told me she'd just come out of a relationship and didn't want me to be seen in her car in Liverpool.

Gary Ablett tried to put me off her. 'I'm sure she's got a kid, her,' he said. She hadn't. It was her niece. Gary knew that. Gary was close with John Parrott. I don't know if the two of them had got together and said, 'We need to put Dunc off Janine!' It didn't work. I'd fallen for her.

Janine's from Norris Green, known as one of the roughest areas of Liverpool. There are occasional shootings there. But Janine comes from a beautiful, lovely family, the Taskers, a nice Scouse family. Theirs must be the luckiest cul-de-sac in Liverpool. Karen married John, of course. Once I was coming out of Janine's house and Everton centre-back Richard Dunne was coming out of another corner of the cul-de-sac. There used to be a nice wee girl in the corner there. There's only six houses in the cul-de-sac! They should put a plaque up!

I was twenty-six when I married Janine, who was a year younger, at the Anglican Cathedral in Liverpool on 26 June 1998. It was a 12.30 kick-off. Janine was late, but definitely worth the wait. She looked stunning. Janine was all in white, tiara, veil kept back and – a lovely touch – she was shielded from the rain by a blue-and-white Everton umbrella as she walked from the Bentley into the church. I was waiting inside, looking (I thought) very dashing in my kilt and full Scottish attire. I'd tied my kilt very tight and was having a bit of trouble breathing. Maybe it was the emotion of the occasion, too. A Highland piper saluted Janine's arrival in the cathedral. And then came the 'Trumpet Voluntary' as her father Tony walked Janine up the aisle. It was lovely to see.

The cathedral was packed, and a lot of my team-mates were there. Dave Watson was an usher. So was John Parrott. Those two went to the Catholic Cathedral by mistake, saw there was no one there and had to rush across the city. Michael Ball and Michael Branch were there. The old chairman Peter Johnson came, got a bit of stick outside. Howard Kendall wasn't there, sadly. Peter had sacked him a month earlier, and that broke my heart. Howard meant the world to me. He was still bitter about his treatment by Peter so didn't come to the wedding – a real pity. We missed him. He phoned me that night to congratulate me. I miss Howard now.

I was waiting at the altar with my best man George Downing. Afterwards we went to Mottram Hall for the reception, and then Janine and I began our new life together. I know she was concerned about me writing this book but I can use these pages to say how blessed I am to have met her, to have fallen in love with her and to be able to spend my life with her.

And we've been blessed with three amazing kids, Cameron, Ross and Evie. My kids didn't know a lot of the stuff they'll read here. As far as they know, I've never even touched a drink in my life. I've just tried to be the best I can be, and tried to give them the best information I can possibly give them so they avoid the mistakes I've made. My two sons won't touch a drop. They're clean-living. My daughter likes a wee dance but she's not a drinker. My kids have never seen me drunk. The house has been a happy house. I've never shouted at them. My younger son, Ross, has never cried in his life. Doesn't swear either. He's so placid. I've got good kids. They know about 'Duncan Ferguson the Footballer' because I still live in the city, and even after all these years since I played I get stopped all the time. They still see it.

I love my kids. I look at Cameron, Ross and Evie and I'm proud of the young adults they are becoming. I'm glad they've not taken the route their dad did when I was younger. I'm proud of their drive and what they are achieving in their lives. I'm proud of their maturity because I never had that. They're certainly not making the mistakes I made, which makes me proud. At least my advice is getting through, because it never got through to me. Keep believing and keep dreaming, kids. It will happen. 'God's good, God's got a plan,' I tell them.

Cameron's trying to make it in football. He was in Everton's academy, went to Tranmere Rovers, then Newcastle in 2021, then Inverness with me and left with me in October 2024. It must be hard for Cameron being my son. Everyone expects him to be like me, don't they? And he's not, he's his own man. If he has a career in football at any level, brilliant. But if he doesn't, no problem. There's life after football.

Not many people are ever going to play in the Premier League, especially if you're British. I checked the numbers. Of the 727 who played in the Premier League in 2023–24, 333 were British. There were players from sixty-seven different countries. The odds are stacked against you. It was a lot easier for a British player to break through when I was playing. Whatever level Cameron reaches, I'll be proud of him.

Ross is at Liverpool University, doing a business course. He wants to earn a few quid – good lad. He's got his head screwed on. He values money, which I never did. I just gave it all away. I didn't care about it at Dundee United. I didn't know what I earned at Rangers. I wasn't bothered. I still don't. It's daft. Janine goes crazy at me. My daughter Evie is working as a fashion buyer, doing well, finding her way.

I'm so proud of my family.

22

MY DAD, MY HERO

My dad was my hero when I was a kid. But I've never heard him say he loves me. To. This. Day. Not once. Who cares? It's just the way the old school are.

I know they're proud of what I've achieved. My dad sits and watches tapes of me all night, every night. My dad's proud as punch, isn't he? He's watching me, he's made up. I know that when he's with his friends he spends his whole time talking about me. 'There's Duncan, he's living his life. He's done great.' Oh, I'm the king of the hill, aren't I? I'm the best, aren't I? He's watching these videos, watching me score. He's Big Dunc, I'm Wee Dunc.

Obviously he does love me, he just never says it. I tell Evie, Ross and Cameron every day, 'I love you.' Every day. I'm always hugging and kissing my kids. They like it. Everyone these days likes a nice hug and a kiss, don't they? 'Love you, son.' Nice, isn't it? It's just that older generation that doesn't, I guess.

I owe my dad everything. I owe him my life. When I was five, I fell poorly with a fever and started choking. I couldn't breathe, I suffered a seizure, I swallowed my tongue, and Dad rushed to my bedside. If I think about it hard enough, I swear I can still feel his big hand at the back of my throat, me biting down on his knuckles, while he turned me on my side, ensuring there was no blockage of the airway until the danger passed. If my dad hadn't been at my side, there's a very good chance I would be dead, gone. I'd have choked to death. He was back from the rigs in the tenement and he saved me. I've thanked him since. 'I'm glad you were there, Dad.'

My dad's always been my hero. I learned a lot from him just being a man, being a leader. I always looked up to him. He was brave, hard, and you always want to be like your dad, don't you? He grafted hard as a rigger at the Mossmorran gas plant in Fife and later at the Solan oil fields west of the Shetland Islands in the North Sea. My dad was stood at pub doors at eighteen. Security. Back in those days they'd carry flick-knives but my dad was good with his fists. You had to be, back then.

When I was a kid playing a match, there'd always be somebody on the touchline shouting 'Break his legs!' because I was their best player. There was always someone having a go at me. I felt protected when I played. My dad waded in and confronted them. There'd be ten of them but it didn't matter. Dad was fearless, and he'd take them all on. I've got nowhere near that bravery. I'd go the other way. I'd never look for confrontation even though it has frequently sought me out.

My dad never hit me. Never. He only attacked me once, grabbed me, flung me across the room. I was fourteen, fifteen, starting to chase birds, trying to get a wee neck off them or whatever. You're walking down the road afterwards smiling, aren't you? I'd be made up, thinking I was a bit of a man now! I'm getting my wings now! But dad had a curfew. Half ten. I missed the bus and had to run, belting down the road, and got in at 10.40.

'You're late,' Dad said. 'You're late every night.'

'I'm early every night, what are you talking about?' I answered him back. 'I'm not out every night.' I pushed him, which I really shouldn't have done.

Dad jumped on me and grabbed me. I tried to get upstairs, got halfway up, and we were struggling, me on top of him, him on top of me, Mum too. He was shouting 'Don't answer me back!' while Mum was trying to get him off me. 'Oh Duncan, Duncan!'

My dad was tough. He was a steel erector. On the rigs, he'd walk on these wee iron girders 500 feet up, working the cranes. No harnesses. They just didn't bother wearing them in those days. They'd be walking along them, the wind would blow in, knock them off, and they'd hit the ground, dead. No Health and Safety back then. Dad felt he had to show everyone. So up he went on to those wee girders, bolting in the big columns with the crane. 'Horrendous work,' he told me. The most dangerous work you could do.

Big Duncan Ferguson was a real man, a hard man, but an amazing man. He could do anything. He was great with his hands. He could build you an oil rig, build you a house, even lay the road outside the house. He was a tar man – the toughest job. The tar would come off the spreader and my dad would rake it in the sun, all day, no problem.

Dad's eighty-three now, still as strong as an ox. He's a working man, still doing the roofs. He recently did a big extension to the kitchen, knocked down walls, everything. 'I've got working muscle, not gym muscle, son.' He's right. Handshake like a vice.

Seven, eight years ago, in his mid-seventies, my dad had a confrontation with a couple of idiots who'd come out of the local pub and were shouting outside our house around midnight. My dad's a light sleeper. He'll usually be up, sitting in the front watching his videos, and these two idiots were in the road, shouting abuse.

My dad opened the front door.

'Get out the road, you.' They wouldn't, so he went out and flattened them.

Me and my dad are very close, which is why it was so painful when we drifted apart for ten years. He took me everywhere growing up. So when we weren't talking for a decade, I felt, 'I've been a bad son and haven't given him enough.' I questioned myself. I started to think I was a bit of a bastard because I'd not spoken to Mum and Dad for so long, that I wasn't a nice person. All those dark thoughts. They had a point: I should have been there for them, I didn't spend enough time with them.

Over the years, we drifted apart. We seemed to be arguing quite a lot. I phoned umpteen times the first two or three years. When my dad got older, he relented and answered.

'Hiya Dad, how's things? Are you all right?'

'All right, son.'

We spoke. I went up to see them in Stirling. Our reunion was very emotional. I told them I loved them.

I haven't spoken to my sister Audrey for about twenty years. She drifted away. It's so sad. Audrey's hardly seen Cameron, Ross or Evie. How many families can say the same thing – drifted apart. My younger sister Iris also never spoke to me for a decade. I get on with Iris now. We met in Dubai, where she lives with her kids, and it was so emotional when I saw her after ten years, an unbelievable moment. She came to my hotel. I saw her walking across the lobby. 'Jesus, it's my sister.' I took the kids to the park and it was great.

But I've never reconciled with Audrey. Mum and Dad struggle with that. They'd like me and Audrey to meet up and clear the air. If I ever met Audrey again I'd say hello and give her a hug.

I think a lot about my dad. He's an incredible man, a real force of nature who learnt life's lessons and channelled his energy accordingly. When I grew older I realised how much my old man was respected in the community – respect that was earned the hard, old-fashioned way. But he knew that real men are clever enough to find another way too.

MY DAD, MY HERO

He often told me the story of how he and his brothers after a week's hard graft went down the pub of a Friday night in their Teddy Boy attire – Maverick lace tie, gunslinger's waistcoat, blue or green Buddy Holly jacket with satin collar and trim pockets and black Winklepicker boots. The Falcon was their local boozer. Each Friday evening they'd pass this man in his garden mowing the lawn, trimming the hedges, tidying up around his drive – real perfection it was. They'd be friendly and say hello, but once they'd walked on by they'd turn to one another and smirk.

'What an idiot,' they'd say, and laugh. 'Wasting away his Friday working in the garden when he could be off down the pub like the rest of us!'

By the end of the night, those pristine Teddy Boy suits with their satin collars and trim pockets would frequently be ripped, torn and speckled with claret and my dad and his brothers would have swelling around their eyes and bloody noses from bouts of fisticuffs down the boozer. Meanwhile, the gardener and his family would be tucked up in bed, with the garden looking immaculate.

'So who was the mug?' my dad would ask me. I should have taken that lesson on board.

As Dad's a proud Mason, when I reached eighteen he wanted me to go through his lodge.

'Look, if we go through your lodge in Stirling I'm not going to get through. I've been in fights with all these young guys in the area. We're not going to get through your lodge.'

'Don't be stupid,' he said, 'it's not like that.'

Guess what happened? We went down for the initial meeting at Stirling lodge, the Grand Masters asked me a few questions like 'Do you believe in God?', and it went to a vote. The place was bulging with people – 400 I reckoned. It was a big occasion. Duncan

Ferguson's son, the football player, coming to their lodge – they wanted to be a part of that. So they voted. If you get three black balls you're out. Three. How many black balls do you think there were in my bag? Go on, have a guess! I'll tell you . . . Three. There were three fellas that my dad or I had come across. So the three of them sat down together and put three black balls in there. I was black-balled. There was murder. They tracked them down, the Grand Master resigned, and it just showed you the jealousy. I was a local boy who got stitched up.

I admit I was a bit bothered. I wanted to join the Masons because my dad was one, there was a tradition there in my family, and my dad wanted me to join. My family were on the lodge and I got refused.

But I've got my rosary beads and I'm proud.

In Scotland, religion runs the two biggest football clubs, Rangers and Celtic, the blue and green football teams. My two best pals were Catholics, and I hated the sectarianism. It's wrong, it's horrible. People tell me it's changed in Glasgow but I'm not too sure. It's still bad. What does it mean being a Catholic or Protestant? Please tell me, I haven't got a clue. Both are Christians. When I married Janine, I crossed myself in the Anglican cathedral and knelt down to lovely music. I had to explain that to my Scottish family who were at the wedding. 'Why is Dunc crossing himself?' That's the way it is up there. It's so unhealthy. That's how it's always been in Glasgow and that's how it'll always be. They'll always hate each other, Rangers and Celtic, Protestant and Catholic.

Janine's Catholic, she loves the Royal Family. Loved the late Queen, loves the King. Janine will tell me, 'Look at that lovely palace, look at what these people do, it's fantastic.' Janine's mum's the same. I hate hearing the National Anthem booed by Liverpool fans. Yes, it's horrible. But there's no religious divide there like in Glasgow. I came from Rangers, and I'm loved here in Liverpool. There's no sectarianism on Merseyside.

When Janine's mum went to Lourdes with the kids, they brought me back some rosary beads. I wear them all the time. Not because I'm religious – I'm not. I wear them because Evie, Ross and Cameron bought them for me, and I love my kids with all my heart.

23

BURGLARS

'Will I phone the police or an ambulance?' Janine was shouting at me.

I was leaning over a burglar who was motionless apart from blood seeping from his mouth. I thought I'd killed the boy. 'Both,' I replied.

It was about 1 a.m. on 7 January 2001. I'd just got home from Watford where Everton had won 2–1, and I was lying on the couch, top off, tracky bottoms on, trainers off. I can't sleep after a game – too much adrenalin, still pumped up. Evie was six months old, in bed upstairs. Janine was upstairs too. I heard a wee bit of noise but didn't think anything of it.

Janine said, 'Come to bed.'

I heard the noise again.

'I'll be up in a minute.'

As I stood up I saw two shadows slipping through my conservatory. My heart went through the roof. When I get a red card on the pitch, I'm not thinking. It just happens. I had time to think about this. They were trying to steal some champagne, a picture and CDs. I went for them. One immediately scarpered, the other one fought, briefly.

I flattened the boy, gave him a terrible hiding. Janine came down and it got to the stage where she was crying and shouting, 'Stop it, Duncan, stop it!' Janine's screaming at me, 'You're going to kill him!' He made this horrendous gargling sound. I thought he was taking his last breath. Eventually the kid stopped breathing.

I looked down and there was blood everywhere. His head must have been three times bigger. I'd pulped him. He had an earring in his brow. Had – I'd pulled it out. I had blood all over me. I thought I'd killed him. I went from giving him a hiding to trying to bring him round. I got him on his side, got the blood out of his mouth.

I started to panic. Why had I kept punching him? Adrenalin, I guess. He was in my house and Janine and Evie were upstairs. He was a big lad and I just wanted to put him down. It was like a primeval instinct – protect my family. I wanted to make sure he was out of action, so I battered him.

'Are you all right, son?' I asked.

He didn't come round. The coppers did. Janine had called them, and an ambulance.

'What have you done, Dunc?' the policeman said. 'Jesus, go and clean yourself up.'

An ambulance came, the medics revived the lad and took him to hospital. There were helicopters overhead, Alsatians running around. Back then, the police turned up when you were broken into. 'We're hearing these boys are going to come back for you,' one of the police told me. 'We can put patrols around your house. This is quite serious.'

'You're all right. Don't be worrying about me.'

At 8 a.m., I phoned Walter Smith. 'Boss, I've had some trouble.'

'Yes, I know. You're ringing me early in the morning.'

'Boss, a burglar broke into my place last night.'

'How bad is he?'

The other burglar was eventually caught. Their names were Michael Pratt and Barry Dawson, I learned later when they went to court. Dawson, the lad I'd thumped, was in hospital for three days. I heard what Judge Anthony Procter told them in court: 'There is no way you can be called hardened criminals but we are dealing with a burglary at night when the house was occupied. Mr Ferguson may give the impression of being a hard man but it is clear he was shaken by this incident, primarily for the effects on his wife and young child.' Pratt and Dawson were jailed for fifteen months, which was harsh on them. They made a stupid choice but again drink played a major role. Remember – 'where there's drink, there's trouble'. I'm sure they've regretted it. I'm sure they've never broken into a house again.

My wife became frightened in the house so we sold up and moved to Formby. Two years later, incredibly, the same thing happened. I was broken into again and my Cristal champagne was targeted again. I'll give the thief some credit – he knew what the good stuff looks like. I was worried about confronting him. I didn't know how many were there. Me being me, I went, 'I'll go in again.' There was only one of them. When I challenged him, he came at me with a vodka bottle. As I ducked, I caught him in the face with a right hook and down he went. I hesitated to phone the police. I was worried about what they would do and what the press would say. So I went back upstairs to check on Janine and the kids.

'You'll never guess what's just happened,' I told her. She said right away, 'You have caught somebody again.'

'Yes, and I've left him to crawl away.'

'I'll call the police. He might die and you will be in big trouble so go out and see if he's still there.'

He was. He'd only crawled a few feet. That's when I phoned the police and ambulance. He ended up in hospital for two days with a broken jaw and three missing teeth.

The police arrested me and questioned me under oath. I told

them what happened and no charges were brought against me. Carl Bishop got four years for trespassing with intent to steal plus a year for failing to return to jail while on licence.

I know there was a lot of interest in the case and I'll just add one thing: everyone has a right to protect their home and their family. Any intruder deserves what they get.

24

MATES

In the summer of 1996, I went to Royal Ascot with my Liverpool mates. We all piled south on a big bus, me and my pals Mark Quinn, Big Terry, Scottish Ged, Fat Stan, Tommy Griff, Sean O'Toole, John Parry, Black-headed Graham and Ginger-headed Graham. I never saw a horse the whole day. I blagged my way into a VIP area, and spotted Kevin Keegan and Terry McDermott. They were Newcastle United manager and assistant at the time. I was in with the horse trainer and former jockey Peter Scudamore and his missus, I had a big cigar in my hand and I was a bit worse for wear, but jovial. I went up to Kevin and Terry.

'You're going to have your hands full,' I told them. 'We've got you in the first game.' Kevin had just spent a fortune on his team, he'd bought Alan Shearer in, and here I was, this Everton striker stood at Ascot, very merry and telling him I'm going to batter Newcastle, his team, at Goodison on 17 August. Kevin was nodding, 'Yes, big man, yes.' Trying to humour me. Kevin must have been thinking, 'We've got this game in the bag.'

That was the only time I drank that summer. I trained hard all through the holidays and through pre-season at Bellefield, I ran round Crocky Park and I was super fit. I was ready for Shearer's debut for Newcastle. Goodison was packed. I had my best game for Everton. I destroyed their two centre-backs, Big Steve Howey and Philippe Albert. I won the penalty off Steve Watson for David

Unsworth to score our first. I then flicked on a ball to Gary Speed, who came from 50 yards deep, came from nowhere. Gary knew I was going to win the ball, he arrived at the perfect moment, and finished it with his left foot. I will never forget Gary's beaming face as he scored his first goal for his beloved Everton.

I was unplayable. I was on a different level. Keegan was sitting on the bench at Goodison thinking, 'Jesus Christ, Big Dunc was right with what he said at Ascot.' I destroyed Newcastle. I shook hands with Kevin afterwards and he shook his head.

The month before, me and my pals had loved our trip to Ascot. Mark Quinn became a close friend but initially it was a name I was wary of. Word had gone round in Liverpool that Mark wanted words with me over something. I had no idea what about. Anyway, we were going to Royal Ascot, getting picked up in a big bus on the dock with all the boys, all good lads, Big Terry, John Parry, the Hardacres, the funeral directors. A lot of well-known faces were on the trip, all dripping in big Rolexes and diamond chains, everyone playing cards. Fantastic. And on this bus was Mark Quinn. What do I do? I better say something.

I asked big Terry Williams, a well-known boy in Liverpool, who owned a big scrapyard in the docks right next to where Everton's new stadium is.

'I have a problem. Is that Mark Quinn down there? I heard he wants a word with me.'

'Who?' Terry looks down the bus.

'Mark Quinn.'

'Mark, do you want to speak to Dunc?' Terry shouted down.

'What are you talking about? I love him! He's Big Dunc! He's one of us, he's a big Evertonian!'

I went down the bus and sat with Mark. Before I knew it, we were best pals. When we got back from Ascot, we'd head to the Retro bar in town with my pals. That was our pilgrimage to the city into the Retro. I would also drink up in the Black Angus on Cantril Farm estate. It was run by Old Mickey Quinn, the father of Mick Quinn, the horse trainer and ex player, and Mark. I would go there on a Sunday and play pool. Loved it. Remember, I was a good pool player and made a few quid. Mark was Top Boy and his best mate Dickey was always in there. One day I was playing pool with this other fella. Ripped jeans, baseball cap on, he looked a bit scruffy, to be honest. He said to me, 'Big man, you looking to buy a house? I'm selling mine.' I was thinking to myself, 'This guy's kidding me.' He then said, 'It's brand new. I will give it to you for a million quid. It's in Sandfield Park.'

I nearly ripped the pool cloth. There's me thinking this fella never had two bob in his pocket to rub together. His name was Robbie. Years later he went on to serve big sentences for importing large quantities of drugs.

At the time I enjoyed being with the lads up in the Angus. In my mind, they were good people and I felt protected. But there were always things going off.

One night I got a phone call about Everton winger Andy van der Meyde's dog, Mac. It had been stolen. Andy was a bit of a boy around town, a Dutchman who ran about with a few naughty people. He was in trouble himself. They broke into his house on the Wirral and took his dog.

So the phone rang and this voice went, 'Dunc, it's about Andy van der Meyde.'

'What about him? I'm not interested.'

'Well, we've got his dog here, and we'll give him back for five grand.'

'Throw it back over the Bellefield fence if you want to give the dog back.' And I put the phone down.

Van der Meyde did get Mac back a few days later.

And I remember once being spreadeagled across the bonnet of a police car, arms pinned down with not a clue what was going down. Flashing lights and coppers were all around me and my mate Tommy Griff as our faces were forced into the steel. Guns all around, pointed at us.

'What's going on?' I shouted.

'Oh no, that's Duncan Ferguson,' I heard one of the coppers say. 'Right, that's not who we're looking for.'

Too right, mate. The police released their grip on me and Tommy and disappeared. Never told us why they stopped us outside the Setter & Vine pub on Queen's Drive. They weren't looking for us. I'd been in Chinatown earlier in the evening with pals and amongst our group was a heavy gangster from London. I don't know whose friend he was. We left the Cockney boy and went off to the Setter & Vine to carry on drinking. They were looking for him, not us.

It's known in Liverpool that some of my pals were a bit lively. I had connections. One day my BMW disappeared from Bellefield car park. 'Have you robbed my car?' I asked Gazza.

'Dunc, I've not robbed your car!'

I called Mark, he put the word out, the boy who stole my car saw sense and agreed to hand it over. The guys I was getting my BMW back off had a car ring. They were thieving all the motors, driving them up to the chopping shop, cutting them into pieces and selling the parts. They'd stolen the coach Archie Knox's car. He went into this garage in West Derby and left his keys in the ignition when he went in to pay. As he came back out, his car was getting robbed. Archie ran to the car, which sped off. He shouted to this boy sitting in another car in the garage, 'Mate, do me a favour, follow that car.'

'Fuck off, I'm with him!' this lad said, and sped off too. He'd dropped off his mate to nick the car.

Archie came back to Bellefield and told me the story. They eventually found his car burnt out.

I was going to get mine back. Mark sorted it. The drop-off was the Daisy, as we called the Deysbrook pub outside Melwood, Liverpool's old training ground. Tommy had come up to nearby Bellefield to sell some jewellery to the Everton players.

'I'm just going with Mark to pick my car up,' I told him.

'I'll come with you,' Tommy said.

So all three of us piled into Mark's car and headed off to the Daisy. We pulled into the car park, and the boys who'd robbed my car came in. Me and Tommy got out of the car, I got my BMW back, and accepted the apologies – all a misunderstanding, OK, no harm done. They drove off.

Months later I was in a nightclub called Shorrocks Hill in Formby and this off-duty copper came up to me and said, 'Duncan, I've got a story to tell you. We had that pub under surveillance and you drove up. We were thinking, "Please don't tell me that Duncan Ferguson's involved in this."' The pub was fine, clean, it was just the bizzies were trailing someone for another big case.

'You know your mates you're running around with?'

I got defensive. 'We weren't running around doing anything wrong. They robbed my car.'

'But you know the boy you're running about with. He's known to us.' I wouldn't listen. Mark was my best pal then. I wouldn't hear a word said against him. I was loyal.

In May 2024 I watched a *Panorama* episode called 'The Crime Bosses Who Terrorised a City' about the Huyton crew. I nearly dropped dead. I knew every one of them, I drank with every one of them, I played pool with every one of them. Some had been at my wedding. They all looked after me. They were my mates. I saw them as good guys. I couldn't believe it when I saw the programme. I was in shock. It was frightening to think the people I'd associated with all those years ago were in this Huyton firm. I didn't know at the time but some of my mates were quite serious players in the underworld. They were all just coming through. Some of them started as armed robbers – balaclavas, sledgehammers through the windows to stop the armoured vans. I never knew any of that until some years later. We just spoke about football. I never pried. They liked me. I was an Everton man, a star player. They were Everton fans and I was one of the lads, I fitted in.

I know I'll be asked why I was drawn to Mark Quinn. I was impressed with Mark. He was tough, respected, feared but also generous, one of the few guys I had to constantly fight to pay a bill, and was good company. He was a big Blue and, at one point, we were inseparable. And I definitely felt I had a level of protection, as long as I never overstepped the mark, which I never did. I'd come from Stirling. I'd never seen this loyalty people had towards each other, the respect for their firms. The North End, South End, or the firms from Huyton, Norris Green or Toxteth. Norris Green is a rough area but there's a camaraderie there, a mutual loyalty; everybody loves each other, they're all together. That togetherness is big for me. Like being on that bus going to Royal Ascot – fifty people all together, a big family.

I guess I'm trying to explain why I hung out with these lads, some of whom appeared in that *Panorama* documentary. I didn't know what they were doing behind the scenes, I only started to get wise to it as the years passed. Some sold drugs, some sold cars and wagons, some even sold cattle. I enjoyed being with them. We were a good group. We weren't bullies, we were loved. They never, ever tried to involve me in anything. They had too much respect for me. Some people who sneaked on to the end of our crowd tried to offer me a line of cocaine or drop a tablet in my drink. They were trying to stitch me up. I wasn't clever enough to take my glass with me when I left the table. But I surrounded myself with good people who kept an eye out for me.

Eventually I did become concerned. Just after I retired in 2006 I was out with Mark and our wives in the Hard Days Night hotel in Liverpool. There was a bit of a queue at the bar, the girls went off to the toilet, and I shouted our order to Mark as he tried to get through.

'Get us a beer and a bottle of wine.'

'Dunc, it can take for fucking ever to get a drink in here, pal.'

The girl behind the bar said, 'There's no swearing in here.'

Mark became confrontational and swore back at her. I'd never heard him do that before. He hardly ever swore – only at me anyway.

She tried to be smart and say something back, so I stepped in. 'No problems, we're getting the drinks.' But the next minute she had the doormen there, five of them. The main one, a big lump, approached Mark.

'Drink up, time to go,' the doorman ordered.

'I'm just going to finish the drink,' Mark said.

Now Mark's small but wide, a neck on him like Mike Tyson, and hard as anything. He had been a boxer and could handle himself. He ran and funded boxing gyms in Canny Farm.

'Drink up, fatty,' the doorman continued.

I was in total shock. I'd never heard anyone speak to Mark like that. Mark changed within a split second. He put his drink down and BANG, hit the doorman with the hardest punch I've ever seen. The boy must have landed a few feet away.

I can still see the wee price stickers on the soles of his shoes to this day. He hit a table with a couple on it, who started screaming. Mark went over and put another one on him. The other doormen froze. They couldn't believe what they'd just seen. He was head doorman and Mark had cleaned him out. I made sure I had Mark's back.

I panicked. 'Just leave it, lads, leave it,' I shouted. I was worried it would escalate. A couple of Scousers came in and said, 'You need any back-up?' We didn't.

The ladies, who'd heard the screaming, ran up from downstairs. I wanted to call it a night. I was in shock. Mark wasn't. 'You're joking? Let's go to that bar there,' Mark said, gesturing to a place over the road. It was just like it had never happened, a passing storm. 'Come on, let's finish the night. Don't be daft, big man, come on.'

So away we went, to this new bar. I was ordering the drinks and the next minute the bizzies came flying in. They'd followed us on CCTV, got all the wagons outside and brought all the Matrix. They pulled Mark out, put him in the back of a wagon and took him away. Mark was known to the police.

Mark, my best pal, eventually became one of the most wanted men in Britain for drugs. He went on the run for seven years and was eventually caught in the Netherlands in 2021, got seven years, and got sent to Barlinnie. I got on great with Mark, he was my pal. All of Mark's mates came on my stag do in Benidorm in 1998. The police followed us to the airport. How we got into Spain, I don't know. A few of my mates got lifted in Benidorm. There was carnage. Later on, after I'd moved abroad and into coaching, I learned some of my mates ended up getting shot and killed. Some went to prison for supplying drugs. But they were all good to me, all good people. I knew they were up to no good but, Jesus, I never thought for one minute how heavy they were.

I was on boards in police stations, in pictures next to some of the Huyton boys, and my solicitors told me, 'Duncan, you need to get away from these people, your face is all over mugshots, it's all over surveillance. Keep away from them.' I wouldn't listen. Mark was my mate. He got fined for that doorman incident.

Mark hitting that doorman was when I began thinking about the drinking, the bad situations it led me into. Mark changed that night, and I think I changed too. Where there's drink, there's trouble. I wished I'd listened.

25

SOBERING UP

I stopped drinking at thirty-seven. I should have just been starting. Any time there's been trouble in my life there's been drink involved. Drink makes you do daft things, doesn't it?

We'd moved to Mallorca, people were coming out to visit, I'd have to take them to lunch and take them for a drink. Before I knew it I was drinking every day. I slipped into an unhealthy routine. Drink, rinse, repeat. I'd never been a daily drinker like that before. I was a binger. If I got a red card, I'd be out on the lash for two days, I'd never come home. When I went to Mallorca, the drinking started to creep in every day. A glass of red wine, a beer; never just one or two, always more.

Hangovers kill you, don't they? Soon I couldn't get out of bed. The kids were jumping on me, needing to go on school runs, wanting to go to football, wanting to jump in the pool, but with hangovers I'd be in bed until lunchtime. It wasn't that I needed alcohol. I had no alcohol dependency issue. I just got sick of alcohol. In the end, I just couldn't take the hangovers. They depressed me. The hangovers put me in a bad place. I'd think, 'What have I done?' That fight with Mark at the bar. I was starting to become a person I didn't want to become. I wanted to be a better person and a better father. Lying in my bed until noon wasn't it.

Some of the things I've done drunk I'm ashamed of. Janine was never happy with my late nights. I was coming in later and later.

The birds were up and singing in the trees by the time I got home, and I was walking up the path, the walk of shame. It's not a good walk, is it? I was a young guy, I had a few quid in my pocket. I ended up doing daft things, embarrassing stuff. Booze made me do things I regretted. I'd forget where I lived.

'What the hell did I do last night? Oh my God . . .'

I was a happy drunk until the few occasions when somebody pushed me and I reacted. I liked the company, going out, having a bit of money about me. It was the culture in football in those days when I had started the behaviour. I'd get drunk and light a cigar. That wasn't healthy. Drinking to excess and then training is not good for you either.

The culture slowly began to change when Arsène Wenger came to Arsenal in 1996. We heard all the rumours at Everton about no booze in the Arsenal players' lounge, no booze on the Arsenal bus. 'What do you mean there's no booze on the bus? That's shocking,' we all said. Foreign players came into the country and changed the drinking culture of British football. Their thinking literally sobered us up. At one point, we were smoking cigars on the Everton bus. We didn't care. The things we planned while pissed. I wish I'd given up earlier. I'd have played more games. It would have helped my football career, no doubt.

Even when I was drunk, I resisted drugs. I never took a line of cocaine in my life. Of course I was offered it, fuck yes – this was Liverpool! As in most cities, sadly. A rumour went round that I was a cokehead but there's not a man alive who ever could say to you 'I've seen Dunc take a line of cocaine'. Never touched it. Even when I retired, I never touched it.

Alcohol was my vice, unfortunately. Drink gripped me even more after I retired. I had to knock it. In the end I woke up late one morning in October 2008 and said to myself, 'I've had enough. I'm going to stay off it till Christmas.' Maybe the first few

SOBERING UP

days I'd pour myself a glass of wine at lunch or dinner. Just habit. Then I broke the habit. It helped that Janine doesn't really drink. She only has a small glass of champagne or wine now and again.

Christmas came and went and I didn't touch a drop. It was on my mind then that I had stopped drinking for good. Janine clocked it immediately. 'Let's wait until New Year,' I told her. 'We'll book a nice restaurant and I might have a drink then.' Hogmanay for a Scot was always going to be the test.

We booked a big restaurant for New Year's Eve. I was opening all the champagne bottles. I did not know but my family were looking at me, wondering whether I was going to touch a drink. I poured the drinks out, then glasses of red wine, and got the traditional twelve lucky grapes you eat in Spain, one with each chiming of the clock. They were all watching. I didn't know, and I went and smelt the red wine. All my family took a deep breath. It smelt like vinegar. I thought it was off. I'm sure it wasn't, I just thought in my mind it was off. I put it down, started chatting, and that was it.

'We knew then it was all over for you with booze,' Janine said a few months later. 'We knew that you wouldn't touch it.'

Once I want to do something, I'll do it. I've always had that strength of character. I get that from my dad. He was a drinker. Dad stopped when he was thirty-five.

I know I've become a better person sober. My kids can't remember the drinking. I just tell them I never had a drink. My two lads don't drink. Once I stopped drinking, I stopped the nights out, I stopped putting myself in dangerous positions. But you know what? I've never actually said, 'I've stopped drinking.' I don't count the days since I last had a drink. I'm not in rehab. Maybe one day I'll start drinking again. Maybe one day I'll be a great manager and Everton will win the Premier League, and if somebody offers me a glass of champagne then I might think, 'You know what? I'll have a nice glass of champagne!' Maybe.

'You'll not do it,' Janine says.

Maybe I'll just have one glass of champagne and think, 'Why did I do that? I've just done twenty years of being off it.'

But I never say never. Maybe when I get to seventy I'll think, 'What am I waiting for? What's wrong with a cigar at seventy, or a glass of brandy at seventy-five or eighty?' We'll see. At least I'll be thinking clearly before making the decision.

26

SKINT

I was kneeling in front of my wife, pulling at her finger. This time I was not proposing. I was going to pawn her beautiful engagement ring. That was one of the lowest moments of my life. How the hell had it come to this?

It was painful to admit that we desperately needed the money because of some bad investments and were selling everything to survive. I'd bought Janine a lot of jewellery when I had the money. I had to flog all my jewellery too. We had Rolexes, sixty-grand diamond rings, hundred-grand watches, and I flogged the lot to keep us going.

We left Janine's engagement ring until last.

'This will have to go,' I finally said to her. I felt terrible as I took the ring off her finger. It felt so wrong. Janine would have sold it because we were trying to survive. But we came round. We couldn't do it, we didn't do it, though we sold everything else. I've not got a watch now. Janine's not got a watch. It's all gone. We had a million pounds' worth of jewellery. But you don't get a million pounds for it when you go to flog it. We managed to get a few hundred grand, and it kept us going.

That period was tough, really hard. We had nothing. We were looking down the back of the seats for money. I sold everything I could, even my pigeons. Seventy grand I got for them. Broke my heart saying goodbye to them. I also sold a lovely piece of land in

Mallorca that I paid £2 million for. Knockdown price for a quick sale. I had some apartments in Albert Dock near Everton's new ground, three or four of them. They went. We got rid of everything we had just to keep going, to keep the kids in school, to keep our heads above water.

How I found myself in a pawn shop in such a wretched financial state is a long, embarrassing story. Back in the days when I had money, Tommy came up to Bellefield one day with a load of jewellery and showed me this beautiful Rolex.

'Here, give me that,' I said. It was lovely, with a great big diamond on it. 'How much?'

'Forty grand. But for you, Dunc, half price. Twenty.'

I had it on my wrist for twenty years. It's on my wedding photos, my pride and joy. When our finances collapsed I went to flog it in the pawn shop and the boy said, 'Duncan, I've got bad news. It's not worth a carrot.'

'What?!'

'It's snide.'

'What?!'

'Sorry, Dunc.'

I phoned Tommy. 'Tommy, this watch is not worth a carrot, mate.'

'What watch? I can't remember giving you that watch.'

Tommy didn't know it was snide. He'd got it off his mate, a middleman. The boy knew that Tommy was in with the footballers so they just passed the gear on. I got buttons for it, a grand. It kept us going for a few days.

I was never great with money. As you know, I'm a generous guy, and I gave a lot away when I was earning big at Everton and

Newcastle. I was a mug. I even gave £250,000 to financial advisers to help them out. It didn't cross my mind that meant they couldn't be very good at their job. I should have kept clear. I went into business with a mate up in Scotland. He ran the property business for me. We bought too many houses and borrowed too much money. The 2008 crash cleaned that little enterprise out. Another £1 million gone. Some years after this, the same mate called me again. 'Dunc, I need £15k for a restaurant I am opening. I will give you 50 per cent of it. Please, Dunc, please, I will get it back to you.' My wife will kill me when she reads this. I was short at the time but gave the guy the £15k. You guessed it. Not a whisper from him since. Nada. I gave plenty of money out to lots of my mates, plenty. If they were struggling or they needed it for a sure thing, I gave them it. Some paid me back, but plenty never did. Too caring, too helpful, too loyal or just a big mug? You can answer that for me.

I was naive. The two worst things I've invested in were a piece of land in Liverpool and getting involved with the film tax scheme. I bought the land for £500,000 and spent another £500,000 on drawings and bills. My mate said, 'We will get permission for 100 houses. There's a councillor who's on board. We stand to make £10 million with a fair wind.' You can guess the rest. The wind never blew. Never got the permission. Another £1 million down. The land's still lying there, and all my money is tied up in it, with sheep still walking about it. When I went skint, they came for everything.

I'd overstretched when the 2008 financial crash happened. I never got the £2.5 million I was owed by the guy who bought my house when I went to Mallorca. The crash came, and he went under. Another £2.5 million gone. I'd been expecting the money so I'd bought that nice villa in Mallorca for €4 million but put down only €1 million deposit, waiting for the rest of this money, and then the crash happened, everything went belly up, and that was the start of the problems.

I got involved in the film tax schemes around 2001. There were supposed tax benefits that harmed so many professional footballers. It went through clubs like wildfire. Hundreds of footballers got caught up in it. Do it, do it – easy money. Because we're all thick, we'll fall for it. Footballers leave school at fifteen. We've got life experience, but I wasn't educated on numbers. We were basically offered tax relief on investments in films. I didn't need to do those film schemes. Like every other mug player, I signed something. One person jumps off a cliff and we all follow. A Scotland player, Billy McKinlay, mentioned it to me and recommended an agent from Glasgow. I spoke to him and he was at the door two hours later, which seemed quick from Glasgow. 'Sign these forms,' he told me, almost ordering me. I should have known then. I should have smelt something was wrong when I smelt the burning tyres outside the house. He'd raced down from Glasgow, chauffeur-driven. The minute I signed the papers, the boy was out the door, counting his commission. I didn't have a clue what it was. Fifteen years later, there was a bang on my door. The taxman was standing there demanding £4 million. I didn't have it.

I was worried sick. I didn't understand the scheme. I still don't. I signed a form, thinking it was a straight plan to save some money. How many people got stung with it? I'm sure other players reading this will agree: this was one of the worst things ever to happen to us. One scheme investigated by the taxman had 129 footballers in it. It was huge. David Beckham, Gary Lineker, Steven Gerrard and Wayne Rooney had to pay tax back. How many people are still paying now? Having sleepless nights? Chris Sutton for one.

Big Sam Allardyce was never off the phone to me – well, he used to be. Big Sam tried to fight it.

Footballers need better advice – or more to the point, I should have wised up. The financial adviser I had disappeared. His phone stopped ringing. He owed me that £250,000 from another deal. He put me into some crazy things, ten grand a month for this, ten grand a month for that. It's all commission. When you're playing football, you've made it, you get a financial adviser. But can you trust them? They all ended up in Dubai, didn't they? Half of Liverpool are in Dubai now. It happens. It's life, isn't it? But the sleepless nights are terrible.

I was sinking. I'd earned well for a decade, but before I knew it the money was all gone, very quickly. Janine was distraught because, once you start getting these brown envelopes through the door from HMRC, it's horrendous. Bills and demands were coming through every day and I was trying to hide them. And Janine was finding them.

Can you imagine, a letter demanding £4 million? That's how much they wanted off me.

I didn't want the stigma of being made bankrupt. That was too humiliating. I got advised to go for an IVA, an individual voluntary arrangement where you try to pay back the money. And I tried hard. I sold everything – property, jewellery.

Eventually I went to Manchester to this insolvency company.

'I was a football player, I had a lot of money . . .' I began.

'Duncan, move on, you made a mistake,' said the tax expert there. 'You know how many football players are coming through this door?'

'I'm trying to pay the taxman off.'

'Duncan, what are you doing? Are you daft? They'll just bleed you and bleed you until you've got nothing. Go bump yourself off and wipe the debt, and you'll sleep a bit easier. There's hundreds in the same boat. I'm dealing with hundreds of clients. I'm telling them the same: "Sign a form, walk away."'

So I did. I declared myself bankrupt. But I'm a proud person, and it hurt. At least Janine still had her engagement ring on her finger. Just.

27

ABSENT FRIENDS

'Shut up, don't say another word, that cannot be true,' I shouted at some of my Under-14s. I'll never forget where I was when I heard that Gary Speed had taken his own life: a tournament in Loughborough, 27 November 2011, in the middle of preparing this bunch of Everton hopefuls for another game. The players were talking about it. 'Shut up,' I ordered them again. It surely could not be true, could it?

I knew Gary well from Everton and Newcastle. I'd made his goal on his debut for Everton against Newcastle on 17 August 1996. I will never forget Gary's big, beautiful, smiling face when he scored. We ran to each other and embraced. I loved Gary, a great guy. I never sensed anything wrong with him, nothing. Gary used to pick me up and take me to training when I first went to Newcastle. 'I'm having a really hard time with the fans, Duncan,' he'd say. Newcastle fans were on his back a bit. I don't think he was quite settled in at Newcastle. This was seven years before he died.

Gary can't be dead, I told myself. He was always so positive, smiling, chatting. It can't be true. Tragically, it was. It filtered through that it was true. It's mad, isn't it? Terrible really. Poor soul. Gary was forty-two when he passed away, far too young.

I had to go out on the pitch with Gary's dad Roger before

Everton's game at Goodison with Stoke City on 4 December 2011. We were all paying tribute to Gary.

I just don't know why Gary took his life. Gary always struck me as a positive person, always happy, a bubbly person with his whole life to live. So it was a huge shock when it happened. In my experiences from drinking – and I'm not saying Gary was drinking – it can put you in a bad place. I don't know what pushed Gary over the edge. All I know is that it's a crying shame. Gary was a good guy and my heart goes out to his family. We all miss you, Gary.

Six weeks after Gary Speed passed we lost Gary Ablett. 1 January, 2012, a horrendous start to the year. Gary was forty-six. He was taken from us so young. To see Gary in the final stages of his illness was heart-breaking. I went to see him when he was dying with non-Hodgkin lymphoma. I went to his house up in High Rufford, on the way to Preston, and I went to see him in the Christie hospital in Manchester. On his sickbed, Gary pulled out a passing drill from under the bed that he had from his time as a Liverpool coach. He knew I was back at Everton coaching. It was the first passing drill I did at Finch Farm. The Gary Ablett Passing Drill. I'll always have it and all my memories of Gary.

On 15 June 2024, we lost Kevin Campbell to a heart condition. Kevin was fifty-four. The club described Kevin as 'not just a true Goodison Park hero and icon of the English game, but an incredible person as well' and he was. Kevin was a legend at Everton, a great centre-forward, who helped keep the team up, and he was always a bubbly and smiling character, always good on a night out. Kevin was a gentleman and always nice company. His kids were breaking through at Man City, so our paths would cross when I took the young academy sides at Everton. Every time I met him at Finch Farm, Kevin was always on form, and looked healthy and strong. It was a tragedy what happened to him. We all miss Kevin Campbell, Gary Ablett and Gary Speed. Everton legends.

28

NEW COACH

I love this club. I couldn't wait to get back. My coaching journey started in October 2011 and I was back at Everton, now at Finch Farm, excited and grateful to David Moyes for the opportunity. 'The best way to learn is to go to the academy,' Moyesy recommended.

I never had a title, never had a position. I didn't even have a desk. Believe it or not, I used to sit on a windowsill in the coaches' room at Finch Farm for months. I didn't care. I just wanted to learn my trade. I worked round the clock, worked all the way through the age-groups up to Kevin Sheedy's Under-18s.

I enjoyed working with the young players and I felt the quality of work I was producing would see me climb the ladder. I was a workaholic coaching the 12s, the 13s, the 14s, the 16s and the 18s. I was addicted to the coaching. I spent every minute I could at Finch Farm – Christmas Day, New Year's Day, every day. I was the first in and the last out and there's not a man on this earth who could say any different. I put the lights on in the morning and I turned them off at 8 p.m. for years. It was pouring down one night and the rain got into the lights and blew the fuse box at Finch Farm. Me and the security boys were trying to disconnect the lights from the generator, smoke everywhere. I've done everything for Everton. I've even picked up litter around Finch Farm, going back to my Dundee United days.

I got to work with so many good young players: Kieran Dowell, Matthew Pennington, Ryan Ledson, Jonjoe Kenny, Tom Davies, Callum Connolly, Antonee 'Jedi' Robinson and Ross Barkley. Everton had a really great academy run by Alan Irvine. Another Scot! Everton also recruited really well back then, a couple of teenagers in particular. On 31 January 2013 Moyesy brought in this great kid from Barnsley. I watched John Stones in the reserves, playing right-back, and saw immediately that Stonesy was a very elegant player, great on the ball, first at right-back, then centre-back and he would progress further. I always liked to be around young people – it keeps me young. They're vibrant, aren't they, especially a player of Stones's likeable personality and huge potential. I'm so proud to see what John has gone on to achieve with Manchester City and England.

Dominic Calvert-Lewin, tall and quick, came from Sheffield United in 2016. We had to work on certain parts of Dom's game like hold-up play, but he's a good goalscorer, lightning quick and athletic. Stonesy and Dom were absolutely good lads, dedicated, the pair of them, and totally focused on where they wanted to go. Everyone at Finch Farm knew they were going to get there. It was good scouting that discovered them and they have fulfilled their potential. Dom joined Stonesy in playing for England.

Finch Farm was full of young talent, it was brilliant to be around it. Eric Dier was on loan with our academy from Sporting Lisbon. He was doing well and Everton were interested but Sporting were asking more than £1 million. So Eric returned to Lisbon. Shokdran Mustafi was recruited from Hamburg into the academy, and was let go on a free to Sampdoria. Both centre-backs went on to have good careers. Mustafi won the World Cup and Eric got to the Champions League final with Spurs and the World Cup semi-final with England. Everton did very well in recruiting younger players back then.

NEW COACH

But it wasn't all perfect. For two years from October 2011 I worked in Everton's academy for free. I got paid nothing for developing their prized young assets, nothing, not a dime. The only reason they eventually gave me money was because big Davey Weir came in as an assistant to the Under-21s and they gave him £500 a week, so in the end they said, 'Duncan, we're giving you £25,000 a year.' I was grateful for the help, although it was not a lot of money. It hardly covered my expenses. I nicked a pool car. I had next to no money at the time and I was struggling to get to Finch Farm. Everyone was scared to say to me, 'That's a pool car.' I never had a desk, or a defined role. I worked hard to be recognised. I started at the bottom. I was even coaching the development kids off the street and I loved it. I did everything I could to be better.

I'll never forget David Moyes's words to me. 'Duncan,' he said, 'I've been thinking about it. I think you need to start getting paid a wee bit of money. At least it will pay for the groceries for you.'

After tax, I was getting buttons. But I kept believing I would climb the ladder. I was working harder than anyone, putting incredible hours in. But also it was Everton, the club I loved.

Janine, bless her, understood. I was trying to make a career for myself. I was trying to show people what I was all about. I knew in the building some people were saying, 'It won't last, he's only coming in for a few months. He'll chuck it.' They thought I'd quit. I never did. I loved it. Janine was always bitter. She felt they weren't valuing me. 'Duncan, they're not paying you enough.'

It sounds crazy but there was no designated space for me, only for the coaches for the Under-18s, Under-21s and Under-16s. In the end, Mick O'Brien, an Under-12s coach I knew who used to play with me, said, 'Duncan, this is ridiculous. Let's go and rob a desk out of the education room and we'll get you set up.' Me and wee Mick went through to the education block, moved cupboards out the way and liberated a desk and chair. We put the desk in the corner, and all my books and my paperwork on some shelves we put up.

Me and Kevin Sheedy were doing incredible work with the Under-18s. We won our league and developed players who've gone on to have careers, like Jonjoe Kenny, Callum Connolly and Ryan Ledson (all made the first team at Everton), Kieran Dowell, Matty Pennington, Joe Williams, Antonee Robinson, and Liam Walsh (now at Luton Town) and Gethin Jones (an Australian international at Bolton Wanderers).

When Moyesy left in June 2013 to fill Alex Ferguson's shoes at Manchester United, Roberto Martínez was appointed. He brought in a large team of staff with him. It's always a good idea to have more friends watching your back. It's also much more expensive for a club to get rid of a lot of staff. So for any aspiring managers out there: take as many staff as you can. Roberto had Graeme Jones, Dennis Lawrence, Richard Evans, Kevin Reeves and Inaki Bergara, the goalkeeping coach. Graeme was a fantastic, detailed coach and very meticulous in his work. Big Dennis was the same. He was an ex-soldier, again very studious. They were good guys and I learnt so much from them. Of course, I'm sure they learned a few things from me like how to play pool and table tennis. Sorry, Dennis, had to get that in! You're good but just not good enough.

I'd started my Pro Licence and Inaki knew people at Real Sociedad, so I went there to do the club part of my Pro Licence. I spent some time in San Sebastián, on my own, for a week. A fabulous city, San Sebastián. I speak a wee bit of Spanish – 'Poco español, amigo, por favor.' The main one was 'La cuenta, por favor'. I quickly noticed this French boy up front for Sociedad. Antoine Griezmann was the last player off the training ground. He just stayed on to practise taking free-kicks. Griezmann obviously went on to be a fantastic player, for Atlético Madrid, Barcelona and

NEW COACH

France. I wrote about him in my Pro Licence book, always last off the training field. I'll never forget him.

I returned to Finch Farm and suffered more frustration. The assistant job to the Under-21s coach Alan Stubbs came up in September. I never got it because the club brought in David Unsworth, who'd just left Sheffield United and was out of a job. I was so frustrated.

'I thought I'd have been coming with you as your assistant with the 21s,' I said to Stubbsy in the corridor at Finch Farm.

'It was out of my hands, Duncan. They wouldn't pay the same wage,' Stubbsy said.

Unfortunately, I'd been blocked. I felt I should have moved up to the 21s. If I'd gone up to the reserves it would have helped my development. And it would have also put me closer to a potential first-team job. Instead it was Unsy. I felt it was not right. I had worked round the clock. Unsy should have gone to the 18s.

Shortly afterwards I was walking through reception at Goodison and Bill Kenwright approached me and said, 'Hi, Duncan, how are you doing?'

'I'm all right, chairman, everything's fine,' I replied, and walked away.

Bill then phoned me and asked, 'Are you really all right?'

'I'm fine.'

'What do you think about David Unsworth coming in in front of you? That was a bit naughty that.'

'Chairman, I felt it should have been me.'

'I'm going to try and get you into the first team now,' Bill said. 'I'll fix it for you. I'll speak to Roberto.' Bill convinced Roberto to take me. I think I was imposed on him. The club probably wanted an Everton man on the bench to give the staff a connection with the fans. Or maybe it was because I was a top coach.

So I started going up to the first team a couple of days a week under Roberto. I got the team training on a Tuesday and watched the training session on a Wednesday. I was running the offside lines, I moved goals, I carried bibs. Eventually I got a passing drill, a wee bit of possession and, once they had confidence in me, got put on to the first team as a full-time coach in February 2014. I still wasn't sure Roberto wanted me there.

But I learned from Roberto. He was known for being a flair manager and certainly added more verve to the side than Moyes had instilled. Moyesy was a bit more pragmatic. Roberto was more attacking. He was a very intelligent man who set his training up brilliantly and went into real detail with his pattern of plays. I was watching things in training I'd never seen before like false full-backs and internal runs. Roberto was the best I ever saw tactically at the time. I took ideas and inspiration from him, his detail, his training, his sessions. They were all relevant to the game-plan going into Saturday.

In the end, my time with Roberto was a mistake. I stagnated as a coach. You can only do so many offside lines. I should have stayed with the 18s or hit the road and made my own path. But I loved Everton that much and Bill had told me, 'You're going to the first team.' Brilliant.

Tactically, Roberto was astute. His sessions were good and I learned a lot from Graeme Jones and Big Dennis about setting up drills. I saw how meticulous they were. I came up with a lot of good drills myself and I was loyal and good at my job, but I found Roberto a bit stand-offish. He was always nice and polite with me, I'd have a bite of lunch with him, and I generally just did my apprenticeship, but I felt I was there under sufferance.

I never complained. I loved Everton Football Club. I'd come back from Mallorca, it was a job, it was at Everton, I was learning my trade, I was going on away games, I was with the players, I was working. It looked good on my CV to be a first-team coach. It

NEW COACH

looked a step up, but looking back now, I was stuck in there and people behind the scenes were probably just killing me saying, 'He doesn't do any coaching, he just stands there, he doesn't do a lot.' Club politics.

I never thought I was going to be a coach. I thought, 'Just be a manager, forget the coaching.' But actually I got addicted to coaching.

That's why I felt I was an authority because I was there. I'd watch Callum Connolly, Jonjoe Kenny, Tom Davies and Antonee 'Jedi' Robinson, all these players that came through. I'd watched them when they were eight. I formed my opinion over years and years.

Roberto came in the canteen one day and said to me, 'That George Green's a good player.' George Green was signed to Everton's academy for a lot of money, around £300,000 with big add-ons, from Bradford City in 2011.

'He's not going to be good enough for Everton's first team. Hopefully, he'll go on to a career elsewhere.'

I had strong opinions on youth players. They liked Hallam Hope. I didn't think he was Everton level either. They rated Luke Garbutt. He was another good player. He just wasn't good enough for Everton's first team, I felt, but who knew, he could go on to have a good career elsewhere.

'The manager really likes him, you know,' Graeme said to me. 'Luke Garbutt's got a lovely left foot.'

'He has got a nice left foot,' I agreed. 'You know what he likes, then, taking free-kicks. He loves taking free-kicks after training. He loves taking corners. Try him on one v. ones against a winger, see how he does.'

I remember it was a nice summer's day, and Garbutt said to Graeme, 'Can I get some extra after training?'

'Yes, we'll do some extra, we'll do some one v. ones.'

So they pulled a goal across and called over Christian Atsu, that poor wee boy who died in that horrendous earthquake in Turkey in 2023, a right-winger. They put a goal on the touchline and Graeme got Atsu to do fifteen one v. ones with Garbutt. Martínez watched, Graeme watched, and I just sat back and thought, 'Here they go . . .' Atsu just went by him, time after time. He scored a lot of goals.

People at clubs go, 'Oh, he's a great player, he's an up-and-coming top player.' But have they really watched them? I made sure I watched everyone, every match. Callum Connolly? I knew him when he was a kid. Jonjoe Kenny? Watched him. I knew he'd have a career. He played for Everton fifty times. I had an informed opinion. You've got to be special to play in the Premier League.

I did my homework. I became an expert on who was good and who wasn't, who was worth sticking with and would train on, and who should be let go. I put the work in. I watched the 21s, 18s, 17s, 15s. At 10 p.m. I was up against the lamppost watching the wee kids, looking to see if one of them had something special. I watched videos at 3 a.m.

One day, Roberto called me into his office and said, 'I got you an increase, Duncan. I've got you an extra £3,000 a year.'

'Fantastic, gaffer,' I replied and walked out.

They even invited me to Roberto's house for his end-of-season party. I wasn't going to go but Janine said, 'You have to.' I was reluctant.

As it happened, my old pigeon mate Albert Tarleton (God rest his soul, he's dead now) was on his way home so I went over to see him. 'Dunc, just go to Roberto's party,' Albert said.

So I went, and Roberto's present to me was a wee wooden-framed picture of me coaching on the pitch. It was signed 'Thanks for all your efforts'.

NEW COACH

Roberto got sacked with one game to go of that 2015–16 season. Norwich City at home. He should not have been sacked like that. But the reason became clear the very next day. I was the last man standing. Finch Farm was like a ghost town.

'Chairman, who are you talking to about Darron Gibson getting a new contract?' I asked Bill.

'I'm not pulling the strings, son.'

'If you're looking for my advice, chairman, I'm here.' I liked Darron Gibson but he was on the downside of his career.

Somebody had a word with Everton's new owner Farhad Moshiri and Gibson got a two-year deal without a manager being in the building. Darron had just come off a season where he'd played only eleven times, partly through injury. But he got a new contract, played twenty-four minutes in the EFL Cup against Yeovil and got offloaded to Sunderland in January 2017.

Mo Bešić somehow got two contracts at Everton. The Bosnian midfielder made thirty-five starts in three and a half seasons and never showed he was worth a second contract. Bešić wasn't good enough for the first contract in 2014, so I was surprised he got a second.

Well, Moshiri bought 49.9 per cent of Everton on 27 February 2016, promised investment, and two days later Bešić got his new five-and-a-half-year deal. For me, it was a bad decision. God knows how much each game cost. A fortune.

It was around this time that Everton invited a young Erling Haaland in to training when he was fifteen, sixteen. But his team back in Norway, Bryne, wanted a couple of million quid. Everton felt that was too much.

Anyway, back in May 2016, who was going to take the last game? Surely me? I was thinking to myself, 'They'll have to put me in for the last game of the season.' I was the only one left. The next minute, Kenwright's walking down the corridor at Finch Farm talking to

Unsworth. He couldn't? I didn't see it coming. I didn't understand the politics. I'm just straight. I'm here, I'll be taking this game. The next minute, Bill came in. I was in the office in my same wee spot. It's a lonely place when you're in there and everybody's gone.

'I've asked David Unsworth and Joe Royle to take the game tomorrow, Duncan.' I was bitter and a bit shellshocked. Surely it should have been me? I couldn't believe it. 'What? What the hell are you on about?' Unsworth and Joe Royle? I knew Joe was close to Kenwright, but why not me? They sacked Martínez because the strategy was to put in Big Joe Royle and David Unsworth, the Under-21s coach.

The chairman came in to see me and tried to explain. He backed Unsy and Joe, and it hurt me. I was upset about it for a long time. In some ways Bill Kenwright broke my heart.

Moshiri had bought into Everton three months earlier and was making his presence felt. I've got no problem with David Unsworth. We'd say hello. It's just the way they did it. That was their plan. I wasn't in that plan so that was that. I was with the manager, I'd stuck by Roberto. I stick next to my boss. 'Be loyal to your boss,' my dad always told me. I'd done that.

Shortly after Roberto left I was in my office at Finch Farm. I never took a day off. All summer I was at my desk doing my wee diagrams and my passing drills and my tactical stuff, no break, nothing. Everybody was away. And then I heard a drilling noise.

I went out and said, 'What's going on?'

It was Dave Harrison, another who had risen up, who'd started as assistant secretary and become director of football operations. He was pulling this name-plate off the door that had been Graeme Jones's office and putting his nameplate on.

'All right, Dave?'

Sawdust was at his feet. The office was right next to the

manager's office. So when Ronald Koeman came in, Harrison was next door. Clever. Be close to power.

There was a vacuum of leadership at Everton. It happens at other clubs. Most of the owners are stretched out on their boats in Monaco or in a gated community in the United States. Nobody knows what's going on at the ground. People exploit that. I've seen it happen for years. Good luck to them. I'm not having a go, it's a game of politics. I didn't play the game. Not only that, I didn't even know what the game was.

29

KOEMAN

We met Ronald Koeman properly for the first time in Hope Street Hotel, all the coaches gathering around a table. By the time I got in they were already there – Ronald, his brother Erwin, David Unsworth, everybody. I knew Unsworth would be there. Whenever a manager came in, Unsy would show him round Finch Farm. I guess he was being friendly and welcoming but it felt like he was trying to ingratiate himself. I wasn't with that gang. I was on my own. Unsy was the board's man. He'd meet Ronald Koeman and later Marcel Brands, help them settle in. I wasn't in their crowd. I felt it was the club's strategy to push and promote Unsy at every opportunity.

I sat at the bottom of the table at Hope Street and listened. I immediately took to Ronald. He could take a joke.

'You Dutch are only good for growing tulips and importing cannabis,' I told him.

Ronald laughed his head off. 'Turn it down, we invented football!'

'You invented tulips!'

I really enjoyed Koeman's company. He's a legend of the game. We spoke about that Scotland game at Euro 92. At the end of the evening I got up to go and saw Unsworth bear-hugging Ronald. Everybody was all over the Dutchman. A manager as experienced as him could see through this mateyness. I took one look at this swarm around Ronald and said, 'Boss, I'm getting off.' I waved because it looked like Ronald was getting choked by Unsy: he was bright red and his eyes were popping. Unsy was a friendly guy.

'Can I see you, Duncan?' He remembered my name! I was also relieved he was able to speak at that moment.

'I'm getting off, boss. All the best.'

Koeman said, 'I'm sorry, it's busy here.'

'No, it's all right, boss, don't be worrying. I'll see you in the morning.'

The next day, when Ronald came in to Finch Farm, I was sitting at my desk as usual doing my thing and keeping out the road. The Euros were on, there were group games in the afternoon, and Ronald was in his office with Erwin, watching some match. I was in my office worrying whether I was losing my job. Unsworth, the Under-21s coach, was running in and out of Ronald's office. 'Can I get you a cup of tea? Can I get you tracky bottoms?' Unsy was there to help Ronald.

Unsy was being Unsy. That was his style. He was trying to get on in the game. We all were. I never had the front. I was more stand-offish. Maybe that held me back.

Eventually Erwin appeared in front of my desk.

'Duncan?'

'Yes, Erwin.'

'Come in the office.'

I went in, and Ronald was sitting there, looking at me.

'Nice to see you, boss.'

'Sit down, Duncan.'

Someone brought sarnies in. My last supper?

'Watch the football with me, Duncan.'

The next minute the door opened and it was Unsworth. 'Do you need any training gear, boss?' Then, 'You're going to the stadium, aren't you, boss? I'll drive you.'

'No, I'm all right.'

Eventually, Unsy left. Ronald asked me loads of questions about the club and players. Hours later, I opened the door and there's Unsworth: 'Are you ready for that lift, boss?'

'No, Duncan's taking me.'

I wasn't. It was just Ronald telling Unsy that I was going to be his man.

Before I left the room, Ronald pulled me to one side. 'Duncan, I'm uncomfortable with what you're getting paid. Your wages are an absolute disgrace and we are going to have to change that.' Ronald got me up to £150,000, and then £200,000. He liked me, he saw I was doing a good job, and that I was underpaid for a coach in the Premier League. I'll never forget how good Ronald was to me. He showed me the respect I felt I deserved for the job I was doing. He got me involved a lot in training.

Koeman was a fabulous player. Remember, I made my competitive debut for Scotland against him in the 92 Euros. Of course, he could not remember me. Ronald was accused of being lazy at Everton and always leaving early to play golf. In all his time at Everton, to my knowledge, he played golf once. I organised it at the famous Formby Golf Course. A four-ball Ronald and John Parrott v Gareth Barry and Phil Jagielka. Ronald played off 11, JP off 2, Gareth off 8, Jags off 7. It was a beautiful summer's day and honestly not a soul on the course. Ronald to this day thinks I booked it out just for us. I can't play golf so I caddied for Ronald. It was fantastic, they were brilliant and Ronald and JP won it on the last hole.

Another thing I should set straight for the record. When he was at Everton, Ronald got stick for having a red Christmas tree. I felt bad because my wife had taken Ronald's wife Bartina to Bents in Manchester for Christmas decorations. They decorated in red – not a good move in Liverpool . . .

I enjoyed being on Ronald Koeman's coaching staff, and I loved coaching Romelu Lukaku. This Belgian kid was raw, quick and strong. He wasn't aggressive, but what a player! I coached his hold-up play. I remember once, me and him were wrestling each other. I'd be the centre-back getting on top of him and pulling him and pushing him. After three repetitions, Rom was on the floor knackered. He was in his early twenties. I must have been forty-two. He wasn't used to the body contact.

'You've got to use your body more,' I told him.

We built Rom up physically and he got used to the contact, to pushing people. Look at the boxer Tyson Fury, who's been so successful because he wrestles people a lot; he's like a big heavy weight on you. We didn't have to toughen Rom mentally. He was already psychologically strong. You've got to be as a striker, to get in there and not be scared to miss. I was a wee bit scared to miss sometimes and that's probably why I wasn't as clinical in front of goal. I didn't have the mindset. But Rom had it. He was ruthless. Size thirteen feet and boom, boom, boom.

Rom loved training and spending extra time on the training ground. When others went in, I'd take him all the time for finishing, and bits of movement. He always had the speed, we worked on his finishing, and he became more clinical. But not always. He once hit my car with a shot at Finch Farm from 30 yards away. Rom struck the ball so hard it dented the front wing.

'You've hurt my car, lad! Look at the state of it!'

Rom just laughed. Never paid for it. It wasn't the pool car either.

When Rom scored against Sunderland on 25 February 2017, he matched my club record of sixty Premier League goals for Everton. I was delighted to hear what he said about me challenging him. 'Duncan spoke to me in a way to keep me sharp and test me. He's been winding me up but he knows it's for a good cause. He wants me to help the team-mates to win, and I want to win.'

Most players always big up their manager. They don't mention the work the assistant manager or coach has done with them. Romelu was different. He was honest. 'I work with Duncan a lot,' he'd tell the coaches or manager. Fantastic! Some managers didn't want me coaching that extra stuff with the centre-forwards. I might get the credit and that might undermine the manager. Rom was generous with his praise.

It was a joy to coach Rom because he wanted to learn and was prepared to put in the graft. I noticed that with all the top players. They're the last off the training field. Any of the great players I've worked with – Rooney, Shearer, Lukaku . . . James Rodríguez, Dominic Calvert-Lewin, Samuel Eto'o and Richarlison later on – they don't stop when training's finished. They do more.

I'd tell Rom, in fact all the centre-forwards I worked with, that they should be listening to the net every day. They should hear the sound of the net so they can imagine the ball hitting it. Different parts of the net sound different. I know that sounds mad but it's true. Hitting the side of the net you get that 'whoosh'. Hitting the bar and the ball going in, or hitting the stanchions – all different sounds. And it's all about repetition. Listen to the sound of the ball entering the net. And repeat, repeat, repeat. Visualising the goal, imagining the sound, building the process and then executing so it all becomes second nature. Centre-forwards like Rom love that. Just getting the ball and bang, getting the ball and bang. 'Whip it in the corners,' I told them. They can't do enough of it. 'Steak and chips, steak and chips,' I'd tell them. I called it 'steak and chips' because it was simple and it was good. There was no shite in it. No fancy runs or fancy talking. When I later worked with the Brazilian Richarlison, he used to come up to me and go, 'Steak and chips?' I'd just laugh.

When Rom left to go to Manchester United in the summer of 2017 we missed him badly. Ronald asked me about players.

Like Gylfi Sigurdsson, who Everton bought for £45 million in the summer of 2017. Gylfi was a great player but the cost was mad. A year earlier we could have got him from Swansea City for, like, £25 million. I could just imagine how the conversation may have gone when the club went in again in 2017.

'He's a great player on the eye, let's bid £30 million.'

'No, £30 million's not enough. He's better than that, let's bid £35 million.' It's like we were bidding against ourselves.

And somebody else would turn round and say, 'Nah, nah, he's better than that, let's bid £45 million.'

While all that was going on I told Ronald Koeman, 'Look, I've got Wayne Rooney here. He's better than Sigurdsson. Take him. He's at Man United. I'll sort him out. Don't be worrying. Get Wayne Rooney.' I kept at it. I loved Wayne – a top player, an Evertonian, who was coming to the end of his career.

I brought Wayne back to Everton. I knew the Everton fans had gone off him after the way he left for United. So I had my plan, and it started about two years before Wayne actually returned. The plan to rebuild the relationship between Wayne and Everton fans was to get Wayne to play at Goodison in my testimonial against Villarreal on 2 August 2015. I rang Wayne and he said he'd check with the United manager, Louis van Gaal.

'Look, I want to play for Duncan in his testimonial,' Wayne told van Gaal. He convinced the United manager it was a good idea for him to put on the Everton shirt again.

'Great!' I told Wayne.

I still worried nobody was going to turn up for the game. I couldn't believe how many did – 35,000 fans (the other 2,000 seats were under construction, and there were no away fans). The biggest attendance Everton ever had for a testimonial. It was so humbling. They'd turned out for a guy who hadn't played for years, which was incredible. I wasn't that fit, I relied on adrenalin and pride to get me through. Wayne played, and that meant the world to me. We briefly thought of inviting Pierluigi Collina to referee but he wouldn't have survived. The club asked Collina if he'd do an interview for the programme but for some reason he wasn't keen! Some of the questions would have been a bit tasty!

When I warmed up, I stopped and had a chat with a couple of fans in the Gwladys Street corner. I came on for the last five minutes, and got a standing ovation. I was desperate to score. I thought I had a chance from a corner but Tyias Browning beat me to it and scored. I had no spring left in my legs.

I took the microphone at full-time. I wanted to thank Wayne for turning out. It was an emotional occasion for him, having left in 2004 and been given a bit of stick by Everton fans since. But he got a great reception. My plan was working. I also wanted to thank Bill Kenwright for bringing me back home to Everton and making this day possible. I gave half the proceeds from the testimonial to charity. I helped the baby hospice Zoe's Place, and the children's charity Variety. I handed out cheques to many people in the community, for minibuses, and kept some of it for myself.

And the plan, of course, worked: Wayne returned to play for Everton in the summer of 2017. The testimonial had definitely helped build a bridge between Wayne and the Everton fans. I convinced Ronald to take Wayne.

'Will you meet Wayne?' I asked Ronald.

'Yes, we'll meet him.'

I sorted a meeting in Alderley Edge and phoned Wayne.

'Look, come and meet Ronald. Say what I tell you to say and we'll get you to Everton.'

Wayne was made up. He wanted to leave United. So I drove to Wayne's and picked him up.

'Tell Ronald you'll train hard. He knows you're Evertonian,

and your family want you there. You want your kids to see you in a blue shirt. Tell him I'll look after you. Tell him I'm your idol. Tell him you've got your hunger back. Tell him you're fit, healthy, you'll score goals for him. Tell him you'll do everything to make the club successful. I'll make sure you don't divert from this path.'

So we went in to see Ronald. His wife Bartina, a lovely lady, raced in and Wayne was really polite. It was all going well, Wayne saying all the right things. He told Ronald that he trusted me 100 per cent and that he would not let me or the gaffer down.

'I've got him, Ronald,' I promised. 'Wayne's under my wing. I'll make sure he keeps on the straight and narrow. Don't be worrying. Stand on me, he'll do it for us.'

Ronald walked away, then turned and said, 'OK, Wayne, lovely to meet you.'

Wayne drove home.

Ronald called. He had his concerns.

'I've heard he's not living the right life. What do you think, Duncan? Can you keep him right?'

'Stand on me, Ronald. He's hungry and he'll do it for Everton. There will be no problems with Wayne.'

'OK. We'll take him.'

I phoned Wayne. 'He's taking you. You're coming back.' Wayne was ecstatic. We got him on a free transfer. He did well, settled fast and scored quickly against Stoke City, Manchester City and West Ham.

Everton still bought Sigurdsson on 16 August. In the end we paid £45 million for a player who'd almost been relegated with Swansea! Nobody in the top six was in for him, so why so much? Bid £20 million for him! Nobody else wanted him, none of the big clubs anyway.

Wayne didn't stay long because Ronald had Gylfi in. Wayne was good. He scored eleven goals in forty games. He was fantastic.

Everton signed a lot of no. 10s but Wayne still had more in the tank. When Wayne scored the penalty against Liverpool at Anfield on 10 December 2017, Janine was so excited she jumped off the couch, smashed a glass and trod on it, cutting her heel. When I got home, Janine was white, and there was blood everywhere. 'Right, hospital, now.' I drove Janine to Southport Hospital, and a big piece of glass was taken out of her heel. We were there all night. She still suffers from it now.

30

STOCKMANSHIP

Strange title, I know, so bear with me. My mate Albert Tarleton was a great pigeon man. He was asked one day to go to a pigeon sale and buy the most expensive pigeons available. Albert went with this wealthy businessman. Albert looked at the pigeons on offer and made his selection. 'But they are not the dearest,' the businessman said. 'They are the ones I like,' Albert replied. The businessman passed on Albert's selection and decided to buy the most expensive pigeons available. Albert decided to buy the ones he liked for himself. They were cheap. Albert's pigeons destroyed the Liverpool pigeon clubs. He won everything. He became a legend in the Liverpool pigeon fraternity. Those five pigeons cost Albert £200. He sold them for over 50 grand in 1983. He bought his house with the proceeds. The businessman never won a thing. If you want a good horse where do you go? (Not to Mickey Quinn's!) You go to Ireland. Greyhounds, the same again, Ireland. My point is, Albert had it. The Irish have it. They've developed it over the years breeding and racing horses and dogs. It's called stockmanship.

Football needs scouts on the grass, out there looking for the next Wayne Rooney. These guys are worth their weight in gold. Alan Shearer, a Newcastle lad, broke through at Southampton. Why on earth was he not at his beloved Magpies? Because Jack

Hixon, the scout, was a good stockman. Shearer went to the other side of the country to break through. Incredible. Newcastle had to pay for that mistake some years later. Howard Kendall built a phenomenal team in the mid-eighties, full of club legends: Neville Southall, Adrian Heath, Peter Reid, Kevin Sheedy, Trevor Steven, Andy Gray. Jesus, I'm sure there must have been a bit of Irish in Howard.

Howard had fantastic knowledge of football. He knew a player, the way they walked and talked and operated. Howard built that great team for Everton in the mid-eighties because of his eye. He could see the potential of youngsters that Everton were developing like Kevin Ratcliffe, Gary Stevens and Kevin Richardson. Howard brought in young players like Trevor, nineteen, and three 22-year-olds, Paul Bracewell, Kevin Sheedy and Neville. He was such a good judge. Pat van den Hauwe, twenty-three, and Adrian, twenty-one, too.

A lot of that craft's gone out of the game because it's all figures now. Data's good but, see, knowing a player and picking a player and using your eyes, that's frowned upon now. And you know why? Because there's not many stockmen left in the game of football. Guys like me, football guys who've been through a career and played with wonderful players and have been out on the grass – we have that feeling.

Like Howard Kendall, Sir Alex Ferguson had stockmanship. Claudio Ranieri is an incredible stockman. He's been on the grass. He's built a team. Pep Guardiola definitely. Pep knows a good player, how he passes a ball. Claudio and Pep can *hear* a good pass. I could tell how good Steven Gerrard would become when he was coming through as a young player because I could hear it. I saw Gerrard play at St James' Park. He hit a pass, and I could hear the pass, I could feel the connection. When you're with top players on the pitch, you can hear it and you can see it. Gerrard was just eighteen but I knew, just like I saw with Wayne Rooney. It's the connection, the sound, the way the ball behaves for them. I was behind Gerrard when he hit this pass and I just knew. When I got home, I told my missus, 'I've just seen a top player there. Steven Gerrard.'

Gerrard's pass, Alan Shearer and Wayne Rooney's strike – each time I heard the ping. I'd always listen to the grass. Sometimes as a coach I tell players, 'Stop speaking, don't talk, don't say a word.' No other coach would do this, because it sounds a bit mad. 'Listen to the grass.' They used to start laughing. 'I'm not telling you to smoke the grass, I'm telling you to listen to the grass. Listen to the crack of the ball when it's struck and how it travels across the grass. That's what a good pass sounds like.'

The grass talks to me in that respect. A bad pass bobbles and bounces like it's been delivered by a Dambuster. Some coaches will hear it if they're as observant as I am, many coaches won't, and people on a laptop definitely won't. They'll not have developed that stockmanship.

I can watch a player walking and say to myself, 'He's good.' Just by his gait. It's not swagger, it's fluidity of movement. They're light on their feet.

I, myself, never had what Albert had regarding the pigeons. But I believe with my experience gained from my playing career and more importantly on my coaching journey, my stockmanship in football is as good as anybody's. I've spent time on the grass with some of the best players in world. Samuel Eto'o, James Rodríguez, Lukaku, Shearer, Rooney. I have been amongst them my whole career and, dare I say it, on my best day I was one of them. In my opinion, I was one of the best headers of a ball there's ever been.

We've all got an opinion about players, and no doubt they're good opinions. As a coach I felt I had an advantage when selecting players because I've been around this top quality. If I ran a club, I'd have an ex-footballer in a leading role as head of recruitment. For me, that would be a must. Unfortunately, I don't feel that's the case.

31

BIG SAM

The best advice my dad gave me wasn't 'Throw the first punch,' it was 'Stick next to your boss, get right next to him and back him to the hilt. Be loyal.' In my coaching years, I swear that's what I've done. I've stood by my managers at Everton – Roberto Martínez, Ronald Koeman and Sam Allardyce, when he came in, to name but a few. Bill Kenwright, Denise Barrett-Baxendale, all the board, were always trying to get bits of information from me about the manager. I never played ball. I never sat with the directors and owners, never ate with them, never drank with them. I stuck with my manager.

I was sorry to see Ronald leave. The day after we lost 5–2 to Arsenal on 22 October 2017, Bill Kenwright and chief executive Rob Elstone spoke to Ronald after training at Finch Farm. Sacked. Unsworth stepped in as caretaker for seven games, five of them defeats.

I was overlooked again. But I expected it. That was the pecking order. Unsy had good relationships with Bill and other people behind the scenes like Denise, who went on to succeed Elstone as chief exec in 2018. They wanted Unsy to become the manager, not me. I got pushed to the side and they pushed forward David Unsworth. He was their man. I respected and expected that. In the end, Ronald got sacked because of results and because behind the scenes they were pushing for their candidate. Ronald got sacked far too early in my opinion. I'll spell that out again: Ronald Koeman got sacked so they could get David Unsworth in. Ronald had come seventh in the league in 2016–17, but the next season began poorly because we played five of the top six teams in the Premier League, and we were playing in Europe so it was tough. I think Everton couldn't wait because of politics behind the scenes. They wanted to give Unsworth another shot at it.

Unsy never did enough before Sam Allardyce came in on 28 November. Everton wanted Marco Silva but couldn't get him out of Watford so they turned to Sam. That evening I bumped into Sam heading to the lecture room for his first meeting with the players.

'Do you want me to come in this meeting with you, boss?'

'Yes, come in with me.'

Big Sam delivered a rallying cry to the players the night of the West Ham match. Unsworth took the game and we won 4–0. Rooney scored a hat-trick, including a goal from his own half. It was a fantastic result and Big Sam had made his mark. The players were all made up and Sam went on to rescue the season.

At that time, I helped a young Anthony Gordon, now at Newcastle, get a taste of the first team at Everton. He was only sixteen but I really rated him. Anthony was fancied in the academy but couldn't break into David Unsworth's 23s. Sam asked me to bring up a player from the 21s, and I pushed Gordon forward and he trained well. Sam then didn't come to Cyprus for Everton's dead rubber against Apollon Limassol on 7 December 2017, and left me and Craig Shakespeare in charge. I made sure Gordon got his debut in Limassol. I then gave Anthony his second game, against Leicester in the EFL Cup on 18 December 2019. I loved his appetite to improve. He wanted to learn and practise, practise, practise. He was addicted to my 30-ball drill. He was fit as a fiddle, took diet seriously but was still going to different boxing gyms and sparring. 'You have to stop,' I told Anthony. 'You can't go to them, you'll get hurt.' He battered me once in the Finch Farm gym, I had a pair of boxing gloves on, he didn't, and I didn't do that again! Anthony's a bright lad, knows what he wants, dedicated and lightning quick.

After Limassol, Everton continued on an unbeaten run. Sam got us organised. I loved Sam. He'd started in management in 1991, been through the process, been a coach and become a manager so he wouldn't take too many training sessions. He became that figurehead, like most of them did – Sir Alex Ferguson, Brian Clough, Martin O'Neill. Sam did the tactical stuff and he was good, really good, and he got good results. Sam liked me because I was honest, straight with him and I had a good eye for a player. Sam knew I was a stockman.

Me and Sam became close because I told him not to sign Cenk Tosun. Everton needed goals with Rom gone. When Sam joined it was clear he wanted Tosun. Me and Sammy Lee, who had come into the club with Sam Allardyce, got called into a recruitment meeting. Normally, Everton didn't want me in there because I tell it how I see it. I went into the meeting, with all of them like technical director Steve Walsh in there, and they were talking about Cenk Tosun of Besiktas, raving about him. 'Let's take him,' they all said.

'Duncan, have you got anything to say here?' Sam asked me.
'Boss, don't take him.'
'Why not?'
'He can't run, but, more importantly, he looks like an old man. How old is he?'
'Twenty-seven,' somebody replied. Everyone else was laughing and going, 'You can't say that, Dunc.'

'Well, I am saying it.'

My point was, Tosun didn't look like he was good enough for Everton. He didn't look vibrant. He didn't look like somebody you wanted to take.

'He doesn't look quick enough to me,' I said.

'We think he is,' one of the coaches said.

'Are you telling me this is going to be the second Turkish player in the history of the Premier League to do well here?' I said. 'I can only think of one other, Tugay of Blackburn. If you've done your homework and you like him then do what you want, but I'm telling you it's a no from me.'

And I left the room.

A lot of the scouts were shocked. They'd done all this work on Tosun, got all the stats. And I'd come in for thirty seconds and been critical.

Big Sam came out the room and said, 'Well, Dunc, who would you sign then?'

I said, 'Off the top of my head, boss, Salomón Rondón at West Brom. Sign Rondón. He can run, he's strong, he's younger. Sign him.'

Sam headed off to his car. On the way home, I rang him.

'Look, boss, I'm going to have one last go at it. Sack Tosun off and sign Rondón.'

'Duncan, I've signed Tosun,' he said. For £27 million.

'All right, boss, fine. Say no more.'

We played West Brom at Goodison on 20 January 2018, and James McCarthy unfortunately broke his leg in a tackle on Rondón. Rondon was upset, but refocused on the game, and played well. We came in after the game, all of us sitting down, and Big Sam said, 'Dunc told me not to sign Tosun. He told me to sign Rondón and I never listened, but I'll listen from now on.'

Rondón was good. He'd have done us a right turn. Sam

gained respect for me then. He came to me personally after three days and said, 'You were right about Cenk Tosun, I should never have signed him.' Sam could tell from training. Tosun had been in Turkey and it was difficult for a manager to assess him properly.

There was another recruitment meeting at Everton that stands out. I was in the coaches' office, sitting at my desk on my own. They wanted to replace Leighton Baines, who was thirty-three and had injured his calf at St Mary's in November 2017. Cuco Martina filled in but he was a right-back. We needed a left-back. I'd heard all the names, like Juan Bernat of Bayern Munich.

Big Sam came in and said, 'What are you doing?'

'Sitting here.'

'Get in here.'

I went in, Sam sat in the seat, and the recruitment people put on footage of seven left-backs. They looked at the first one, and then it went quiet. I've come into the meeting cold.

'Dunc, what do you think?' Big Sam said.

'No, not for me. Next one.'

'Why not?'

'He's not quick enough.'

'You can't say that,' one of the scouts said. 'You've only seen a clip.'

'He's not quick enough, and I am saying it. If you don't want me to speak, stop asking me.'

One of the seven was the Ghanaian Kwadwo Asamoah, whose contract at Juventus was expiring that summer.

'He's a midfield player!' I said.

'Yes, but he's converted from midfield to left-back.'

'He's a midfield player.'

On it went, arguing about the players. One of them wanted £85,000 a week.

'No to the seven of them,' I said when it was all over.

Big Sam rolled back in his seat. 'Yeah, I agree with Duncan, let's go.'

Sam had learned, but the rest of the recruitment office were all sitting there open-mouthed. Seven left-backs, and I'd killed every one of them in twenty minutes. The scouts had done months and months of work on them. They probably thought right away, 'Dunc's done us again in the neck.' Seven left-backs, but not one of them had ever played football at top level, except for Asamoah at Juventus. Anyway, Leighton Baines played another two years on £65,000 a week. They wanted a left-back at £85,000 who was nowhere near the level of Baines. So, why are we thinking about signing him?

They stopped pulling me into recruitment meetings. I don't blame them! They were only trying to do their jobs. I'd notice details from the clips like a player's shirt hanging out to cover his arse because he was a bit overweight. Some players with big arses are good players, like John McGinn at Aston Villa, even world class, like Kenny Dalglish. They always had their shirts tucked in, and looked great.

Our results picked up under Sam but Everton fans weren't having him. They didn't like the style of football, which was totally unfair on Sam. We beat Huddersfield Town 2–0 at the John Smith's Stadium on 28 April 2018, and Everton fans held up an abusive banner along the lines of 'get out of our club' and chanted against Sam. I was going crazy at them on the touchline. It was hurtful to hear the animosity towards Sam – 'WE WON!' My mates were behind the goal arguing with some of those fans having a go at me.

As my dad had demanded, I stood by my manager. I stood next to Sam when he was getting destroyed. I probably fractured my relationship with some Everton fans because I stayed next to my boss when they were booing him and didn't want him. Sam got Everton to eighth but the fans never took to him. He didn't play 'sexy football' according to the press and they fuelled the fire. Big Sam unfortunately got the bullet.

32

MARCO

Marco Silva was at Finch Farm within a fortnight of Sam going. Marco was a very dedicated man and a good coach. His sessions were really long and intense. We were conceding from set plays all the time so we'd head out at Finch Farm and do two hours of set-piece work. We still kept conceding. I watched the training, and was itching to intervene. For me, it was about the mindset at set-pieces. It was about being aggressive and attacking the ball, making sure we got the first contact. Marco was very meticulous and rightly so. We went over things time after time; corners, free-kicks, even throw-ins, over and over. That was Marco.

I was never involved under Marco. He inherited me. He had his own people around him: João Pedro, Hugo Oliveira, Antonis Lemonakis and Pedro Conceição. I did next to nothing under Marco. I ran offside lines, set up pitches, moved the goals, took some shooting work with the strikers. I wasn't involved in any tactical work, and I wouldn't have expected to be.

There was a wee line in my office window when I closed it, and when the players walked past I could hardly see the tops of their heads. That used to make me laugh. 'He's got no chance,' I'd mutter as another short player went past. Marco Silva brought in the Brazilian Bernard – 5ft 4in and weighed just over 9 stone. Big money, never going to do it. Eight goals in eighty-four games. He was a lovely footballer but not for the Premier League. You can get away with one small player but not a gang of them. Everton had some small players and a big wage bill.

When Marco smelt that I knew a player, he was on to me during recruitment meetings. Marcel Brands was now the director of football and Everton were interested in Moise Kean from Juventus. I made it quite clear what I thought of the 5ft 11in Italian: I just never rated him as an Everton player. They never asked me about Moise Kean. That was strange as I was a striker. Maybe they didn't ask me because I'd been killing players in recruitment meetings. I saw clips of him playing and just didn't fancy him for Everton. Other people in the building thought he was the best young striker in Europe. On 4 August 2019, Everton signed Kean for £30 million. I watched him closely in training, which confirmed my original view. I didn't think Kean was good enough for Everton. He had potential but he was just not ready to lead the line for Everton.

Dan Purdy asked me about Kean after training. Purdy was the lad who was the performance analyst intern made manager of scouting and operations by Brands. Purdy asked me, 'How did he do, Dunc?'

'Not very well.'

'What do you mean?'

'Not for me in my opinion.'

I got on well with Kean. I put time into him.

'Moise, what about finishing?'

I'd take him somewhere quiet to help him, like I did with Richarlison, James Rodríguez, Romelu Lukaku, Dominic Calvert-Lewin and Gylfi Sigurdsson.

Moise probably had a lot of good things about him, and he'd won Serie A twice with Juventus and was getting touted all around, but he wasn't for me, and I said that. I was proved right because he wasn't good enough for Everton. Recruitment for Everton has not been right for a very long time. It was around that time that we let Antonee Robinson go. 'Jedi' was a bit behind the rest in the academy technically but he had that pace that hurts you. What 'Jedi' had was physicality, he could run, he was aggressive, strong in the one v. one duels. He wasn't the best crosser or passer and Marco Silva sold him for £2 million. He eventually did really well under Marco at Fulham.

Marco Silva! What is it with these managers and restaurant bills? Marco kindly asked me to join his staff for some food. I was to organise the restaurant. So I book the Greek restaurant, Eureka, in Wavertree. Lovely food, the lad put a great spread on. The waitress had come in to help out on her night off. The bill was not dear, around 250 quid. I had 40 quid in my pocket, not thinking for one minute I would have to pay. This was the first time I had seen this: everybody pulled out a credit card and all started to pay individually. I never owned a credit card. I threw in my 40 quid on the table. Marco said, 'You've paid too much.' And gave me a fiver back. 'Jesus, fuck me!' I thought. The girl had come in on her night off probably thinking she'd get a good drink out of it. I was embarrassed. I sent my mate up the next day with 100 quid for her. After the meal I said to Marco, 'I'll walk you to your car. It can be a bit lively round here.' So I did around 9.30 p.m. We heard the next day on the news there was a shooting in Wavertree, around 10 p.m. 100 yards from the restaurant. Lucky escape.

Marco could be a negative guy. He's intense. I felt he was too negative towards Dominic Calvert-Lewin. Dom was a young player and Marco drained his confidence. He dropped him against West Ham on 19 October 2019, and even brought Moise Kean on ahead of him. Marco gave Dom some encouragement but not enough. Dom will tell you that. Marco chipped away at him and eroded his confidence. There was nothing positive. If somebody continues to say negative things to you, guess what? It eats away at your confidence.

Marco was a great young coach but he couldn't see some things. We played Liverpool on 4 December at Anfield with Gylfi Sigurdsson, a central midfielder, overlapping on the left-hand side against the best counter-attacking team in the world. I was sitting there in the first half thinking, 'Counter-attack, goal; counter-attack, goal; counter-attack, goal; counter-attack, goal.' Marco played five at the back and Liverpool ripped us apart. Dom was isolated on his own up front, Richarlison was wide. I saw the players arguing with each other. We lost 5–2, our biggest derby defeat. It was sad, and a total shambles.

The next day we were all in at Finch Farm. Farhad was there, the chairman was there, Denise the CEO was there, Marcel Brands was there. All the board. They spoke to all the players in the lecture room. Me, Marco and all his staff were in our offices, waiting to see what the outcome would be and whether we'd be working for the next game, against Chelsea. We all thought, 'we're all losing our jobs here'. Me included. It's not a nice place to be when you are sitting there waiting to lose your job. Unfortunately, Marco and his staff lost their jobs. I never got sacked, which I was grateful for. But I could have been. I was walking up the corridor going for a coffee, and I bumped into Farhad. 'Hiya Dunc, how are you doing?'

'Not very good, boss, to be honest.'

'Why not?'

'I'm worried about losing my job.'

'You're not losing your job tonight.'

'Thanks very much.' I was made up, a big relief.

'If theoretically you were in charge against Chelsea, Duncan, how would you play?'

I had only a split second to think. 'I'd play Dominic and Richarlison up front, go back to 4–4–2, be hard to beat, be compact.'

So that was my interview for the job, in a corridor. I think Farhad got taken aback with what I said. Right away he said, 'Duncan, come into the boardroom and tell the rest of the board members what you have just told to me.' Marcel, Denise and the chairman all looked at me as I came in.

'I think I have found our new manager,' Farhad said. I will never forget their faces. They were in shock. 'Duncan, just repeat what you said to me in the corridor,' Farhad continued.

'Look, boss, there's a tactics board, let me show you on there.' So I put up my 4–4–2 set-up, how we were going to be off the ball, how we were going to press, how we were going to play on the ball and who I was going to play. The board were quiet, never said a word. They had been in that office discussing every option they had. It was running late on that night and I'm pretty sure they weren't discussing me.

Farhad looked incredibly impressed with my presentation. When I finished, Farhad said, 'Right, Duncan, can you just give us a minute.' I went back to my desk, and a few minutes later, Bill Kenwright came in.

'Duncan, I've got you the job, you'll be the manager against Chelsea on Saturday.' That was Bill for you! Bill never got me the job. It was Farhad who gave me that job.

The board basically put me in temporary charge while they looked for Marco's successor. I knew I still didn't have a chance of being put in permanent charge. But I was determined to show what I could do.

33

CARETAKING AND TAKING CARE

I had forty-eight hours to prepare the lads before Chelsea on 7 December 2019. Nobody gave us a chance. Everybody thought Everton were stuck in a spiral towards relegation. Attack. I couldn't risk losing so I went for it, 4–4–2 with Dom and Richy up front. Marco and his staff never saw it. They just played one up. To me, it was obvious. Pair them, get them to bring the best out of each other, cause the other team problems.

I was more the players' helpful friend, an older brother guiding them. I did the opposite to what Marco did to Dom. I said positive things. Before the game, I told Dom, 'You're my man, you're my main man. You're my number nine, you're the centre-forward, you're going to lead the line and you're going to batter Chelsea. You get up there and show people what you're all about, son. Continue shooting, lad. The fans love you, because you're in the tradition of an Everton number nine. Be physical in the box, score headers.' I felt I was almost talking about myself.

Dom needed that. He hadn't scored since October so he needed that confidence. Doesn't everybody like a pat on the back? Everybody needs that, and in this day and age, more and more people need it. All the best managers I've worked under – Walter Smith, Howard Kendall, Carlo Ancelotti – they were all positive. None of them were big shouters. Well, guess what? Their players tried harder for them.

Putting Richarlison in with Dom was a bit of a gamble. It left us a bit light in midfield but I wanted to go for the jugular. Me and Richy had a love/hate relationship and to this day I don't know if he hated me or loved me. I introduced a scoring system at Finch Farm. I put a table on the wall for points from exercises like 'Last Man Standing', which is not what you might think it is. It's not fighting! Last Man Standing was a shooting exercise for everyone in pairs. I'd put the players in pairs. I'd smash the ball to one, shout 'Set!', he'd touch it to his partner, I'd shout 'Steak and chips!' and he'd shoot. It was called Last Man Standing because if one pair scored, the pair behind had to score. If they didn't, they had to walk in. It was fun but competitive as they played for points, which went up on the board for all to see.

I had another exercise called '30-ball Finish' for the strikers. I'd get thirty balls – ten to one side of the 18-yard box, ten to the other and ten in the middle. There was plenty of 'Steak and chips'. I'd get attackers like Gylfi, Dom, Richy and, earlier, Lukaku. Gylfi was best at 'Steak and chips'. He got twenty-four out of thirty once. If Richy scored twenty goals out of thirty, I'd write 66 per cent on the board. The players were competitive, but Richy was the worst. He had to be top. If we did 30-ball Finish, I'd give them a point to add to their total on Last Man Standing. It would go up on the table.

Richy would come in, shouting 'Point! Punto!'

'No, you never got a point for that.'

He'd go crazy. 'I did get a point!'

'You never.' I'd intentionally not put one up to blow his head off.

Richy thought I disliked him but I really liked him. He used to get a delegation to come and see me to complain. Later on, Richy got the wee boy from Napoli, Allan, a good player who came in under Carlo, to come and see me.

CARETAKING AND TAKING CARE

'Duncan?'

'What is it, son?'

'Richy says you don't like him and you're favouring all the English boys.'

'I am favouring all the English boys,' I replied. 'Dominic, Tom, Mason are my favourites.' Richy would go nuts but I was only winding him up.

I'd wind up Dominic Calvert-Lewin, Tom Davies and Mason Holgate too, giving others extra points. I'd wind them all up.

I loved mixing the training up. Another variation of Last Man Standing I introduced was if you scored, you picked which pair were eliminated. Say one pair scored, they could go, 'Right, Richy, in.' And Richarlison would have to walk in with his partner and there'd be murder! I had to stop it in the end because players were falling out.

I introduced all of these games and they loved them. It's competition, see. Top players love seeing their name up in lights, king of the hill. Adding scoring systems into training definitely gives an extra motivation. The players loved it. I also felt good, my innovations were working.

I felt I had a chance against Chelsea. I loved Richy's competitive nature and was sure he'd work well with Dom. They'd go as well together as 'steak and chips'!

Speaking to the press at Finch Farm the day before the game I got very emotional. I'd seen my kids earlier. Cameron, Ross and Evie were season-ticket holders in Gwladys Street and I knew how much this meant to them. Everton were fighting for their lives. We needed the points. One of the reporters asked whether the players were hurting as much as me. 'Is that possible?' I replied. 'We all hope it is. That is the kind of message we gave the players this morning. We have to bleed for this club. We have to bleed on that pitch.' Just as I'd done as a player.

I couldn't sleep that night. I actually had a bath at 2 a.m., I was so nervous. But having John Ebbrell, Franny Jeffers and Alan Kelly as assistants was good. I trusted them. Sound football men who loved Everton. Before the match, Lily, Howard Kendall's widow, gave me Howard's watch. It was broken, but it was to be my lucky charm. I was booted and suited, smartly dressed for the big occasion.

There was big controversy over my suit. I was trying to pick my tactics on the Friday night but all I was getting from the directors was I was not to wear my suit. As I got off the bus, surrounded by screaming fans, I got another message that I was not to wear it. When I went into the boardroom, they told me not to wear the suit and told me categorically that I was caretaker for only one game. I was worried sick as I had only these 90 minutes. They must have another manager lined up. Maybe my old sparring partner David Moyes? My head was swimming. That bloody suit, I was determined to wear it. I knew if we got beaten, I was out the back door and how many people would have stood up for me? I would have been finished. I was determined to do it my way. So I got the suit on, Howard's watch on my right wrist, blue sweatband on my left. The sweatband originally came from a sick kid who gave it to me when I visited Alder Hey. It deteriorated over the season, so I'd get a new one each year and at the end of the season, I'd be walking round the pitch at Goodison and give it to a disabled kid. It was superstition and identity. The players went out and 'Z-Cars' blasted out as I waited at the bottom of the steps for my call to go. I got the tap on the back and I bounded up the steps into the roar of the crowd.

I was so emotional at the reception the Everton fans gave me that I struggled at first to concentrate on the game. This was everything I had dreamed of, managing the club I loved and doing it my way.

I've always tried to manage with my head, staying focused, but my heart was racing overtime with pride. I couldn't control myself

CARETAKING AND TAKING CARE

when we scored, first Richy with a header I'd have been proud to call my own, then Dom twice. For his second, which made it 3–1, I went wild on the touchline, sprinting down and hugging a ballboy who jumped into my arms and then hugging another ballboy on the way back to the dugout. Dom ran over and I embraced him. This was what Everton's about: togetherness, local people, kids, players, manager, ballboys, all in it together.

We were fired up. The players – my players – made thirty-seven tackles, the most Everton had managed for a decade. They played with passion, they played for the famous blue shirt, and that meant the world to me and the Everton fans. I watched the game back later and heard the commentator greet the final whistle with these words: 'Duncan Ferguson has inspired and guided Everton to victory this afternoon. They've shown exactly what Duncan Ferguson wanted – desire, passion, commitment, the Ferguson DNA.'

I shook hands with Frank Lampard, and got so carried away I kissed him. I kissed the opposition manager! I realised what I'd done afterwards and was embarrassed. I really respect Frank. I rang up John Terry. 'Look, John, you are going to have tell Frank I'm really sorry. I was kissing and hugging everybody!' But to kiss the opposition manager was a bit too far. I'm not sure Frank appreciated it. John laughed. 'Don't worry! I'll tell Frank.'

Back on the pitch, I walked across to shake hands with the referee Craig Pawson. As I crossed the pitch, I couldn't focus. All I could hear was 'Duncan, Duncan Ferguson!' all around Goodison. Music to my ears! I soaked it all up. I really appreciated the fans' reaction. Some of the players came into vision, and I hugged them and congratulated them all on putting such a superb shift in. My heart was still racing, and it was because of the performance, the result, and because of the love I felt for Everton fans and the love I knew they felt for me. I punched the air in front of the Everton fans in the Bullens Road and Gwladys Street. It was electric. It was a different emotion. I've never experienced that at Goodison Park before. The memory of their overjoyed faces and their songs will stay with me to my dying day. All I wanted was to make them happy, to make them proud of their team again, to make them smile knowing that their team represented them – honest, hard workers.

Afterwards I had a word with Dom. What a shift he'd put in. He'd played a part in Richy's goal, he'd fought for the ball for his two goals.

'Well done, fantastic, Dom, you've been brilliant for me today, mate, your work ethic is amazing, I'm so proud of you. You were a proper Everton number nine today and they love you for it, son.'

Dom himself spoke publicly about wanting to make me proud, repaying me. I loved hearing that. Whenever I see Dominic, he tells me he loves me. He told Cameron, 'I love your dad, he helped me so much.'

In the Goodison boardroom afterwards, everybody was delighted. Marcel Brands, Everton's director of football, wasn't over the moon. I think actually he was over the horizon – he'd disappeared early. I couldn't see him. He must have been flaming. He didn't want me in the caretaker role. Fair play to Farhad Moshiri. He went up to Janine and said, 'Your husband's been neglected at this club, he's been neglected and ignored.' People at the club had been telling Farhad that I wasn't a coach, that I was just a cheerleader, I was just Duncan Ferguson. They didn't tell anybody I was coaching and I was good at it. Farhad had this wrong image of me and, obviously, he then saw what happened against Chelsea, and everybody celebrating. Some of the Everton fans had doubted me. I showed everyone what I was all about as a coach.

I knew then this was my time to push my claim, to get a chance for a bit longer or an increase in my salary. That one game became a string of games because whoever Everton had lined up as manager suddenly wasn't too keen on coming. He'd want to come in on a poor performance or result so he could get a lift. It wasn't Carlo Ancelotti then. He didn't leave Napoli until 11 December, four days after our win over Chelsea.

On 15 December we went to Old Trafford with a lot of players out. We had Covid but didn't really know about it. I just thought it was flu going through the squad. Gylfi and Morgan Schneiderlin were out, Djibril Sidibe and Theo Walcott, too, so I took a look at Mason Holgate in central midfield in training. He hadn't played there in his life. Mason knew I was short. 'I'll play anywhere for you,' Mason said. Mason and Tom Davies were going to be my two no. 6s and neither of them were. It was a massive gamble, a big ask for them but my God did they deliver. They covered every blade of grass. Everybody remembers the game for another decision I made, my bravest decision as a manager. No, not that I never wore a jacket in the freezing cold wet weather. More than that. We were winning 1–0 when I took Bernard off after seventy minutes and put Moise Kean on. 'Centre-forward,' I told him. 'Richy going left.' It was simple. But Kean ran out to the left, and right away my back was up. I was thinking, 'I just told him to go centre-forward.' Kean didn't have a clue. The atmosphere, the noise, my language, the pissing rain, who knows? Maybe it was me. Scottish.

I was standing there thinking, 'This is not working.' United equalised within seven minutes. I thought to myself that I could keep running with it and we'd get beat, it wouldn't matter and nobody would say a word. I knew full well if I took Kean off and United scored again, which looked likely, I was finished.

Totally finished. The press would slaughter me. 'Out of his depth.' 'Terrible decision. Sub on, sub off, got beat. Shambles.' I knew that Marcel Brands would destroy me for doing it and being naive.

This was the moment I actually realised what type of fella I really was. I probably knew it anyway, but this was a reminder. I asked myself, 'What does Howard Kendall say to you? What does Walter Smith say to you? Be yourself.' OK. 'I'm in.'

My heart was pounding out of my shirt. I turned to John Ebbrell and said, 'Come here, get him off.'

'Who?' Ebbrell asked.

'You know who.'

'Duncan, you know the consequences of us doing this?'

'I do. Get him off.'

They put the number up – 27. I was subbing a sub after nineteen minutes. It was humiliating for the lad. Kean off, Oumar Niasse on.

'You know this is serious, Dunc?' Ebbrell said.

We got the result, 1–1. Big point. I can't put all the blame just down to Moise Kean. It must have been tough for him. I did feel for the lad. I still got stick for it and people tried to spin it round, saying I'd humiliated a young player, but a manager can't be sensitive to individual feelings when the game, possibly the season, is on the line. I know Kean looked devastated as he walked past me when he came off, and in hindsight I should have been more caring to Moise Kean. I was too focused on the game. It was a bad look that I blanked him on the way off. I should have shaken his hand. But in my mind I was right to sub him. Kean had nine touches in nineteen minutes. Niasse had four in two. Kean lost the ball six times and didn't make a tackle. Niasse never lost the ball and made two tackles. Do the maths. They added up to the right decision.

In my Sky interview afterwards, I explained to their reporter Geoff Shreeves why I'd subbed a sub. 'I was just doing it for fresh

CARETAKING AND TAKING CARE

legs,' I told Geoff. 'Unfortunately he was the one I decided to bring off. I see why he's upset, but it's about the team. I just needed to make a substitution to kill a bit of time. I've got so many strikers on the bench, I just decided to make that change. It was nothing personal to Moise Kean really.'

I took Kean off because he was struggling to get to the pace of the game and was out of position quite a bit. Of course, it's not an easy task to come on as a sub and hit the ground running. He was costing me, but I couldn't say that. That really would humiliate the lad. Kean was out of position. I dragged him off and I was right. Geoff led me to the Everton fans in the corner, and they were singing my name. I felt brilliant. A couple had a banner of me with the blue nose on lifting the FA Cup in 1995 with the words 'Spirit of the Blues'. And that's what I'm about, doing everything for the good of Everton Football Club.

I came back in the dressing room. I'd been on the pitch giving it big licks to the fans. I was pumped up, made up with a point at Old Trafford – another battling performance, and a decision that took real balls paying off. I found twenty players there, sitting quietly, all disappointed as we'd conceded in the last ten minutes. 'It's a great point,' I told them. They wanted so much more. One player was missing. Moise was upset and had gone in the shower. The kid's head had gone and I understood why.

'Duncan, go in and speak to him,' Brands said.

'No. He should be sitting here with the boys. You go in and speak to him. You signed him.' And I walked away. I was in a strong position because I'd got the result.

Of course, I talked to Moise later. I care for my players. He was really upset, and I understood. I worked with him after it. I tried to help the kid. I cared for him as a human being. He was a good young player. He just wasn't ready for Everton.

I look back on that Old Trafford game and the Moise decision with pride at my guts. My whole career was on the line. Brands would have come down from the stand and I'd never have taken another game. I'd have been out the club. All those years doing all my coaching badges, all that time developing training sessions and developing myself as a coach would have gone up in smoke if United had scored a second that day. It would have killed me. It worked out well for me, but I still had an enemy, didn't I? I had an enemy in Marcel Brands.

I'd subbed a £30 million star.

'Maybe you can go and learn about substitutions,' suggested chief exec Denise Barrett-Baxendale. What?! Who's the football person in this exchange? That's what Everton was like. People behind the scenes, spinning their web and trying to cover themselves. She made sure she moved in the right direction. When I first met her she was running Everton in the Community, and very good at it she was. She had a lot of ambition but that didn't give her the right to tell me about substitutions. Stick to the CEO stuff. It's a big step from running a community department to running a major football club. Denise is very talented at what she did and she did politics well. But I was fuming to be given a lecture by her on football.

As I headed home, I knew some people were criticising me for what I'd done to Moise. Big Sam said I should have hugged or consoled him as he came off. It is embarrassing for a professional footballer, I understand that. But I could see that United were going to score if I didn't change it. I had to be decisive. I will live and die by what I do and not be scared to make a decision. I have that character in me to make decisions.

Three days later Everton were getting beat 2–0 at half-time by Leicester City in the quarter-final of League Cup. So I put Kean on for Bernard, and this time he played well, he was running around like a good 'un for me. I will never forget the atmosphere in that second half. Davies pulled one back then Leighton Baines hit one of the best goals I'd seen at Goodison, left-footed, bang in the corner. 2–2. Took us to penalties. I thought our name was on the cup, especially when Jordan Pickford saved James Maddison's penalty. Brilliant, Jordan, here we go. I got on well with Jordan, typical goalkeeper, a wee bit mad. Jordan's not a big guy. He's had to be fantastic at other aspects of his game, his kicking and reaction saves, and he showed his quality against Maddison. Our first two takers were Cenk Tosun, who took pens for Turkey, and Leighton, who took them for Everton. They rarely missed. They did here. Both of them. I was devastated. We went out, 4–2 on pens.

We then drew 0–0 with Arsenal in the league, and this time I subbed a sub, Cenk Tosun, for Kean. Tosun wasn't happy but it was a different situation to the Kean one at Old Trafford. Tosun had played most of the game and was tiring. So that was five points from my three league games in charge after Everton had lost three on the spin under Marco.

After the Arsenal game I was absolutely delighted. I went into the dressing room and poured my heart out to the players. 'I'm made up for you. You've done me proud. You've done the club proud.' I knew that was me done as caretaker as Carlo Ancelotti had joined. He was standing there with Brands, listening. He'd only just left Napoli and it was a real coup by Everton to get him.

Séamus Coleman stood up, very emotional, his voice breaking. Séamus is a lovely guy and a great servant to the club so everyone listened. 'Dunc, you got us going again. You gave us our identity back. You've given us something to build on. It's fantastic. Thank you.'

I thanked Séamus and the players and then turned to Carlo.

'Well, we've got the best manager in the world now. I love these players, Carlo. I love how they fought for me in these four games. Over to you, Carlo, son – good luck, my friend!'

I was buzzing, right? I was undefeated. Follow that, Carlo!

Carlo was laughing. He must have thought, 'Jesus, they don't need me.' But we did, Carlo, we did. My Don.

34

CARLO FANTASTICO

Carlo Ancelotti didn't waste any time as Everton manager. He congratulated my players (now his players) for a 'great, fantastic result, great game' and headed off to his new office. I followed.

'Duncan, great work,' Carlo said.

'You're the don, lad! Don Carlo. If you want me working with you, brilliant. If you don't, the fans will destroy you!' And I started laughing. 'Good luck with the fans!'

'Duncan, my friend. You're with me, no problem.'

We went into the manager's office with Marcel Brands. Carlo was straight down to work.

'Right, who are the good players, Duncan?'

'At the moment, the three best players are Richarlison, Dominic Calvert-Lewin and Lucas Digne.' Obviously Séamus and Leighton are club legends. 'They're all good players,' I said to Carlo. 'They've been great for me.'

'The club have signed some poor players, in my opinion,' I added.

'Come on, Duncan, you can't say that,' Brands said.

Carlo, to this day, says to me, 'Dominic Calvert-Lewin, Richarlison, Lucas Digne – Everton's three best players.'

Then Carlo asked, 'Moise Kean, Duncan?'

'Look, Moise has not done it for the club and I don't think he will do. But you're the man.'

'I tried to sign him at Napoli!'

'Well, luckily for you, you didn't. But you're the expert. You obviously see something in Moise Kean that I don't.' Then I thought I'd better be diplomatic for once. 'To be fair, you're Italian, he's Italian. I'm sure with your coaching you'll get the best out of him.'

Brands was jumping up and down. 'Come on, you can't say that about Moise Kean. He's only young, Duncan.'

'I know he's young, but Don Carlo asked me and I'm telling him he's not for me, that's it. It's my opinion and hopefully I'm wrong. Hopefully he will do it for Everton for years to come.'

Four weeks later, Carlo said to me, 'Moise Kean, no, he has to go.' Carlo felt Moise was not the right fit for Everton. Maybe his game suits the Continent more than the Premier League.

When Carlo came in to the club, Brands pulled me into his office. 'Right, Duncan,' he said, 'it's a new start, there are four things you've got to do. First, you're not to go on the touchline. You sit down in your seat, don't move.

'Second, I don't want you clapping the fans so don't you go to the fans. It's not your job to go to the fans and clap. You don't do that, you stay where you are.'

Brands hadn't finished. He had two more points.

'Stop talking down about the players we sign, stop telling people we're not very good – that's just your opinion. We are good. I want you to tell Carlo that we've signed a lot of good players. Don't be negative.'

I'd just rescued Everton, and I'd got five points, but I let Brands talk on. His last point I found hilarious.

'By the way, since I'm at it, go and clear your desk up. Your desk's a mess.'

CARLO FANTASTICO

I managed not to laugh out loud. It was like being back at school and getting bollocked by the supply teacher! Brands did have a point, I suppose. I had paper, diagrams, pens all over the place. I'm a messy guy that way. So that was the four things I had to do. But one of them I pushed back on.

'Right, you've had your say, now I'm going to tell you straight so you know: if anyone asks me for an opinion on a player, I'll tell them straight, end of.' I was not covering Brands' back if the players were not up to it. He was getting £1 million a year for whatever he was doing. And then having a go at the state of my desk. Afterwards, I looked on the internet and found a picture of Albert Einstein's desk. He was a brainbox and his desk was absolute chaos. I was desperate to send Brands a picture of it but I never did. Brands just wanted to clip my wings. I'd done so well and I felt he'd never wanted me. He tried to bring me down to earth after the Arsenal game.

The main thing about Brands was he was sick how well I'd done as caretaker. There was always a tension between us. Around this time Everton released my son Cameron, a striker in the academy, which was fine, but they should have had the courtesy or respect to alert me. They could have said, 'Look, Duncan, what do you think about your lad?' But no. We went into the meeting and Marcel said to me, 'I'm releasing the lad.'

'Without a discussion?' I replied.

My three games in the league at the end of 2019 turned Everton's season around. I changed the formation to 4–4–2 and Carlo kept that going. 4–4–2 isn't sexy or sophisticated but that was the system that brought the best out of the players. That was good tactics, not me being old school.

Carlo saw the way I spoke in the dressing room after the Arsenal game and then saw the way I could coach. Carlo and his son Davide clapped me off the training ground after watching me coach one day. Carlo then came in with his electric fag and said, 'I like your tactics, I like your set-up, and we're just going to continue that. And, Duncan, do you mind taking the training? Do you mind talking at half-time? Do you mind taking the tactics?' He was half joking. All this after Marcel Brands had clipped my wings!

'Yes, I do mind! I'm not getting paid £10 million a year! I'm not getting paid for that. You're going to have to do it!'

Anyway, Carlo came in and kept the same formation. I was to do all the training.

'Duncan, I see you as a manager now. Stand next to me and we'll let the young ones take training.'

'What are *you* doing?' I'd say to him. 'You have to do something!'

'Ah, Duncan,' Carlo laughed.

I stood next to Carlo during games.

On 8 March 2020 we were on the side of the Stamford Bridge pitch getting tonked 4–0 by Chelsea. 'Duncan,' he said to me, 'what are we doing? What do you think?'

'I haven't got a clue what to think, boss. We're getting stuffed, I just hope the game finishes soon. And I am getting hungry.'

'So am I.'

People thought we were talking tactics but we were thinking, 'Let's hope this whistle blows very quickly.' Carlo looked at me with a wry smile.

Sometimes Carlo stood up and said, 'What are we having tonight? Pasta? Meat?' Carlo always knew what to say at the right time. He wasn't worrying too much about formations in those moments.

It was an education being close to Carlo. He's what you see on the touchline – calm, very rarely shouts. Tactically he's very good and gets his point across. Sometimes he'd raise his voice but never really that much. He was not cut from the Jim McLean cloth. Carlo had this quiet authority and if he said something, you listened. He had the players' instant and deep respect. Carlo won the European Cup twice as a player with AC Milan so that gives him that extra credibility with players. And with what he's done as a manager – in 2024 he won his fifth Champions League – that guarantees players' respect right away. He was always good with people and a nice man. Carlo never, ever gave the impression that he was too big for Everton. I mean, obviously he'd mention the drop in the standard of players as we were talking to each other. 'Jesus Christ, Duncan, why are they not passing to the player?' Obviously, the level of player at Everton was not the level Carlo was used to working with at Milan, Real Madrid and Bayern Munich. He couldn't understand why they were giving the ball away so much. 'Jesus Christ, these players,' he'd say to me. To be fair, Carlo got a tune out of them because he was such an experienced and inspiring coach. They did well enough.

Being around Carlo was fun as well as an education. I used to sit next to him on the bus. On one trip I stopped him getting stung by one of those Indian scams. He was on the phone going, 'How much? £2,000? . . . I owe you £5,000?' The next minute it was £500,000. 'I'm Carlo Ancelotti and you need my account details?'

'Give me that phone,' I told Carlo. 'Hey, you, get off the phone, you dirty robbing bastard. Fuck off.'

How dare they try to scam my manager on the team bus.

I also gave Carlo some advice when he was being chased by the taxman in Spain in 2020. The authorities there claimed Carlo owed them €1 million relating to image rights revenues when he was at Real Madrid in 2014–15. Carlo mentioned the situation to me. He told me he was absolutely innocent and that it was daylight robbery.

'Don't talk to me about tax, Carlo, they crucified me. They crucify everybody in this country.'

'They say I owe a million euros.'

'What about it? Have you got it?'

'Yes.'

'Well, pay the taxman his million euros and walk away. It's going to cost you with the solicitors in the end anyway.'

'No, I'm going to fight it,' Carlo insisted. And he carried on fighting it. The last I heard about it was in March 2024 when Carlo was on the news saying he was calm about the whole tax thing. Good luck to him.

I really liked Carlo. We used to go for dinner together . . . which reminds me, I'm still to see him with any money! I suppose when you get to Carlo's level it's a bit like being a king. And Carlo is the king. You don't see them with any money, do you? Carlo was living down in Crosby, and when his house got broken into, I said, 'They robbed the safe, but there was nothing in it!' I did feel for Carlo, though – not a pleasant experience. He needed me waiting for them in the front room.

I took Carlo, Davide, his son-in-law and daughter out to a restaurant in Liverpool and gave them a good night.

'We're going to a wee jazz bar round the corner called the Puffin Rooms,' I said afterwards.

'No, Duncan, I have to be rested.'

'No, come on.'

I'd never been to the Puffin Rooms before but I made sure an area was boxed off for Carlo. It was his first night out in Liverpool for ages so I brought security with me. The boxer Tony Bellew got me a boy. So we went to L'aperitivo and it was fantastic. I bought him a whisky and couldn't get Carlo out of the place. Two boys came on and started singing 'Nessun Dorma' and Carlo was made up. He's a good singer, Carlo, and great company. He liked a glass of wine or a beer on a Friday night.

'Is it all right if I have a small beer, Duncan?'

'Yes, of course it is, Carlo.'

If we were in a restaurant in Liverpool, he'd sometimes go, 'Can I light my cigarette, Dunc?'

'Yes, light your wee electric one.'

He's very humble, Carlo. And a world-class manager, who for that 2019–20 campaign calmed everything down and sorted the team out. Everton finished twelfth and Carlo got a £2 million bonus for keeping the club up. I don't think Everton were keen on paying him, though. He had to go through a bit of litigation to get his money. Anyway, I'd been the one who got Everton out of the relegation mire. We were in the bottom three when Marco Silva left and fifteenth when I handed over to Carlo, four points above trouble.

'You took my bonus!' I told him, laughing. He saw the funny side.

He was very close to me, Carlo. We just clicked. He knew how loyal I was and how straight I was. Carlo did a lot for me. He recommended me for the Blackburn job in 2022.

At the end of the season, he said to me, 'Where are you going on holiday?'

'I've been invited on my mate George's boat in Croatia,' I told him.

'I'll come. I'll get a boat.'

So I was in Croatia on my mate's boat, we were anchored up somewhere off this wee island and my phone went. It was Captain Carlo! Somewhere on the high seas.

'I've got my boat! Where are you?'

We gave him the coordinates. It was like Captain Pugwash coming over the horizon. I guarantee you Carlo thought his boat was the dog's rollocks. He'd paid like £100,000 for it for the week. I saw him waving in the distance, but as he drew closer I could see his face dropping. My mate's boat was massive. Carlo anchored in our shadow and stayed on our floating palace for the week with his wife Mariann and her daughter. We had a great time. I couldn't wait to get stuck into the new season with him.

Carlo rebuilt the midfield with James Rodríguez, Allan and Abdoulaye Doucouré, who I'd recommended when we were on the boat. James was a real statement of ambition when he arrived for £20 million from Real Madrid on 7 September 2020. Wonderful player. In his very first training session I hammered him. I went for the kill. I rarely do that but we were doing a possession session, James was walking around and I nailed him. I stopped the session.

As you know, I speak some Spanish. 'La cuenta, por favor.' (The bill, please. I was always left to pay the bill!) Well, I thought I could speak some Spanish, but I couldn't. I still laid into James. 'Are you going to run? Venga! Venga! Vamos! Vamos!' I didn't even know what 'venga' meant. 'Come on', apparently. I'm not kidding you, James gave me that look of 'Who the hell is this guy?' Carlo's face went white. He had his wee electric cigarette, and he nearly swallowed it whole. Probably nobody had spoken to James Rodríguez like that ever, at Porto, Monaco, Real Madrid or Bayern. He was a superstar, a two-time Champions League winner, a Golden Boot winner at the World Cup too.

I put him in as a floater in a possession session, which means he only played for the team with the ball. He turned it on, and looked world class. 'Campeón! Campeón, amigo!' I shouted. 'Estupendo! Estupendo, James!' He smiled, everybody laughed.

James and I became close. He understood what I was doing. I always only wanted to help players. I don't mean help them tactically or give them too much information because it's crazy to tell a top player what to do. Top players like James are always practising so I put time in with him. After training, James would come to me – 'Entrenador, come on.' I'd take him for shooting and just spend a bit of time with him.

CARLO FANTASTICO

James was brilliant on his debut when we opened the 2020–21 season by beating Tottenham 1–0. Dom scored a great header. On the bus back I was sitting next to Carlo when he took a call from the directors. I heard them shouting, 'This is wonderful! We beat Tottenham and we haven't beaten Tottenham for years! We have to give you a present!' I was thinking a nice bottle of after shave? A nice Armani suit? Next minute there's a big black Rolls-Royce Cullinan in Carlo's spot at Finch Farm. It was huge. When I arrived, Carlo was working out how to open the door.

'Duncan, look at this!'

Four hundred thousand pounds' worth of car, orange roof, Swarovski crystals all through the roof, and Carlo struggling to open the door.

I really wanted that Rolls-Royce. I had my eye on it. I was thinking, 'I could get this Rolls-Royce because I've helped Carlo, and he's been on my mate's boat, I've treated him like a king. This boat if hired would have been £200,000 a week. She had all the toys, all the jet skis, the whole thing, and we paid for everything. So he'll leave me this Rolls-Royce, won't he?'

I went in to Finch Farm when he left to discover the car had gone as well as Carlo.

'Where's that Rolls-Royce?' I asked one of the staff.

'It's gone, Dunc. He's sold it.'

I daftly thought Carlo would give the car to me. I'd have given it to one of my staff if I'd been in Carlo's position. There you go.

The Spurs game got us going and we won the next six in all comps. Everton fans loved Ancelotti. 'Carlo Fantastico, Carlo Magnifico, olé, olé!' We were top briefly, and then slid to tenth. On a freezing February night in 2021, we were playing Spurs and I genuinely began to worry about Carlo's well-being in the cold. Carlo was in a bad way, almost turning into a snowman, totally white and shaking. 'Are you all right?'

'Duncan, I am freezing. I cannot move.' I went to the doc. 'We're going to have to get Carlo a drink, he's freezing to death.' The doc got me a coffee and I handed it to Carlo. He was made up. When Bernard scored the winner at 5–4, I was jumping around and Carlo was still standing there, blowing on the coffee to get the warmth up into his face. Up the Coffees!

The last few months of his reign were terrible. I knew Carlo was leaving. He'd told me two or three months before that he'd had enough. His ex-wife Luisa was dying and Carlo was in pieces; they'd split a few years ago but remained friends, and they'd been childhood sweethearts. It was a tough time for Carlo. Davide was, obviously, devastated at his mother's illness. He was flying back and forth and missing training.

Carlo's last game as Everton manager was a 5–0 loss at Man City on 23 May. I was fuming because Marcel Brands had been having meetings with players at Finch Farm before and after the game and I felt that was wrong. In one, he'd criticised Richarlison. He told Richy that he'd not been doing well enough.

It was shocking, so I spoke to Carlo before the game.

'Why's this guy meeting your players? *Your* players. Are you allowing this? It's wrong. He's overstepping the mark.'

'Come on, Duncan, one game to go.'

No, I was steaming.

Afterwards, Carlo and all his staff were distraught at the defeat. 'Duncan, it's football, it's Man City,' Carlo said.

'I know, but he's in there talking to the players, man. You've got Marcel Brands and Leighton Baines addressing our players, *your* players. They're in the dressing room talking to them right now.' I knew Leighton's heart was in the right place but it was not his role. It was Carlo's role, my role.

'Ah, Duncan,' Carlo just sighed.

I went in and Leighton was talking to the players. Leighton had never said two words in his whole life in the dressing room. Leighton overstepped the mark. Brands was trying to take everything over. It was horrible.

'What do you want me to do, Carlo? Do you want me to go in there and sort this out? I'll tell them to turn it in and get out?'

'Ah, Duncan.'

They were in there, telling the players they'd let the club down. They said something to Richarlison and he got pulled apart from Brands. Brands and Baines overstepped the mark. I was livid. I had no authority to say anything, but I told Carlo what I would tell Brands. 'Do your job,' I'd tell him. 'Your job's to go and buy some good players. Don't do other people's jobs, do your job. The dressing room is for the manager and for the coaches, not for you.' Carlo told me not to say anything.

What could I do? I loved Carlo but I knew he was leaving.

Why look for confrontation? Carlo showed his experience. I was a bull in a china shop. They were thinking of Luisa. After the game they flew back to Italy to be with her in her final hours. Luisa passed away on 25 May, God rest her soul.

Carlo resigned on 1 June 2021. I knew he had other plans and was not surprised when he turned up back at Real Madrid within twenty-four hours to succeed Zinedine Zidane. I feel honoured to have met and worked with Carlo Ancelotti and I count him as a friend. I text him before some Champions League games and I can see him walking out of the tunnel texting me back.

I went to see Carlo at Real Madrid in 2023, and he stood up in front of everybody and said, 'This is the best coach I've ever worked with.' Davide was sitting there. Raúl was sitting there. Then Carlo started coughing and saying, 'One of the best coaches.' Carlo maybe was trying to big me up but he wouldn't have just said it for nothing, would he? He liked me as a person and I'm proud of that. He was being respectful to say he rated me as a coach. Carlo knew I loved him. I stayed in his villa on 24 August, the night before he was going to Istanbul to pick up his big award as UEFA Coach of the Year. Me and Carlo were in this big mansion on our own. He took us for dinner with a couple of his staff, and that's the only time I've seen him dip in his pocket. I was ready to pay the bill but he just looked and went, 'No, Dunc, I'll pay it this time.' I felt I'd made it.

35

BENÍTEZ

What on God's blue earth were Everton Football Club thinking in appointing Rafa Benítez? The Spaniard was a former Liverpool manager who once described Everton as a 'small club'. Gwladys Street and Bullens Road were never going to forget or forgive that.

Everton used a big boat in Sardinia and helicoptered people in for interviews after Carlo left. I think Rafa got the job on the strength of a big laptop presentation: 'and these are the 3,000 players I'm going to get you'. That's what convinced them. Obviously Rafa's been a fantastic manager, a Champions League winner, but still it was a ridiculous appointment by Everton. 'Former Liverpool manager' – that's all the board needed to know not to appoint him.

Moshiri backed Benítez, and appointed him on 30 June 2021. I always tried to get on well with my managers and always tried to help. I got on well with Rafa, no problem at all – a great manager and a great tactician – but every time I looked at him I saw 'This Is Anfield'. It just wasn't right.

I never mentioned the Liverpool problem to Rafa. But he knew. That was around the time when I thought they could have given me the job, but they never did. I never thought the board would be crazy enough to hire Rafa. But they did. I felt a bit for Rafa, who was managing on an absolute shoestring. He brought Demarai

Gray in for £1.7 million, Vitaliy Mykolenko for £17 million, and Andros Townsend, Salomón Rondón and Asmir Begović on frees. His big mistake was getting rid of Lucas Digne, our best left-back. They fell out, Mykolenko came in that January 2022 but losing Digne to Villa, one of our relegation rivals, made it even worse. I hoped it wouldn't come back to haunt us.

Rafa was good to me. He let me coach. I did all the training. I'd run the patterns of play, the possession, passing, crossing and finishing. Rafa did all the tactical work. He loved the phases of play. He'd take attack and defence. Rafa's sessions were good, all tactical. But his man-management wasn't great. Rafa didn't have a real warmth about him. What people didn't know was that Rafa wasn't a well man at the time, he was struggling with some kind of stiffness or arthritis. But he turned up, never complained and he trained.

We got on well. He knew I was an Everton man. But it was never going to work. Rafa could have won every game and then if he'd lost two or three the Everton fans would have been on his back. He always said to me, 'Duncan, football is a lie.' It got me thinking. What did Rafa mean? People think you've got a great secret, that you've got the golden ticket and that you're a tactical genius. I've been around half a dozen top managers and two have won Champions Leagues. There's no real secrets that I've seen. They are all very good at a number of things but that statement is right. 'Football is a lie.' Rafa was clever and always wanted to show how clever he was. 'If you want to get better at something,' he'd say, 'well, you always use your fork in one hand, so try the fork in the other hand.' I found him difficult to read at times.

He was very cold. He did poor things, like sacking people before Christmas, but I suppose that was just Rafa being decisive. Dan Donachie, our director of medical services, was at Everton for seventeen years in two spells. Dan was a lovely fella and very good at his job. Rafa got rid of him in November 2021. I didn't understand it. He got rid of Lucas Digne too. I mean, he wanted to leave, but Rafa's comments about his commitment to the team didn't help.

Digne was sold two days before we played Norwich on 15 January 2022. That 2–1 defeat at Carrow Road spelled the end for Benítez. Everton fans sang, 'Get out of our club.' One fan tried to get at him. We had lost nine of the last twelve Premier League games, slipping from fourth to fifteenth, and Rafa, after just six months at the helm, had to go.

Everton asked me to be caretaker for the game against Aston Villa a week later. Carlo phoned to wish me luck. 'Be yourself. You know what you're doing and you've got the experience on the training ground. You're ready.' Grazie, Carlo! Top man. That helped. Carlo believed in me. I felt different from when I was put in charge after Marco Silva left. I knew I didn't have a chance of landing the job full-time back then, but now I did.

I was harder on the players. I demanded higher standards. 'It's not been good enough,' I told them. I gave them a few home truths. The gloves were off. They'd been losing and losing. 'That stops now. Everyone here knows the performances haven't been good enough. Everyone in the city knows that. Everton fans expect better. Everton fans deserve better. We're here to play for them. Never forget that. We play for the Everton fans.'

The day before we faced Villa, I first had to face the press. They asked me all about what I'd learned from Carlo.

'Obviously Carlo was calm, wasn't he? He's seen it all. Tactically he was fantastic, and I picked up loads of things from him, but you have to be yourself. That's what you'll see tomorrow and that's what you see on the training ground.'

I wanted to send a message through the press about what I wanted from my team, and that I wanted the Everton job.

'The club are looking for experience, aren't they?' I said. 'I believe in myself, and I believe one day I'll become a great manager. I know I can do the coaching. Hopefully one day, whenever that day is, I'll become the permanent Everton manager. Of course they are always going to be looking out for the top boys, the guys with the big CVs and the guys who have won trophies. And so they should. At the end of the day we are one of the greatest clubs in the world. Why not look for one of the greatest managers in the world?'

Still, I wanted to grab this opportunity to show what I could do. I needed Everton fans up for it – as they usually are, but absolutely breathing fire this time. So I went on Everton TV and made my point very clear: 'We are Evertonians. We love our club and fight as hard as we can for it. We need everyone in our corner.'

I knew they would be. I also knew Digne going to Villa might cost us. He returned on 22 January 2022. The atmosphere at Goodison was fantastic, and I hoped I'd played a part by putting a few quid behind the bars of nearby pubs. We were in first-half stoppage time, and I turned round to the assistant when Villa got given a corner and asked, 'How long?'

'Eleven seconds.'

'This will be the longest eleven seconds of my life.' Digne whipped in a corner and Emi Buendia, the smallest boy on the pitch, headed in. Second half we absolutely battered Villa but couldn't break through. Fifteen shots. If I'd got the draw I think I would have got the other two games. We were up in the boardroom and my missus was sitting with Tony Bellew when Bill Kenwright came up and said, 'It's not quite the result we were looking for.' We'd only just lost.

With Rafa gone, Everton fans focused their anger on the board, and especially Bill. A plane flew over trailing a banner reading

'22 YEARS OF FAILURE BILL @TIME2GOBILL'. The mood was angry.

We'd actually played OK. I was meant to get three games. But I never did. Our stats were all right against Villa. I kept a screenshot of them on my phone. Yet I was in Marcel Brands' office when he got out stats that he said showed how terrible I was. That only made me even more determined to try and become Everton manager, to show I could do it. My club, my dream.

36

HEARTACHE

'If Bill Kenwright is asking me to go down to London for an interview, I must have this job,' I thought to myself. They were putting me in a terrible position if I didn't get it. I wouldn't be able to stay at Everton. It would be too humiliating, and whoever the new manager was wouldn't want me there. I wanted desperately to be Everton manager, to sit in the Big Chair. I knew I was up against Frank Lampard and the Portuguese guy who went on Sky Sports News and made a fool of himself, Vitor Pereira, a bad move. But I felt I had a real chance.

The interview was such a classic I wish it had been videoed. It's the reason why I left Everton. When either Frank or Pereira were getting interviewed that day I was sitting outside, and suddenly Farhad appeared. He'd walked out. He came out to see me, sat down and had a wee coffee.

'What do you think of Wayne Rooney?' Farhad asked. I mean, I was in for the job, trying to get it, and the owner was asking me about someone else?

'Wayne's good,' I said. What else could I say? I couldn't slag Wayne off. I'd never do that. Wayne's a diamond, a great fellow, a good manager. I'd always bump Wayne up. I've got total respect for him, a big Evertonian, one of us – once a Blue, always a Blue. But it was a weird moment.

When the time came for my interview, Farhad walked out of

that as well. Apparently he often did that in meetings. I had no presentation, because I only got the shout the night before. I just went in, focused on not swearing, and did my spiel. Tim Cahill was in there, bizarrely. Denise Barrett-Baxendale and Graeme Sharp were in there too, so was the finance director Grant Ingles.

In the middle of my spiel one of them announced, 'We're signing Donny van de Beek from Man United and we're signing Dele Alli. What do you think of them?'

I was stunned. 'You've got to be joking me, haven't you?'

'What do you mean, Duncan?' one of them asked.

'Everton need a holding midfield player. They're not holding midfield players, neither of them. And they're not good enough.' I wasn't swearing, I was controlling myself and talking nicely.

'Who do you suggest we sign?'

'Off the top of my head, Matić. You know, the big Serbian boy at Man United? Did well at Chelsea, wasn't quite getting a game at United, left-footed. Out of contract. Get him. You can sit him right in front of the defence.'

'I'm quicker than him,' Farhad said.

That's when I flipped. 'You're signing a holding midfield player, he doesn't need to be that quick. He just needs to be in the middle of the pitch with his left foot, and Matić is a great player, big and strong. He'd be a great player for us.'

They shrugged.

And that's when I swore. 'Farhad, this is your fucking problem, you don't fucking listen. Listen to what I'm fucking telling you.'

The whole room went dead. Farhad just looked at me.

After the interview, I came out. Bill followed, smiling and shaking his head.

'I've got to say, Dunc, I've never heard you speak like that, but I tell you what, I guarantee nobody has ever spoken to Farhad like that before.'

'I had to say it, chairman. He had to be told.' They were about to make another two poor signings, in my opinion. But they didn't listen. I was starting to worry that my chances of getting the job were looking slim. There was more chance of Coisty the pigeon turning up.

Needless to say, I never got the job. But I think, deep down, Farhad respected me for giving him an honest opinion. He realised I was trying to help and that Dele Alli was not the answer. Van de Beek was certainly not the answer. And I was right. Van de Beek came on loan on 31 January 2022 and played only seven games. Dele came the same day, started one game, and got loaned to Besiktas. See, José Mourinho took Nemanja Matić, didn't he? Matić went to Roma, had a good season, played fifty games and played in the Europa League final.

On my way back north, Bill called to tell me I'd not got the job. It was going to Frank Lampard. I knew I had to leave. When the chairman phoned I felt I'd been stitched up. I used a lot of expletives in our conversation. I was struggling. The chairman told me it was a legitimate interview.

'You were in the frame,' Bill said. But I never thought I had a chance. Was this a way to ease me out of Everton?

Some of my mates were cynical about it: 'Kenwright's stitched you up there.' The board, it seemed, were using this as an opportunity to get rid of me because I couldn't go back into the ranks when somebody else came in. With what I'd done for Everton Football Club, Farhad couldn't take the fans on. There'd be war. Anyway, afterwards me and Farhad became closer. Because everything I'd said to him over the last five years, especially on recruitment, came true.

When Bill told me I hadn't got the job, I tried to resign that night. 'Look, you're not resigning, we want you there,' Bill said.

'You've put me in a terrible position now, chairman. Frank's

HEARTACHE

coming and I'm sitting next to him and I've interviewed for his job? It doesn't look right. I'm not having it. I'm away.'

'You must stay. Frank will phone you.'

'I'm not interested in talking to Frank Lampard, I'm not that bothered. You've stitched me up.' I then screamed at him. 'You've fucked me, Bill!' It wasn't nice what I said. 'You've asked me for an interview, you've got me down there, you've put me in a terrible position and it's down to you. I didn't want to get interviewed for the job. I never asked to be interviewed. You could have given me the job for the caretaker role and you never did it, you never did it, did you? Now you've stitched me in an interview and I was actually never getting the job, was I?'

'You were getting the job, Dunc. I brought you down in good faith.'

I don't know if Bill did or not. I do know he blocked me in the past for the caretaker role. I had the experience.

I felt I needed more support from the chairman. I loved Bill but he probably turned me over. He hindered me. Bill still loved me because the fans loved me and I'd done so much for the club and the city. The security boys at Everton once told me, 'There's one picture of a player up in the chairman's house and it's you.'

I always loved Bill Kenwright. Bill gave me a testimonial, he got me back at the club, helped me get back up to the first team coaching. Bill put a hell of a lot into Everton, mortgaged his house, and did so much for people in the community. He was a fantastic Evertonian, who used to hitchhike up to Goodison from London as a kid. It was an absolute outrage he couldn't go back to Goodison in the last few years of his life. Some people always look for somebody else to unleash their anger on and it just happened to be the chairman. Graeme Sharp also got stopped from going to games. He was part of that board. It got a bit messy. It was wrong that a guy like that, a famous no. 9, who scored a load of goals, who gave so much to Everton, couldn't go to games. He and Bill were in exile. Bill was the man who brought Farhad Moshiri, a billionaire, to the football club. Farhad didn't want to blow a billion pounds on players who never delivered. It's incredible how some fans can treat people who have put in billions. Some people slaughtered Bill and Farhad. They delivered a £1 billion stadium on the banks of the famous River Mersey. They did so much for the club. It broke my heart that Bill couldn't come to games. I did go to his funeral.

But I was still bitter about that Norwich game. After he told me Frank Lampard was coming to Everton, it all came pouring out of me. 'And, chairman, I wouldn't have signed Dele Alli and Van de Beek.' They were Frank's first signings. Frank later told me the recommendation to buy Dele came from Harry Redknapp, Frank's uncle.

'You stopped me being caretaker for one game of the season, you put Unsworth and Joe Royle in. You backed Unsy, not me. When you did put me in as caretaker, there were great results, and you brought in Carlo Ancelotti. All right, it was Carlo Ancelotti, but you weren't shouting, "Put Duncan in!" Now this. You just don't want me here. I need to leave, end of.'

Bill was upset as well because I was saying a few bad things.

'Just talk to Frank. Please, Dunc.'

Because I respect Bill, and Frank, I agreed. When Frank got into his office at Finch Farm he called me in. I explained what had happened and why I had to go.

'I know,' Frank replied. 'But I've asked a few people about you, Duncan. Everybody talks so highly of you.'

'Look, Frank, I interviewed for your job and I'm sitting next to you now. It looks terrible to the fans, to the press, to the players. I'm not going to be stabbing you in the back and wanting you to fail but it's not a good look me still being here.'

'I know you're not like that, Duncan. I've asked people about you.'

'Frank, I'm upset. I should never have gone to that bastard interview. They asked me to go.'

Frank's smart. He'd quickly picked up the politics. 'I know they asked you to go.' Frank didn't know the ins and outs of things, but he said, 'I've asked people. You're loyal, you're straight and I want you.' Frank's honest. He then said, 'I understand your point of view. Will you stay with me?'

I thought long and hard.

'All right, I'll stay,' I eventually said. 'It'll be good for the fans,' I added.

Frank was genuine. He knew it made sense to keep me. If it looked like he'd got rid of me, and his results never went right, Everton fans may have jumped on him a lot quicker. He wanted a massive career at Everton, didn't he?

Frank got the people around him that he wanted: Ashley Cole and Paul Clement, wee Joe Edwards and Chris Jones, the first-team coach and head of performance, a nice sports science boy. I just kicked a can up and down the place. I liked Ashley. He was like me, obsessed with football and coaching. Ashley would talk about throw-ins for two hours.

'I've got this throw-in,' he would begin.

I'd almost fall asleep. 'What?'

'We've got this great throw-in. Lock this guy and block that guy.'

Frank would come in and Ashley would present this throw-in for about twenty minutes and Frank would go, 'All right, Ash, we'll have a think about that one, right?' Frank was as enthusiastic as I was. It's a throw-in. Throw it to somebody's feet, throw it down the line. But Ash had a pattern of play for throw-ins. Still, I got on well with all of Frank's coaches.

I backed Frank all the way but those first couple of weeks were tough for me. I had missed out on the top job again. I'd watched Dele and knew I was right. They'd signed him on a big contract, big money, and he reminded me a bit of Gazza. When I played with Gazza, Gazza was gone, his body was weak. Dele was the exact same. He came on the training ground and looked fragile. He couldn't compete in the Premier League.

One day I was in the coaches' room with Ashley, Paul and Joe and they mentioned Dele.

'He's miles off it, lads,' I said. 'He's not the same player he was.'

This was after about two or three days of watching him, falling over and tripping up. I didn't know Dele had issues, which he eventually spoke about, all the difficult stuff from his childhood, and obviously I felt for him when I heard. I did know that he'd once been a great player but wasn't now.

At that point, Frank walked in. He'd heard the raised voices.

'What is it, Duncan? You're talking away there.'

'As it happens, boss, we're talking about Dele Alli.'

'What are you saying about him?'

'Well, I'm saying he's struggling in training.'

'You know what, Duncan? You could be right.' Frank knows players and he'd seen it too. Everton were interested in Dele prior to Frank but it must have been his final decision to sign him in January 2022, and it proved a mistake. As we know, it was Harry Redknapp's recommendation.

I liked Frank. I've worked with a lot of fantastic coaches and managers and I'd put Frank right up there. The work I saw of his on the training ground was as good as anybody's. I never understood why Frank wasn't considered for the England job when Gareth Southgate left after Euro 2024. Tactics – he's very good. Communication – second to none. Frank's got respect because he's been a tremendous player, with good staff around him, and he's a very intelligent man. Frank's got choirboy looks but I saw another side of him that made me realise why he'd been such a top player. Salomón Rondón and Frank had a right set-to one day in training. Salomón wanted to leave and he felt Frank was blocking him. They were shouting at each other, and the argument continued into the changing room. I followed as I could see what was happening. Frank had changed. He'd rolled back the years to him being a player. It was getting naughty. I could see Frank becoming the aggressor with Salomón, who's a big lump, so I stepped in between them. I managed to get Frank away from Salomón. I thought, 'That's why guys like Frank were such great players.' You'd think butter wouldn't melt in his mouth. Frank's tough. He had that edge. He's a warrior, a fighter. And he's a very good manager. So why not England manager?

The guy who's managing England should be English. Scotland, Scottish. We should not have foreign managers managing our national teams. It's about identity. British managers have not done a lot of winning because they've not been given jobs where they can win. Why did the FA not give the job to Lee Carsley?

Look what they did with Gareth. They built a big place at St George's Park, got a good pathway for coaches, Southgate did a great job with England. Lee took the same pathway, Under-21s, into the first team, won five games, had a great record, lost one game against Greece at home, got slaughtered, and, yes, it was a disappointing result. Why should Lee's whole coaching journey come down to one game? I'm sure Thomas Tuchel has had loads of poor games. Lee Carsley's name is not exotic enough, but Lee has done the hard yards. The FA should respect that. Come on, put one of your men in. Back your system. Back what you're preaching. Lee Carsley should have been England manager, or Frank Lampard, Graham Potter or Eddie Howe. Any one of them managers would have done a fantastic job, an even better job than Tuchel. To go for a German coach managing England doesn't sit right with me. Do you think an English coach would ever manage Germany? No chance.

Frank kept us up. Before the Crystal Palace game at Goodison on 19 May 2022, we stayed in the Titanic! We were worried about going down! Frank did an inspirational presentation about big moments, big players and big games. He left pictures by the players' seats in the dressing room, pictures of loved ones, and messages from kids. Séamus Coleman organised it. Everyone knew how important this was. It was the biggest match in Everton's recent history. Leading up to the stadium, all the fans were out with their blue flares and flags, all of them singing. It was like Boca Juniors against River Plate. I've never seen an atmosphere like it. At 2–0 down, Frank stepped up. He got us going again. Dominic was superb in the second half. Séamus was magnificent. The history of the club weighs heavily on you, especially when you are captain. Séamus has been under so much pressure and strain over the years, I have total respect for him. He keeps on fighting for the club, as I did. He loves Everton so much, a really lovely man, great servant to the club, works his socks off, drives the dressing room and sets the standard. He really is an Everton legend. He deserved to stay up. Dominic made it 3–2 with five minutes left, the fans invaded the pitch at the final whistle, and we'd survived.

There was one game left, Arsenal away, and I was determined to stay until the end of the season to help Frank settle in. He's a good guy and a good manager. But it wouldn't have been right to stay. I'd not got the job. It would have been wrong to stick around hoping for another chance. I wanted the best for Frank and his coaches so I did the right thing and moved on. I needed to go away, start a managerial career and crack on.

I rang Frank. He was in Dubai with his wife Christine.

HEARTACHE

'Look, Frank, I'm leaving.'

'What? Duncan, I'm just getting ready for my dinner. I'll phone you back in a minute.'

He phoned back an hour later.

'Duncan, you're not leaving? It hasn't registered, say that again.'

'I'm leaving. I've had enough.'

He was on the floor. 'Duncan, I'm back in a couple of days. Let's talk then. Don't leave.' But I had to go.

I was sad to leave Frank. He'll be a very good manager one day. He is certainly one of the best managers I've worked with in terms of communication, tactics, presentations and presenting himself. He's fantastic, and it will work out for him one day. Frank's already done good work as a manager. He got Derby County in the Championship play-offs, got Chelsea to fourth in the Premier League and to the FA Cup final. He came to Everton at the start of February 2022 and kept us up. But twenty-four losses in forty-four games was always going to kill him and Frank himself left on 23 January 2023.

I was long gone. I'd left in the summer of 2022. Everton were very good to me and gave me a generous severance pay, which I was incredibly grateful for. My heart was breaking as I drove out of Finch Farm for the last time. I travelled and learned. I spent three days at Real Madrid, watching Karim Benzema train and talking to Carlo. It was time I became a manager.

37

JUST ABOUT MANAGING

'What are you doing tomorrow?'

Jesus Christ! This was Sir Alex Ferguson on the phone, the greatest manager in British history. I gulped, and replied, 'Feeding my pigeons, Sir Alex.' I was in the back garden with my pigeons at the time.

'Get yourself over to see me.'

That was it. End of call.

I rang Big Sam Allardyce to thank him – he'd sorted it out for me. 'Good luck,' he said. 'Alex will get on well with you.'

I met Sir Alex in a café in Wilmslow. I brought a cake for Lady Cathy and a case of red wine for Sir Alex. It's nervy buying wine for Sir Alex. He's such a connoisseur, isn't he? I don't know if he drank it. He probably threw it away. I was made up to meet him. Only my second time. He's got a presence. And I got on really well with him. We talked about life back in Glasgow and his upbringing and a wee bit of my upbringing and we talked a lot about football. I listened and listened.

Sir Alex talked a lot about family, about background, about where you come from, and to *remember* where you come from. He also spoke about how tough his road has been. He spoke about the shipyards of Glasgow. I was in the presence of greatness, incredible wisdom and knowledge that he gained over eighty-odd years. It was a privilege. I knew he'd tried to sign me in 96, after I had that good game against United. I knew one of the secrets behind Sir Alex's success was that he adapted. He mellowed in time with his man-management from a really strong approach back in the day. Jim McLean would never have survived in the modern age.

These guys like Sir Alex . . . well, how do I put it? Unfortunately, when these guys pass away, a lot of the stories will go with them, won't they? I wish Sir Alex many more years on this earth but I also know what a privilege it was to have three hours listening to him and learning. And it was free. Six months before, I'd been at my mate Andy Bell's charity event and my pal George paid £100,000 to have lunch with Sir Alex.

He was so encouraging.

'It's your time,' Sir Alex said. 'Be you. I'll support you. And surround yourself with people you can trust.'

Now I just needed somebody to give me a chance at management. I'd got my Pro Licence at Largs, I'd coached under prestigious managers, I felt ready. Some of the greatest managers we've had in this country have been Scottish. There is that respect for Scottish managers but not just because of tactics. Sir Alex Ferguson was tactically clever. There's no great secret to being a good football manager: just choose the right players and motivate them to play. Just! Sir Alex was a master at that. Give me Lionel Messi, give me Kevin De Bruyne, give me Thierry Henry and I'll be a world-beater. The better players you get, the more chance you've got. Sir Alex had the hunger to keep going. That's what separated him from mere mortals.

I just needed that first door to open to the top flight. Some managers have doors opened for them into the Premier League. I've had help, too, but I went to League One. Mikel Arteta played under Arsène Wenger and then learned under one of the modern greats in Pep Guardiola. I'm not sure Mikel ever had to pick a team until he went to Arsenal as manager at the end of 2019.

He got a good leg up. Good luck to him. Mikel had tremendous support from Pep, just as I did from Carlo Ancelotti. But obviously Mikel was a fantastic coach. He built his knowledge and reputation working for Pep, who was bringing in the results. People take different routes. My direction was through the academy route. Some people start at the top. I started at the bottom. 'Go and serve your apprenticeship,' David Moyes told me. Mikel interviewed for the Everton job. He was sought after by Arsenal because of his connections and being a fans' favourite there.

I've found it's not been as easy to get a Premier League job. But look at who I've worked with. I've been in the privileged position of working under two Champions League-winning managers, Rafa and Carlo. Carlo took me over to Real Madrid and made a big fuss of me. He's the best of them all. People love Carlo. Roberto Martínez, he's worked with Belgium and Portugal. Ronald Koeman – Barcelona manager, Netherlands manager, elite level. They all trusted me to put on training sessions. Ronald's brother, Erwin, is never off the phone to me.

I was a caretaker manager at Everton. I got results at Everton. But I went to Forest Green Rovers, bottom of League One. I went to Inverness Caledonian Thistle and life on the breadline. These foreign guys aren't doing that. You don't see the likes of famous foreign players learning their managerial trade in the Highlands with no budget. And rightly so.

Sporting directors think I'm this big hard case who shouts and screams at people. I didn't have a cross word with anybody in Finch Farm in my ten years working there, never raised my voice at anybody. Certainly at Forest Green and Inverness I never raised my voice. It's not me.

I'd have hoped with my coaching CV that I'd possibly have more opportunities. When you hear the name Duncan Ferguson, would you hire him? I always worried that these younger sporting directors hear my name and it may frighten them. You, as readers, can answer that. I always think it's how I am perceived – 'the hardest football player who ever walked this earth'. It's embarrassing, I've never been able to get away from it. My CV is intimidating to some people because I've worked with the best managers in the world. I've probably got one of the best CVs in the country, but my first opportunity was in League One, bottom of the league, my next opportunity was up in Scotland, bottom of the Championship. I hope in these pages you see a truer reflection of the person I have become, and what a serious coach I am. I did have a few interviews. I got close at Middlesbrough because Michael Carrick didn't take the job and I went for a chat and think I did well. They told me, 'You've basically got the job,' and then Carrick came back. I interviewed at Blackburn too. The new sporting director came in and stopped that. I spoke to Huddersfield, Wigan, Hull. No joy.

I sat in the house for six months and got impatient, then I got a phone call from an agent: 'I've got you the Forest Green job, £6,000 a week, you should take it.' The agent and my assistant, Tony Grant, put me under a bit of pressure to take it. Grant needed a job too. His last one was at Everton, which I got him. But I was a big boy and I made the decision to go to Forest Green on 26 January 2023. I didn't think the phone was going to ring again. I was won over, too, by the enthusiasm of the owner, Dale Vince, and by his green spiel. I had a vegan curry there which was decent. Dale's right: we have to look after the environment, for our kids and grandkids.

When I agreed to take the job, I knew the club were four points off safety but I'd hardly looked at the table. 'Dad, you see how far off they are?' my son Ross said. 'They've played four more games.' It was an impossible task. But I still wanted to go. I should have waited for the phone to ring again with another job offer, but I got impatient. I should not have gone to Forest Green. But Dale convinced me and I was promised a rebuild. All that hard work I'd put in, all the work on the Everton training ground, all these years and years with the 12s, 14s, 16s and 18s, managing in the Premier League, and I took the Forest Green job. Absolutely nuts. I knew better, didn't I?

I thought I could turn it around, even though it was an impossible job. The players were just not good enough. When I went in there, I think I made them competitive. But Dale never gave me time. If he had given me more time and a bit more support, which he said he was going to do, we'd have built a great thing. I was ready to bring a lot of good players in. I always liked Dale. He's passionate, loves his club. I never went out for a meal with Dale, he was too busy thinking about gluing himself to the M5! I didn't agree with throwing orange paint at artwork but they certainly have a just cause. Eating the veggie burger for the cameras when I joined didn't bother me. I was laughing my head off. It was hilarious. Later on, Dale called me up in Inverness and said, 'Duncan, look, we have decided to sell the Big Dunc Burger! It's 30 per cent bigger than the rest. Are you all right with that?' Dale was asking me if it was all right to use my name, did I want a few quid. 'Don't be daft, Dale, you can sell the Big Dunc Burger.' I must have made an impression there.

I was ready. But Forest Green weren't a great club to go to. I think my reputation also preceded me. The young players there were afraid of me, it seemed. Charlie Savage, Robbie Savage's lad on loan from United, plucked up the courage to approach me one day.

'Gaffer, I've been designated to come and speak to you.'
'What is it, son?'
'Do you mind if we train at 2 p.m. tomorrow? The boys have

put me forward to ask.' Fair play to Charlie, and yes, we could switch training.

We got off to a good start too, at Shrewsbury, Jordon Garrick scoring a worldie. We led going into injury-time, then Shrewsbury scored twice in the ninety-fourth and ninety-eighth minutes. I couldn't believe it. Where did those extra minutes come from? It wasn't the World Cup in Qatar where they'd been playing fifteen minutes of injury-time.

'Are you sure it's not the World Cup you're officiating?' I said to the fourth official. She was a Scouser. Fifty-fifty whether she was a Blue or Red. Yes, you guessed it, another unlucky break.

We never recovered after that. We won one game of my eighteen in charge. The team was on the slide. I got on all right with Dale, but things were a bit odd at the club. In May 2023 they brought a boy in from Brentford, Allan Steele, as director of football. He sold them the Brentford model. But it's never all about analytics and stats on potential recruits. Brentford know what they're doing, they've got football men backing up their data on players. You need to get eyes on them. We fell out in the summer because they never brought in the players I wanted and brought in Steele. He told me he'd built Brentford.

'Really, you built Brentford?' I asked. 'Do you know Thomas Frank?'

'Of course I do.'

'Do you?'

I let it go. Next time I was with Steele, my phone rang. It was Thomas Frank, Brentford's manager.

'Oh, Thomas, how are you doing? You all right, mate?'

Steele melted.

'I've got a fella here telling me he built Brentford, Thomas.'

'Duncan, I know him, but he was in a meeting twice in twelve months with twenty other people. I know the guy but there are other guys there.' He was certainly a part of it.

Steele kept out of my way after that.

Anyway, good luck to him. He did a fantastic presentation. Well done. He wouldn't even listen to what I was saying about stockmanship and picking a player. I tried to work with him for a few months and tried to get players in but it didn't work. Beware of the guy who sits next to your owner. He's the one who has the real clout. Owners in the main don't have much of a clue. I went to Forest Green knowing it was a near impossible task. I put my career in the hands of Dale Vince. I liked him. I believe we could have done great things with the club. But, nope, he listened to someone else. Forest Green were relegated out of League Two the following season. And had a big budget to boot. So, let's be fair, Houdini could not have saved them in League One.

Steele got the run of the club and they made poor signings. In the end, it was me who suggested, 'I think it's time for me to move on.' I started the ball rolling. I left on 4 July 2023. Steele didn't last much longer.

38

INVERNESS

I wonder if José Mourinho would have accepted his wages being reduced on his first day in the job. Inverness Caledonian Thistle F.C. did mine, on 26 September 2023. But, to be fair, I'm not José Mourinho.

I went for the interview at Inverness with their chairman, Ross Morrison, a local property developer, because I thought to myself, 'I need to get straight back into work.' Ross offered me £3,000 a week. 'That's as high as we can go,' he said.

'OK, I'll take it. I'll take the job.'

Ross came to see me the next day. 'Look, Duncan, we're really sorry, we've overstretched ourselves on the salary. We can't afford the £3,000 a week. Will you take £2,000?'

I just wanted to crack on, get back into football. I was psyched to be working again. 'Yes, I'll take the £2,000 a week.' I was geed up to go. Maybe I should have clocked there and then about the state of Caley's finances.

Eight months later, after we dropped down a division through losing the play-off final, the chairman phoned me and said, 'Unfortunately, money is tight. Will you now take £1,000 a week?'

I had to accept. Why? Because I was worried sick that I wouldn't get another job, and I had to stay in the show. At least I was still in football, trying to get results. It was costing me to be there though, bearing in mind I spent £20,000 on hotel bills because

Inverness wouldn't pay for away trips. And Inverness ain't near anywhere. At one point I'd lost just three games in eight months away from home in the league. The record was excellent. But at Caledonian Stadium we were poor. The pitch was bobbly, it was wide open, and the facilities were shocking. There was no hot water half the time. The drains backed up and stank the place out. The physio's room leaked when it rained. There was no proper food, no canteen, only a wee sandwich place in the corner. I brought the players some food two or three times a week. The club paid for that in the end.

I considered leaving in the summer of 2024. I spoke about Inverness to people I trust. 'Walk away from it,' they said. 'Your record is good. You've got forty-one points in thirty games since you've been there, which gives you the fifth best points tally in the league, with all your injuries.' But who's listening? We got relegated.

What really got me was the level of officiating. I was doing my nut as Caley Thistle manager at how few decisions we got. Referees found infringements all the time. It was like I was still paying for my reputation of thirty years ago. All the hard work I did on the training ground, it was for nothing. One decision can kill you. The referee's got so much power to do you in, intentionally or unintentionally. It felt intentionally quite often. I thought about Rangers v. Celtic and whether it had anything to do with that. I was standing on the touchline seeing pens given against us. I continued to rack up red cards. Some things don't change.

We got beat at Hamilton Accies in the play-off in May, and Caley Thistle should have had a penalty and never got one. The next game at home, we conceded a penalty. The ref could not wait to give it. He saw that one clear enough. Then the opposition didn't get a red card. That's it. I got annoyed.

I don't want to complain. Having returned to Scottish football for the first time in almost thirty years, I'd never want to criticise it. But the officiating is not great. There's not a lot of money and not many fans – but then there's not a lot of people in Scotland. There are only five and a half million, aren't there? So you're not going to have big crowds, are you? Most people in Scotland support Rangers and Celtic, and a wee bit with Hearts or Hibs in Edinburgh, or in Dundee, or 15,000 or so at Aberdeen. A lot of Scottish supporters watch the English Premier League and Championship. I was listening to talkSPORT about how two Scottish fans from Fort William travelled to Leeds home and away. To Elland Road! That's a 600-mile return journey.

After six months at Inverness I started to feel isolated up there. It was great at the start. The club put me in this beautiful house right on the River Ness, close to the Fort George training ground. But as the season wore on, or the money ran out, they kept downgrading me. They'd lured me in, showed me round the training ground, talked of their plans to build this and buy that, but nothing happened. I felt I was in the middle of nowhere in a club going nowhere and I got a bit down.

It's a stunning area, but I found some of the fans problematic. There's not many of them for a start – Inverness's average attendance was only around 2,200 – and it only took two or three to kick them off. I had a good relationship with them when we were winning.

We played at Partick on 30 March 2024. They were third top but we battered them with ten men: 55 per cent possession, 454 passes to 337, nine free-kicks to one. All over them. Cammy Kerr got a yellow for simulation when it was a clear foul on him, and then another for a foul, and we were down to ten. That's what happened to Inverness: we got bad decisions against us. It was never a sending off. We did everything but score, and got beat 1–0. I backed my players up because they were brilliant. The

Partick manager came in after the game and said we'd played them off the park with our ten men. I went with the players to clap our fans who'd come all the way down to Glasgow and the players and I got slaughtered. It was only four or five barracking me, and they might have been drunk, and they didn't know football, but I flipped and reacted.

I had a go back. 'We were down to ten men, give the lads a break!' By the way, Kerr's red card got rescinded. He never dived.

After that for the rest of the season I got the hump with the fans so I didn't go over to them to salute them, which was a shame as there were a lot of good fans. That's really unusual for me. Those four or five Caley Thistle fans were completely and utterly out of order. Why should I be abused like that? I lost connection with the fans then. With the fans round about the dugout, all the kids, I made a fuss, but I didn't clap the other Caley Thistle fans. They soon cottoned on to it. 'He doesn't come near us now,' they said. My style of football was not what they were used to. They liked long balls. I liked us to play through the thirds. My teams play football. I think they preferred tossing the caber.

Away from the ground, Caley Thistle fans were great. They all loved me because I took time with them. I'd go to Tesco – the highlight of my day – buy some stuff and they'd all talk to me, quite happily. But there are always a few idiots, aren't there?

Caley Thistle fans were all made up when I first came, having a name up there, but that experience at Partick turned it into a bit of a stand-off.

Inverness actually finished the season well with three wins and a draw in our last five, but we still dropped into the Championship play-offs. We played at Montrose in the semi-finals on 7 May, a tough game, but we got a 0–0 draw. The players went over to the fans and got abused again. One of the players came into the dressing room afterwards shouting and screaming. He was really flaming. It was the same handful of fans. We got to the final, lost to Hamilton and got relegated, and then the fans were all talking about a boycott. It was a shambles.

I think it must have been one of the worst conditions that any manager has worked under, certainly up there. Forest Green's facilities were poor but they were St George's Park compared to Inverness. It was basically a rugby pitch, with a football pitch at the side and a container where you put your stuff. There were no showers, no gym (that was in a tin hut at the stadium). Ross Morrison was putting money in but it was unsustainable. The situation wasn't helped when the events company they'd set up lost money on concerts they'd hosted at the stadium; some were successful like Andrea Bocelli and Duran Duran, others weren't. The company went into liquidation. We lost the play-off final to Hamilton 5–3 on aggregate and were relegated to Scottish League One partly because of a really poor refereeing performance; the opposition player should have got a straight red. Inverness under Duncan Ferguson did not get any little decisions going our way.

Our predicament was made worse by the uncertainty off the pitch. The club wanted to move training 130 miles to Kelty Hearts' base in the Central Belt. Inverness fans felt it was an insult to their city. The way it was explained to me by Ross Morrison was that it was financially unviable for Inverness to carry on training at Fort George. They'd not got the money for accommodation for players, which was quite pricey in a tourist haven like Inverness. They couldn't attract players up to League One in the north-east of Scotland. Going to the Central Belt between Glasgow and Edinburgh, where most people in Scotland live, offered a much cheaper option. I saw the logic. Recruitment would be easier. Players would stay in their own houses in the Central Belt.

Caley Thistle had planned to make the move regardless of relegation but the cost of going down made them think twice. They were spending £250,000 on accommodation, and to them that was massive. My entire budget for 2024–25 was meant to be £500,000, now half of that was going on accommodation. It was hard for Inverness in the Championship, never mind League One. Who's going to go to League One in Inverness if you're getting a few hundred quid a week? Where players lived was not really important. Look anywhere: Everton players don't walk about Liverpool city centre. Well, I did, but most don't. They live out, some of them over towards Manchester. They just drive in to Finch Farm, which is on the outskirts of Liverpool. It was just that the Caley Thistle fans felt abandoned in the city. I sort of understood. Fans might look forward to bumping into players in the garage or in Tesco and having a wee bit of interaction.

Morrison called. 'We're moving to the Central Belt. You'll have a budget, but can you drop your money to £1,000 to help us with the budget, and we'll get promoted out of League One,' he said. I felt positive for the future. I went on holiday to Florida with the kids, then Morrison called again. He'd resigned on 1 June because the board went against him on the move to the Central Belt. They'd buckled under fan pressure and petitions stoked by the local press. I felt for Ross. Inverness had struggled financially for years and then got a chairman in Ross who put a lot of money in. He basically got sick of losing money – up to £2 million – and got no thanks for it. He was sticking that money in and still getting abused. He's an Inverness fan, comes from the area, made a few quid in property and whisky warehouses, and wanted to give back to the club he loves. Imagine losing £2 million quid and getting slaughtered. It was probably a relief for him to step away from the coconut shy. Two days later, Inverness announced they were staying at Fort George for the foreseeable future and were hopeful of bringing in new investors and owners.

I came back from Florida to no players, no budget. I had eight young players left. I went into the boardroom looking for answers. Five of them in there. 'Duncan, we've got no money,' they told me. Inverness had gone from Ross paying all the wages, and all the staff keeping their jobs, and having a budget and players lined up, with everything getting funded for twelve months, to now, four weeks later, facing administration.

'What are you going to do?' I asked them.

'Administration,' they replied. I didn't want administration so I said, 'I'll put £50,000 of my own money in the club account tomorrow, if yous all put in £50,000 apiece. That £300,000 will keep the club going until we find a backer.' They all started looking down, fiddling with their laces, as not one of them would put a penny in. They all resigned in the end.

There was a bad atmosphere. Someone at the club was telling the players every Friday, 'You're all losing your jobs.' How could the players concentrate the next day? I felt someone at the club didn't want the team winning. They wanted administration. They got a consultant in, Alan Savage, a local businessman who hired the administrators BDO, who looked at the books and said the best step was administration. So they did that, bumped all the debts, and we lost fifteen points right away. Local suppliers and small businesses were all owed money. It was horrendous.

I was buying all the players their breakfast every morning, £50 a day. I was giving them money for petrol. They were starting to struggle. I helped them. But I was finding it incredibly difficult to keep the whole thing going. I felt, on my own, I had little or no support especially during the 2024–25 season. Although we went into administration, who was still paying for many things? Again, it was me. I wanted to help the players.

What really hurt me during the 2024–25 season was that I'd signed my son, Cameron, who was returning off the back of an injury, and he came off the bench against Kelty Hearts on 24

August and got terrible abuse. It was disgusting what they were saying to Cameron, a young man trying to make his way in the game. Sickening. The fans were a disgrace. I don't mind a bit of stick, but for people to go out of their way to hammer my son, that, for me, was the end. I was not interested in them any more.

I knew exactly what was going to happen to me for the last few months. It wasn't a nice environment the last two or three weeks. And when the club went into administration, that was it for me. I lost my job. I look back on my points return and it was good. I managed forty league games and lost eleven, not bad given what we all went through.

The players were devastated when I left. Every single Caley player messaged me. It was emotional. They knew how much effort I'd put in and how much money I'd spent on them because I cared. I never received any messages from any of the senior staff. Considering I was buying all their breakfasts, no class.

39

BROTHERS AND SISTERS

In April 2024, Farhad Moshiri phoned me. 'What do you think of Beto?' he asked.

'I'm not too sure, Farhad,' I replied. 'I haven't seen a lot of him, because he's not playing many games. The manager mustn't fancy him. Beto's profile does suit a traditional number nine at Everton. But at the moment it looks like he's struggling. It does take time to adjust to the Premier League. I hope and pray it's not another expensive recruitment mistake. Time will tell. But to be honest, I'm not sure if he will cut it.'

I get on well with Farhad. I like him. He eventually sold up to the Friedkin Group in December 2024, and he deserves a lot of credit for what he did for Everton Football Club. He spent hundreds of millions on players, and hundreds of millions on a new stadium. I never understood why Farhad got so much stick. But unfortunately it didn't work out for him. The main part of that was down to poor recruitment and that's happened to Everton for far too long. He probably saw through all the crap. I once went to meet him in London. We had a good discussion and I told him straight: 'The players you sign are not the profile Everton are looking for.'

It frustrates me that Everton continue to struggle with their recruitment. I always follow what's happening at Everton. I desperately want them to do well. When they were struggling and

Sean Dyche was getting criticised, I wanted them to recover even more. I respect Sean Dyche, who had his hands tied in the transfer market and had to deal with points deductions. Everton broke Profit & Sustainability rules, and that was bad senior management at the club.

I look back on my career with pride for what I achieved, a wee boy from St Ninians, breaking the British transfer record, playing for the mighty Glasgow Rangers, playing for my country, finding my home at Everton, becoming the Everton captain and going on to manage them, playing alongside the best players in the world like Rooney and Shearer and scoring more English Premier League goals than any other Scotsman. But there's a BIG but. What was that horse of mine called again?! No Regrets. Jesus, if only. Because I have many regrets. I am sorry for turning my back on my country. I am sorry for headbutting John McStay, and I regret all those stupid red cards. But I hope I've become a better person as time has moved on. And a special thanks has to go out to my Blue Everton Army.

Everton will always be a part of me, even when I am 450 miles away in Scotland. Every time I heard 'Z-Cars' as a player or coach, the hairs stood up on the back of my neck. Sometimes now I hear the tune ringing in my head – such a distinctive sound, taking me back to Goodison, and scoring in front of Gwladys Street, back in the embrace of my beloved Everton family.

I think of my goals against Liverpool at Goodison. Games against Liverpool are what make or break you in front of Everton fans. It's local pride. It matters the earth. Everton have been the underdogs against Liverpool since the 80s. So I always especially got up for the derby. I consider myself an honorary Scouser. When I was at my lowest, incarcerated inside Barlinnie, Everton fans wrote to me, their letters a lifeline from the outside. I'll never forget that. I salute you, my brothers and sisters. You made me feel special, you made me feel like family. I hope and pray I gave you back some memorable moments in your lives.

   Take care, God bless,
   Dunk.

ACKNOWLEDGEMENTS

Thank you to my wife, kids and family for putting up with me and for supporting me through the good times and the bad times. I love you all.

INDEX

Aberdeen FC, 81, 91–2, 128
Ablett, Gary, 153, 216, 217, 252
Adams, Tony, 89, 167
Albert, Philippe, 232
alcohol, 11, 13, 39, 41–2, 83–4, 111–12, 130–33, 145–6
    drink driving offence (1994), 140–42, 150
    Huyton Firm and, 232–40
    sobering up, 241–4
Alder Hey Children's Hospital, 208, 210, 213, 270, 292
Allan, 290, 308
Allanbridge, William Stewart, Lord, 52
Allardyce, Sam, 14, 249, 277–83, 318
Alli, Dele, 319, 320, 322, 324
Amokachi, Daniel, 146, 156–7
Ancelotti, Carlo, 14, 178, 289, 295, 299–300, 301–12, 322, 330
Ancelotti, Davide, 304, 306, 310
Ancelotti, Luisa, 310–11
Andersson, Patrik, 110
Anderton, Darren, 149
Anstruther, Fife, 40–41, 43, 97
Apollon Limassol, 278

Ardiles, Ossie, 136
Arsenal FC, 56, 163, 167, 242, 299, 326
Arteta, Mikel, 14, 199, 200, 203, 206, 329–30
Asamoah, Kwadwo, 281, 282
Ascott Bar, Dundee, 39
Aston Villa FC, 119, 315, 316
Atkinson, Ron, 119
Atsu, Christian, 260
Austria national team, 113
Ayr United FC, 67

Baines, Leighton, 281, 282, 299, 301, 310–11
Baird, John, 42, 51
Ball, Alan, 207
Ball, Michael, 218
bankruptcy, 245–50
Bannockburn High School, Stirling, 62, 68–9, 73–4
Barcelona FC, 133, 183
Barlinnie Nine, 12
Barlinnie prison, Glasgow, 1–9, 11, 12, 14–15, 17–33, 45, 47, 54, 158
    drug use in, 17, 18–20
    hospital wing, 19–20, 22, 23–5

INDEX

Barlinnie prison – *cont.*
   letters of support, 26–8, 189, 344–5
   mental health in, 18, 23–5
   pipe smuggling system, 18–19, 30
   top boys, 5, 20
   weakness, displays of, 20–23
Barmby, Nicky, 159
Barnes, John, 81
Barrett-Baxendale, Denise, 277, 287, 298, 319
Barry, Gareth, 266
Barton, Joey, 162
Barton, Warren, 178
Battle of Bannockburn (1314), 57, 60, 61
Battle of Britain game (1992), 117, 129
Battle of Stirling Bridge (1297), 57
Batty, David, 120
Bayern Munich, 38, 40, 114
Beattie, James, 198
Beckham, David, 156, 248
Begley, Tam, 21
Begović, Asmir, 314
Bell, Andy, 329
Bellamy, Craig, 183
Bellefield, Liverpool, 32, 139
Bellew, Tony, 316
Benítez, Rafa, 14, 313–15, 330
Bennett, Steve, 165, 171
Bent, Marcus, 201
Benzema, Karim, 327
Bergara, Inaki, 256
Bergkamp, Dennis, 109
Bernard, 284, 295, 298, 310
Bernat, Juan, 281
Bešić, Muhamed, 261
Beto, 343
Bishop, Carl, 231
Blackburn Rovers FC, 76, 118, 171, 331

Bobic, Fredi, 165, 166, 193
Bocelli, Andrea, 339
Bollan, Gary, 74, 75
Bolton Wanderers FC, 159, 160, 165
Bone, Alex, 67
Bonner, Packie, 96
Borestone Primary, Stirling, 60
Bosman ruling (1995), 87
Bosnich, Mark, 180
boxing, 63
Boyd, Tom, 112
Boys' Brigade, 62, 65, 68
BP Boys' Club, 67
Bracewell, Paul, 148, 274
Braehead Primary, Stirling, 60
Branch, Michael, 218
Brands, Marcel, 264, 285, 287, 294, 296–8, 299, 302–3, 310–11, 317
Brechin City FC, 80
Bremner, Billy, 64
Brentford FC, 333
Bridge of Allan, Stirling, 133
Bristol City FC, 148
Brown, Craig, 64, 107, 111–12, 113–14
Browning, Tyias, 270
Bruce, Steve, 154, 156, 167
BT Sport, 162–3
Buchwald, Guido, 112
Buendia, Emi, 316
Bulgaria national team, 95
Bullard, Jimmy, 169
Burns, Robert, 57
Buzzy Wares, Glasgow, 131

Cadamarteri, Danny, 169
Cahill, Tim, 319
Calvert-Lewin, Dominic, 14, 254, 268, 285–8, 289–94, 301, 309, 326
Cameron, Kenny, 70–72, 78
Campbell, Kevin, 161, 252

INDEX

Campbell, Sol, 176, 178
Canada national team, 108
cannabis, 13, 132
Cantona, Eric, 31, 120, 156, 158
Capello, Fabio, 180
Carrick, Michael, 331
Carse Thistle FC, 66, 67–70, 73, 101, 118
Carsley, Lee, 325
Case, Jimmy, 163
Catholicism, 4–5, 27, 226–7
celebrations, 148
Celtic FC, 5, 25, 69, 96–7, 110, 113, 337
   Rangers, rivalry with, 4–5, 110, 129–30, 132, 166, 226
Central Boys, 66, 67
Channon, Mick, 105
Chapman, Lee, 120
Charles III, King, 151, 154
Charles, Ray, 94
Charlton Athletic FC, 168, 185, 187, 192
Charnley, Chic, 98
Chelsea FC, 146, 160, 172, 287–95, 304, 327
Chimbonda, Pascal, 169
Clark, Darren, 96
Clark, John, 80, 83, 96
Clark, Kenny, 46, 48, 49
Clark, Lee, 148
Clarke, Steve, 177
Cleland, Alex, 90, 93
Clement, Paul, 323, 324
Clough, Brian, 279
Coach of the Year, 312
coaching, 213–14, 253–87, 301–27
cocaine, 242
Cole, Ashley, 323, 324
Coleman, Séamus, 299–300, 301, 326
Collina, Pierluigi, 14, 200–201, 270

Collins, John, 112
Commonwealth of Independent States (CIS), 109, 110
Conceição, Pedro, 284
Connolly, Callum, 256, 259, 260
Conville, Eddie, 40, 41, 83
Cooper, Davie, 128
County Cup, 68
Court of Session, 56
Coventry City FC, 160, 183
Covid-19 pandemic, 295
Cowdenbeath Racewell, 89
Cowie Colts, 65, 66, 68
Coyne, Tommy, 96–7
Creaney, Gerry, 107
cricket, 121, 175–6, 180
Croatia, 307
cross-country running, 62–3, 66
Cruyff, Johan, 89
Crystal Palace FC, 118, 326
Cullen, Eric, 23
Cunningham, Willy, 64
Cyprus, 164, 278

Dabizas, Nikos, 165
Dailly, Christian, 74, 83, 90, 93, 94
Dalglish, Kenny, 114, 118, 213, 282
Davies, Tom 259, 291, 295, 299
Davro, Bobby, 154
Dawson, Barry, 229–30
De Bruyne, Kevin, 329
Delaney, Mike, 48
Dennehy, Stephen, 21
Derby County FC, 148, 163–4, 193, 327
Dicks, Julian, 55, 163
Dier, Eric, 254
Digne, Lucas, 301, 315, 316
Donachie, Dan, 314
Doucouré, Abdoulaye, 308
Dowell, Kieran, 256

INDEX

Downing, George, 149, 218
drug testing, 132
Dublin, Dion, 143
Dundee United FC, 4, 14, 34, 37, 40, 44, 63, 64, 66, 77–99
    Anstruther incident (1992), 40–41, 43, 97
    four-plus-four contracts, 87, 89–90, 91
    labouring work at, 87–9, 124
    quitting incident (1990), 92–4
    signing (1990), 69–76
    transfer negotiations (1993), 117–24
    wages and fines, 82–3, 92–4, 97–9, 127
Dunfermline Athletic FC, 95
Dunn, Steve, 164
Dunne, Richard, 218
Duran Duran, 339
Durie, Gordon, 109, 111, 130, 134
Durrant, Ian, 111, 122, 128, 137
Dyche, Sean, 344
Dyer, Kieron, 181

East Fife FC, 94
East Fife League, 66
Ebbrell, John, 150, 154, 292, 296
Eccles, Sandy, 48–9, 51, 52
Edwards, Joe, 323, 324
EFL Cup, 278, 298–9
Elizabeth II, Queen, 102
Elleray, David, 171
Elstone, Rob, 277
England national team, 324–5
English First Division, 122
Estonia national team, 113
Eto'o, Samuel, 268, 275
Euro 1992 Championship, 78, 108–10, 264, 266
Euro 1996 Championship, 113–14

Euro 2024 Championship, 324
European Cup, 81
    see also UEFA Champions League
European Under-21 Championship (1992), 107–8, 110–12
Evans, Richard, 256
Everton FC, 3, 11, 14, 26, 27–33, 48, 51, 55, 56, 94, 115, 180–81
    ambassador offer (2011), 212–13
    bookings at, 163–71
    Champions League (2005–06), 200–201
    coaching, 213–14, 253–87, 301–27
    FA Cup (1994–95), 148–55
    League Cup (2002–03), 190, 192
    loan to (1994), 136–9, 140–46
    manager stint (2019), 287–8, 289–300, 303
    manager stint (2022), 315–17
    philanthropy, 208–10
    Premiership season (1996–97), 158–9, 232–3
    Premiership season (1997–98), 159–60, 161
    Premiership season (1998–99), 161
    Premiership season (2000–01), 185
    Premiership season (2001–02), 194
    Premiership season (2005–06), 202–3
    resignation from (2006), 202–6
    testimonial match (2015), 269–70
    transfer negotiations (1998), 172–4
    transfer offer (1993), 119
    transfer to (1994), 147
    transfer to (2000), 182–4
    wages, 146–7

FA Cup 1994–1995, 148–55
FA Cup 1999–2000, 178

INDEX

Fallin, Stirling, 35–6
Farm, The, 150–51
Ferguson, Alex, 81, 115, 152, 154, 163, 180, 274, 279, 328–9
Ferguson, Archie, 104–5
Ferguson, Audrey, 58, 60, 126, 224
Ferguson, Cameron, 219–20, 221, 224, 227, 291, 294, 303, 341–2
Ferguson, Duncan Sr, 2, 5, 21, 42, 57–60, 62, 63, 65, 68, 74–5, 221–6
   Dundee signing (1990), 71–3, 78
   Freemasonry, 133, 225–6
   McLean, relationship with, 79–80, 84
   McStay incident (1994), 134–5
   pigeon fancying, 101, 102
   Rangers, support for, 90–91, 122
   transfer negotiations (1993), 117, 121, 125
Ferguson, Evie, 219, 220, 221, 224, 227, 291
Ferguson, Iris Jr, 57–8, 60, 215, 224
Ferguson, Iris Sr, 2, 5, 42, 57–8, 62, 69, 78, 84, 134, 223
Ferguson, Janine, 175, 181, 182, 210, 215–19
   alcohol and, 241–4
   bankruptcy and, 245, 249, 250
   burglaries, 228–30
   coaching and, 255
   Qatar visit (2004), 197
   religion, 226–7
   wedding, 218–19
Ferguson, Ross, 219, 220, 221, 224, 227, 291
Ferguson, Sarah, 61–2
ferrets, 103
Ferris, Paul, 175, 179
Feyenoord, 29
fighting, 1, 13, 34–43, 74–5, 162–71

Anstruther incident (1992), 40–41, 43, 97
McStay incident (1994), 1, 13, 44–54, 113, 134–5, 344
film tax schemes, 248
financial crash (2008), 247
Finch Farm, Merseyside, 208, 212, 253–63
Finch, Clifford, 28, 29, 137, 146
Findlay, Donald, 52, 55
fishing, 103, 104
Flo, Tore André, 159
Football Association (FA), 164, 166, 168
Football League Cup (2002–03), 190, 192
Forbes, Derek, 129
Forest Green Rovers FC, 12, 330, 331–4, 339
Formby, Merseyside, 192, 206, 230
Forth Valley, 67
four-plus-four contracts, 87, 89–90, 91
Francis, Gerry, 102
Francis, Trevor, 89
Freemasonry, 133, 225–6
Freund, Steffen, 165–6
Friedkin Group, 343
Fulham FC, 193, 286
Fury, Tyson, 267

Gallacher, Kevin, 76, 109
Garbutt, Luke, 259, 260
Garrick, Jordon, 333
Gascoigne, Paul, 186–7, 235, 324
Gemmill, Archie, 64
Germany national team, 38, 107–8, 110, 112–13
Gerrard, Steven, 248, 274–5
Gibson, Darron, 261
Giggs, Ryan, 148
Gillespie, Keith, 149

INDEX

Ginola, David, 187
Glasgow, Scotland, 131–3
  sectarianism in, 4–5, 27, 132
Glenafton Athletic FC, 48
goalkeeping, 65
golf, 266
Goodwillie, David, 64
Goram, Andy, 110, 111, 122, 129, 134, 152
Gordon, Anthony, 278
Gough, Richard, 91, 110, 117, 122, 186
Gower, David, 175
Grant, Tony, 331
Gravesen, Tommy, 150, 170, 185
Gray, Andy, 137, 274
Gray, Demarai, 313–14
Great Ormond Street Hospital, 209
Greece national team, 113
Green, George, 259
greyhounds, 104
Griezmann, Antoine, 256–7
Griff, Tommy, 149–50, 232, 235–6, 246
Guardiola, Pep, 206, 274, 329, 330
Gullit, Ruud, 78, 109–10, 172, 173, 176–8, 179

Haaland, Erling, 261
Hagen, David, 130
Halcrow, Mr, 68–9, 73–4
Hamann, Didi, 176, 178
Hamilton Academical FC, 336, 339
Hamilton Thistle AFC, 70
Hansen, Alan, 186
Harford, Mick, 163
Harrison, David, 166, 262–3
Hart, Robbie, 163
Harvey, Colin, 207
Hateley, Mark, 122, 127, 134
Hawkins, Alan, 31
headers, 143–4

Heart of Midlothian FC, 48, 66, 67, 69–70, 337
Heath, Adrian, 274
Hegarty, Paul, 80, 81, 117–18
Helmer, Thomas, 112
Henry, Thierry, 174, 329
Herrlich, Heiko, 107
Hess, Rudolf, 18
Hibernian FC, 66, 337
Hickson, Dave, 138
Higgins, 'Shotgun', 85
Hinchcliffe, Andy, 142, 146, 148, 153, 160
Hixon, Jack, 273–4
Hoddle, Glenn, 89, 118
Hodgson, Roy, 110–11
Hogg, Graeme, 48
Holgate, Mason, 291, 295
Hope, David, 52–3
Hope, Hallam, 259
Horne, Barry, 150, 153
horse racing, 105–6
Howe, Eddie, 325
Howey, Steve, 232
Hreidarsson, Hermann, 168
Huddersfield Town FC, 282, 331
Hughes, Mark, 89, 153
Hughes, Stephen, 185
Hull City AFC, 331
Hunter, Norman, 163
Hutchison, Don, 169–70
Huyton Firm, 232–40
Hyypiä, Sami, 167

ICI Caley, 66, 67, 68
Ince, Paul, 153, 160
Ingles, Grant, 319
Inglis, John, 37
injuries, 13, 39–40, 92–5, 98, 115, 130, 152, 176, 179–80, 184, 187–9

INDEX

Inverness Caledonian Thistle FC, 66, 67, 68, 330, 335–42
Irish Republican Army (IRA), 27
Irvine, Alan, 214

Jackson, Darren, 39, 90, 95
Jackson, Matt, 152
Jagielka, Phil, 266
James, David, 142, 144, 159
Jeffers, Francis, 146, 168, 292
Jensen, John, 163
Jess, Eoin, 107
Jewell, Paul, 205
Johnson, Grant, 83
Johnson, Peter, 28, 29, 137, 172, 173, 184, 218
Johnston, Mo, 97, 119
Jones, Chris, 323
Jones, Gethin, 256
Jones, Graeme, 256, 258–60, 262
Jordan, Joe, 162
Juventus FC, 152

Kanchelskis, Andrei, 158
Kane, Harry, 143
Kean, Moise, 285, 286, 295–9, 301–2
Keane, Roy, 152, 162
Keegan, Kevin, 232, 233
Kelly, Alan, 292
Kelty Hearts FC, 339, 341–2
Kemp, Ross, 18
Kendall, Howard, 119, 138, 159, 160, 163–4, 193, 205, 206, 218, 274, 289
Kendall, Lily, 292
Kenny, Jonjoe, 256, 259, 260
Kenwright, Bill, 184, 257, 261–2, 270, 277, 288, 316–17, 318–22
Kerr, Cammy, 337
Klinsmann, Jürgen, 112, 149
Knight, Barry, 165

Knox, Archie, 117, 170, 173, 235
Koeman, Bartina, 266, 271
Koeman, Erwin, 264, 265, 330
Koeman, Ronald, 14, 78, 109, 263, 264–72, 277–8, 330
Kohler, Jürgen, 112
Köpke, Andreas, 112–13
Krivokapić, Miodrag, 94
Kuszczak, Tomasz, 204

Lambert, Paul, 107–8
Lampard, Frank, 14, 293, 318, 320–27
Largs Thistle FC, 48, 68, 329
Last Man Standing, 290
Laudrup, Brian, 129, 133
Law, Denis, 114
Lawrence, Dennis, 256, 258
League One, 330, 331
Ledson, Ryan, 256
Lee, Rob, 149, 175
Lee, Sammy, 279
Leeds United FC, 120–23, 129, 146, 185, 337
Leicester City FC, 165–6, 278, 298–9
Lemonakis, Antonis, 284
Levein, Craig, 48
Limpar, Anders, 153
Lineker, Gary, 248
Liverpool, Merseyside, 138–9, 140–42, 144–6, 149–50
Liverpool FC, 113, 140–45, 159, 171, 227
Livingstone, Graham, 69, 70
Lukaku, Romelu, 14, 267–8, 275, 285, 290
Lukic, John, 120

MacDonald, Alex, 69
Macfadyen, Donald, 56
Maddison, James, 299
Mallorca, 205, 206, 212, 241–2, 247–8

INDEX

Malpas, Maurice, 80, 81
Manchester City FC, 138, 184, 206, 310
Manchester United FC, 66, 113, 131, 143, 148, 152–5, 156, 180, 256, 295–8
Marić, Silvio, 176
Martina, Cuco, 281
Martínez, Roberto, 14, 256–63, 277, 330
Mason, Ian, 69
Materazzi, Marco, 47
Matheson Cup, 68
Matić, Nemanja, 319, 320
Matthäus, Lothar, 112
Maze prison, Northern Ireland, 27
McAllister, Gary, 120
McCall, Stuart, 110, 122
McCarthy, James, 280
McClair, Brian, 109
McCoist, Ally, 14, 90, 97, 102–3, 109, 122, 128–9
  drinking culture and, 111, 131
  Hateley, partnership with, 127
  McStay incident (1994), 49
  World Cup (2006), 115–16
McCoy, Paul, 206
McCullough, Lee, 169
McDermott, Terry, 232
McFadden, James, 203
McGinn, John, 282
McInally, Jimmy, 96
McKinlay, Billy, 75, 90, 248
McKinnon, Ray, 75, 83, 85, 94, 95, 107
McLaren, Andy, 75
McLaughlin, John, 64
McLean, Jim, 14, 70–73, 77, 78–84, 86, 87–9, 95–9, 100
  death (2020), 99
  fines, issue of, 82–3, 92–4, 97

four-plus-four contracts, 87, 89–90, 91
honesty box incident, 86
labouring work, 87–9, 124
transfer negotiations (1993), 117–24
McLean, Tommy, 96
McLean Court, Stirling, 60
McLeish, Alex, 54
McMahon, Steve, 163
McManaman, Steve, 159
McNeill, Billy, 96
McPherson, David, 110
McStay, John, 1, 13, 44–54, 113, 134–5, 344
Menzieshill, Dundee, 38
Messi, Lionel, 329
Michels, Rinus, 110
Middlesbrough FC, 331
Miklosko, Ludek, 55
Milan, AC, 305
Miss Scotland, 132
Miss Tunisia, 156
Mitchell, John, 52
Montrose FC, 338
Morgan, Blair, 29
Morris, John, 175
Morrison, Ross, 339, 340
Mortimer, James, 44–5, 54
Moshiri, Farhad, 261, 262, 287–8, 294, 318–20, 322, 343
Motherwell FC, 72, 96, 204
Mourinho, José, 320, 335
Moyes, David, 165–6, 169, 191–8, 202, 203, 205, 292, 330
  coaching and, 253, 254, 255
  falling out with, 192–8, 212–13
  resignation (2013), 256
Mulholland, Lee 31
Mulholland, Tony, 31
Mullin, Keith, 151

INDEX

Murray, David, 122, 126, 127, 132
Mustafi, Shokdran, 254
Mykolenko, Vitaliy, 314

Narey, David, 80, 81
Netherlands national team, 109–10
Neville, Phil, 163
Nevin, Pat, 108
Newcastle United FC, 14, 32, 148–9, 172–81, 191, 193
Nicholas, Charlie, 96–7
Nolan, Kevin, 165, 193
Normand, Andrew, 47–8
Norris Green, Liverpool, 208–9, 217
Northern Ireland, 27
Norton, Franny, 105
Norwich City FC, 148, 183, 202, 261, 315, 322

O'Brien, Mick, 255
O'Neil, John, 76, 94, 95, 96
O'Neill, Martin, 279
O'Neill, Michael, 83
O'Toole, Sean, 232
Oliveira, Hugo, 284
Osborne, Kenneth, 52
Osman, Leon, 170, 202–3

Pallister, Gary, 154, 156, 158, 167–8
Palmer, Sue, 28, 173
Parkinson, Joe, 150, 153
Parr, Ray, 149, 156
Parrott, John, 191, 216–17, 218, 266
Parry, John, 217, 232
Partick Thistle FC, 337–8
Pattullo, Alan, 12
Pawson, Craig, 293
Pearce, Stuart, 162
Pedro, João, 284
Pennington, Matty 256
Pereira, Vitor, 318

Perry, Mark, 78
philanthropy, 208–10
Pickford, Jordan, 299
pigeon fancying, 100–103, 245, 273, 275
Pistone, Alessandro, 177, 178
Portsmouth FC, 205
Potter, Graham, 325
Pratt, Michael, 229–30
Premier League, 14, 143, 158, 219–20
Preston North End FC, 194
Pro Licence, 256, 329
Procter, Anthony, 230
Professional Footballers' Association, 196
Prosser, William, 56
Protestantism, 4–5, 27, 226–7
Purdy, Dan, 285

Qatar, 197, 333
Quinn, Mark, 232–40, 241
Quinn, Micky, 105–6, 234

Raith Rovers FC, 1, 44, 45, 48, 49, 134
Rancel FC, 67
Rangers FC, 2, 3, 14, 24, 25, 42, 66, 68, 113, 125–33, 337
  Celtic, rivalry with, 4–5, 110, 129–30, 132, 166, 226
  drinking culture at, 130–33
  Dundee United matches, 90–91, 97
  Everton transfer deal (1994), 147
  Everton, loan to (1994), 136
  Freemasonry and, 133
  McStay incident (1994), 1, 13, 44–54, 113, 134–5, 344
  Scotland national team and, 110
  transfer to (1993), 3–4, 40, 44, 59, 73, 98, 117–24, 130
  wages, 127–8

INDEX

Ranieri, Claudio, 274
Raploch FC, 67
Raploch, Stirling, 58, 64
Ratcliffe, Kevin, 213, 274
Rathbone, Mick, 189
Real Madrid, 305, 311, 327, 330
Real Sociedad, 256
Redknapp, Harry, 205, 322, 324
Reeves, Kevin, 256
Reid, Peter, 207, 213, 274
Retro, Liverpool, 145–6, 155, 233–4
Richardson, Kevin, 274
Richarlison, 14, 268, 285, 287, 288, 289–91, 293–5, 301, 311
Rideout, Paul, 144, 153, 154
Riedle, Karl-Heinz, 112, 113
Rijkaard, Frank, 78, 109, 110
Riley, Mike, 168
Roach, Dennis, 44, 89, 97, 117, 121, 127, 146, 172, 173, 182–4, 197
Robert I 'the Bruce', King of Scots, 57, 60, 61
Robinson, Antonee, 256, 259, 286
Robson, Bobby, 178–80, 182, 184
Rock Bar, Dundee, 38–9, 40, 130
Rodríguez, James, 14, 268, 275, 285, 308–9
Roma AS, 180
Ronaldo, Cristiano, 187
Rondón, Salomón, 280–81, 314, 325
Rooney, Coleen, 190
Rooney, Wayne, 14, 27, 131, 174, 189–92, 248, 268–72, 273, 275, 278, 318
Roxburgh, Andy, 112
Royal Ascot, 232
Royle, Joe, 28–9, 32, 53, 140–42, 146, 150, 159, 163, 184, 262, 322
    FA Cup (1994–5), 151, 154, 155
Ruddock, Neil, 142, 149
Rufus, Richard, 186

Rummenigge, Karl-Heinz, 38, 114
running, 62–3, 66
Rush, Ian, 145

San Sebastián, Basque Country, 256
Savage, Alan, 341
Savage, Charlie, 332
Scales, John, 142
Scharner, Paul, 168–9
Schmeichel, Peter, 148, 158
Schneiderlin, Morgan, 295
Scholes, Paul, 152
Scholl, Mehmet, 107
Scotland national team, 38, 64, 107–16
    Under-21s, 89, 95, 107–8, 113
Scotland Schoolboys, 68–9, 73, 91
Scottish Central Boys, 66, 67
Scottish Cup, 68, 94, 126
Scottish Football Association (SFA), 48, 55–6, 67, 113, 115, 214
Scottish League Cup, 128
Scottish Premier Division, 81, 94, 97, 122
Scudamore, Peter, 232
sectarianism, 4–5, 25, 27, 132, 133, 226
Shakespeare, Craig, 278
Sharp, Graeme, 137, 207, 213, 319, 321
Shaw, Phil, 112
Shearer, Alan, 14, 172, 174–7, 178, 190, 232, 268, 273–4, 275
Shearer, Lainya, 175
Sheedy, Kevin, 253, 256, 274
Sheffield United FC, 118, 254
Sheffield Wednesday FC, 118
Shepherd, Kenny, 191
Sheringham, Teddy, 149
Sherwood, Tim, 171
Shreeves, Geoff, 296–7
Sidibe, Djibril, 295

INDEX

Sigurdsson, Gylfi, 269, 271–2, 285, 287, 290, 295
Silva, Marco, 14, 278, 284–7
Simmons, Jack, 211
Skelton, George, 70–72, 78
Smith, Charles, 41
Smith, Walter, 44, 70–72, 75, 97, 115, 130, 132, 133, 187–8, 193, 289
   burglary (2001), 229
   Everton, move to (1998), 170
   transfer negotiations (1993), 117, 120, 122–4, 125
   transfer negotiations (1998), 172–4
   transfer negotiations (2000), 183, 184–5
   UEFA Champions League (1993–4), 126–7
Sopwell House, St Albans, 151
Sorín, Juan Pablo, 200
Souness, Graeme, 122
Southall, Neville, 110, 152, 166, 213, 274
Southampton FC, 118, 150, 178, 198, 273
Southgate, Gareth, 324, 325
Speed, Gary, 120, 160, 175, 176, 178, 233, 251–2
St Johnstone FC, 37, 95
St Mirren FC, 67
St Ninians, Stirling, 58, 61, 67
Stam, Jaap, 180
Steele, Allan, 333–4
Steven Rae Cup, 68
Steven, Trevor, 104–5, 122, 274
Stevens, Gary, 122, 274
Stirling Albion FC, 67
Stirling University, 70–72
Stirling, Scotland, 5, 13, 20–21, 34–8, 58, 132
Stobie Bar, Dundee, 78
stockmanship, 273–6

Stone, Michael, 27
Stones, John, 14, 254
Strachan, Gordon, 120, 121
Stretford, Paul, 191
Stuart, Graham, 153, 154, 160
Stubbs, Alan, 198, 257
Sturrock, Paul, 80, 81
Sugar, Alan, 136
Sunderland AFC, 176–7, 261, 267
Sutton, Chris, 248–9
Sweden national team, 110
Switzerland national team, 111

Tally Ho pub, Dundee, 84
Tarleton, Albert, 260, 273
Taylor, Dick, 68, 69
Terry Hurlock, 163
Terry, John, 293
Thomson, Billy, 85
Tiler, Carl, 164
Tosun, Cenk, 279–81, 299
Tottenham Hotspur FC, 136, 149, 176, 178, 309
Townsend, Andros, 314
Tranmere Rovers FC, 213, 219
transfer record, 3–4, 59, 73, 98, 123–4, 125, 130
Tuchel, Thomas, 325
Tunisia, 156–7
Tyson, Mike, 102, 238

Udinese Calcio, 343
UEFA Champions League
   1992–93, 117, 129
   1993–94, 126–7
   1998–99, 152
   2005–06, 200–201
UEFA Coach of the Year, 312
UEFA Cup
   1986–1987, 80, 81
   1999–2000, 180

INDEX

UEFA European Championship
  1992, 78, 108–10, 264, 266
  1996, 113–14
  2024, 324
Under-14 Scottish Cup, 67
United States national team, 108
Unsworth, Dave, 153, 232–3, 257, 261–2, 264, 265, 277–8, 322

Van Basten, Marco, 78, 109
Van de Beek, Donny, 319, 320, 322
Van der Hoorn, Freddy, 96
Van der Meyde, Andy, 234
video messages, 211
Vieira, Patrick, 162, 168
Villarreal CF, 200–201, 269–70
Vince, Dale, 331–4
Vogts, Berti, 115–16

Walcott, Theo, 295
Walker, Jack, 118
Walker, Mike, 137, 139, 150
Wallace, William, 57, 61
Walsh, Liam, 256
Walsh, Steve, 279
Wanchope, Paulo, 164, 184
Warrington, Cheshire, 150
Warriors, The (1979 film), 67
Wars of Scottish Independence (1296–1357), 57, 60, 61
Watford FC, 228, 278

Watson, Dave, 149, 152–3, 155, 159, 218
Watson, Steve, 232
Weir, David, 198, 255
Welsh, Brian, 93
Wenger, Arsène, 242, 329
West Bromwich Albion FC, 203–4, 280
West Ham FC, 159, 184, 278, 286
Westerveld, Sander, 178
Whitehurst, Billy, 163
Wigan Athletic FC, 168–9, 205, 331
Wilkinson, Howard, 120–22
Williams, Joe, 256
Wimbledon AFC, 174
World Cup, 47
  1978 Argentina, 64
  1982 Spain, 81
  1986 Mexico, 78
  1998 France, 116
  2006 Germany, 47
  2022 Qatar, 333
Wörns, Christian, 107
Wrexham AFC, 190
Wright, Ken, 31

Yeovil Town FC, 261
Young Player of the Year, 40, 44
Youngson, Alasdair, 49
Youth Cup, 79

Zidane, Zinedine, 47, 311